For David and Ruth with
very best wishes to you both

Peter Walker.

Mungu awabariki
(God bless you both)

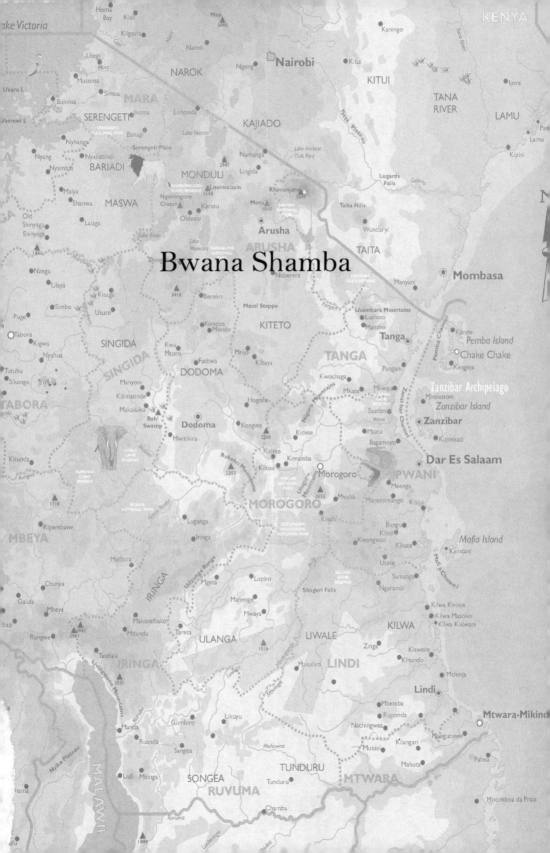

Bwana Shamba
('Mr Agriculture')

The autobiography of a Field Officer (Agriculture) in Tanganyika
Territory (now Tanzania) during the closing years of the
British colonial era in Africa

BY

PETER M WILSON

The Pentland Press
Edinburgh – Cambridge – Durham – USA

First published in 2001 by
The Pentland Press Ltd
1 Hutton Close
South Church
Bishop Auckland
Durham

manuscripts@pentlandpress.co.uk
sales@pentlandpress.co.uk
www.pentlandpress.co.uk

ISBN 1–85821-907-8

Typeset in Bell 11 on 13 by
Carnegie Publishing
Carnegie House
Chatsworth Road
Lancaster

www.carnegiepub.co.uk

Printed and bound by
Antony Rowe Ltd
Chippenham

This book is dedicated to the many friends, African, Asian and European, whom I met and made during my life and career in Africa, who contributed so much towards giving me eighteen happy years on that continent, thirteen of which were spent in Tanganyika/Tanzania.

All profits earned from the sale of this book are being donated by the author to the British and Foreign Bible Society (Stonehill Green, Westlea, Swindon, SN5 7DG) as a 'thank offering' to the Lord for those wonderful years.

Acknowledgements

I wish to express my heartfelt thanks to the following for their assistance in completing this book:

To Almighty God, without whose help and strength I could never have found the enthusiasm, energy and clear thinking to complete such an undertaking after a major stroke.

Also to my brother André for his meticulous proof reading and advice.

Also to Rob Brimson for so generously giving of his professional expertise to enhance my fading and diminutive old photographs to bring them up to standard for use in this book.

I would love to hear from any friends from Africa with many of whom I regrettably lost touch. In particular, I long to re-establish correspondence with my Zaire friend, Denis Songolo (Saxo-Songolo).

Peter M. Wilson, PO Box 304, Horley, Surrey, RH6 7NE, UK.

Books by the Same Author

Simplified Swahili – 1971 & 1985 Longmans, (Addison-Wesley-Longman)

Le Swahili Simplifié – 1970 – East African Literature Bureau, Nairobi

Classified Vocabulary – 1967 – East African Literature Bureau, Nairobi

Swahili Picture Vocabulary – 1972 East African Literature Bureau, Nairobi

'Almasi' – 2000 – Pentland Press, Bishop Auckland

[N.B. The East African Literature Bureau has now been taken over by the Kenya Literature Bureau in Nairobi.]

Contents

Acknowledgements		vi
Illustrations		ix
About the Author		xi
Foreword		xiii
1	In the beginning	1
2	Into Tanganyika	6
3	Orientation	11
4	Dizzy Heights	17
5	It's Those Hens!	24
6	Game	26
7	My First Posting	31
8	Kilosa District	42
9	Wadudu - Insects and Creepy Crawlies	58
10	Fun and Games	65
11	Reunification and Multiplication	71
12	Triple Christening	77
13	Tea break in the Southern Highlands	81
14	A Shilling a Tail!	86
15	Stop Thief!	92
16	Railway Construction	97
17	Road Construction	100
18	Bridge of Sighs?	109
19	Witchcraft	113

20	Preaching to the Unconverted?	115
21	Village Safaris	118
22	Hitch-Hiking the Trains	125
23	A Musical Soirée	127
24	Don't take it for Granted	129
25	Cottoning On	132
26	Filmrover	135
27	Film Making	138
28	Ox Ploughing	140
29	Half an Onion	145
30	Spots Before the Eyes	147
31	Snakes Alive!	149
32	Kwa Heri Ulaya! Jambo Ulaya!	153
33	Swahili Tutoring	161
34	Singing for Joy	173
35	Dolly	175
36	Scouting for Boys	181
37	On Top of Africa	188
38	Lock, Stock and Kitchen Sink	199
39	Dar es Salaam and Home	205
40	For Afters	220
	Glossary of Swahili Words Used in the Text	229
	Glossary of Abbreviations Used in the Text	233

Illustrations

Sketch map of regions visited   xv

Map of Tanzania   xvi–xvii

Sketch map of the Kilosa district   xviii

Approaching mount Meru's peak   20

The Kilosa boma or government office block   36

My Landrover stuck up to its axles in *mbuga* mud   46

The somewhat precarious looking bamboo bridge leading
   onto the Juani estate   51

Author and his wife with Daphne and Bjorn Graae   51

Most of the Ilonga staff with some wives   56

The Kilosa rugby team   66

The interior of Kilosa's church   77

The three proud mothers with their newly
   christened babies   79

The completed bridge at Kisanga   106

Some of the devastation caused by the disastrous
   flash flood   111

The Ulaya cotton grower prizewinners   134

The sum total of Kilosa's agriculture department staff   140

The ox ploughing demonstration at Gairo   142

The local tribesmen at Gairo preparing for their dance
   in our honour   143

Shopping on Arusha market   162

Lecturing to agriculture students in the new large
   lecture theatre at Tengeru   163

Peter M Wilson
Bwana Shamba

Teaching agriculture students on my museum plots   164

One of my smallest VSO Swahili classes at Tengeru   166

My home at Tengeru, near Arusha   167

Dolly awaiting her next game of 'squash'   176

With the Lane family by one of the Momella lakes   183

Sir Charles Maclean talking with local scouts   184

Bryan Down, Tengeru's Principal, entertaining the
    Tanzanian President, Mwalimu Julius K. Nyerere   190

My complete family just before we left Dar   206

The completed permanent ministry exhibition hall
    on the Sabasaba ground, Dar es Salaam   216

About the Author

Peter M. Wilson, a member of the Society of Authors, was born in 1931, in Chelmsford, Essex, in England. He lived and worked in Africa for 18 years, of which 13 were in Tanganyika/Tanzania. For some years in Tanzania whilst working for the Ministry of Agriculture, he was editor of that ministry's Swahili journal *Ukulima wa Kisasa* (Modern Farming). He conquered mount Kilimanjaro in 1961. Working as he was for the Ministry of Agriculture, he established a very close working relationship with the Tanzanian Africans, thereby quickly mastering the Swahili language, the common tongue throughout East Africa. As a result of his mastery of the language, he has written a definitive book, *Simplified Swahili*, which was originally published in East Africa in 1970. It was later published by Longmans in 1985 since which date it has sold in excess of 35,000 copies. It has also been translated into French and is published in this form by the Kenya government. He has also written two smaller books concerning the Swahili language, which are also published in Nairobi.

Being brought up bilingually by his French mother and English father, he was caught in France at the outbreak of the second world war. After attending a French school in Arcachon for a year, he was fortunately able to escape being overrun by the Nazi invasion of France aboard a British unladen collier, the S.S. *Alresford*, arriving back in Falmouth in June 1940.

By this time, having forgotten all his English, he had to re-learn it through a private tutor before being able to enter Cressbrook preparatory school in Kirkby Lonsdale. Having completed his schooling there, he moved on to public school education at Sedbergh School in what is now Cumbria.

His chosen career being in agriculture, he worked for some six years on a traditional hill farm in Westmorland, before eventually attending Harper Adams Agriculture College (now

Peter M Wilson
Bwana Shamba

Harper Adams University College) in Shropshire. Having qualified there he took up an appointment as farm manager on a
mixed farm in Buckinghamshire, later moving to Tanganyika
Territory in 1958 to work in their Ministry of Agriculture for
13 years before leaving to take up a teaching post at the
Botswana Agriculture College.

Returning to Britain in 1975 he worked as a bus driver for
London Transport for a while before moving up into manage-
ment. During this time he was awarded a membership of the
Chartered Institute of Transport, the MCIT.

In 1983, he ran the London Marathon, completing the course
in 3 hours and 57 minutes, collecting sponsorship for the Guide
Dogs for the Blind Association, totalling just over £2,300.

His hobbies include philately, photography, making finely
detailed models of transport vehicles, and classical music. He is
also a passionate railway enthusiast. He has, since the major
stroke he unfortunately suffered in June 1994, taken up water-
colour painting through the auspices of 'Conquest Art', an
organization specializing in encouraging disabled people to
paint, using their methods.

A devout born-again Christian, he has experienced many
spectacular answers to prayer since his stroke, including a
remarkable measure of recovery from his stroke. Forcibly retired
on health grounds and now living close to Gatwick airport, he
has now turned his attention to writing. His first novel *Almasi*,
was published in 2000.

He has three daughters, all of whom are married, who have
given him 7 grandchildren between them.

Peter M Wilson
'Mr Agriculture'

Foreword

When I was going through the draft of the author's autobiography, I realized one remarkable thing about the author that we both proudly share despite the distance that separates us. Both of us in our different roles and capacity were witnesses to the birth of the United Republic of Tanzania, my country. As responsible adults, we therefore had a moral obligation to make sure that our new born country received all that it needed in terms of education, health services, food security, infrastructure etc. to develop it into a mature adult.

I chose to make my contributions through politics and Mr Wilson, the author, chose to make his contributions through *Bwana Shamba*.

During those early years of independence, as a politician, like any other politician, my voice was heard more than Mr Wilson's although our objectives in the development of the country remained the same.

I formally retired from politics in 1993 and Mr Wilson, so he says, retired from active service in 1994 after experiencing a massive stroke which completely paralysed the left part of his body. I for one completely disagree with Mr Wilson's retirement pronouncements. The reason being, that ever since he declared himself as a retiree, Mr Wilson, inspired by his love of my country, as evidenced by his publications *Simplified Swahili*, *Almasi* and now *Bwana Shamba*, just to mention a few, continues indirectly to make enormous contributions in promoting the heritage and the hidden treasures of the country he helped nurture from its infancy. In other words, Mr Wilson has now assumed the role of the politician and I have in the reverse assumed his role as a farmer. Mr Wilson's voice is now more heard than mine.

For those Tanzanians born immediately after our independence, Mr Wilson's publications, particularly this autobiography for which he has given me the honour and privilege to write a

Peter M Wilson
Bwana Shamba

foreword, I hope would go a long way to remind them of where our country came from and who were responsible in their small way for what it is now. For those born in the 21st century and those in the diaspora, it is my hope that Mr Wilson's publications will once again serve to demonstrate to them the richness in our heritage and the dire need to glorify it and its preservation. Thank you and God bless you for a job well done.

RM Kawawa

Rashid Mfaume Kawawa
London
13 May 2001
Former Vice President of
the United Republic of Tanzania
and Prime Minister of Tanganyika

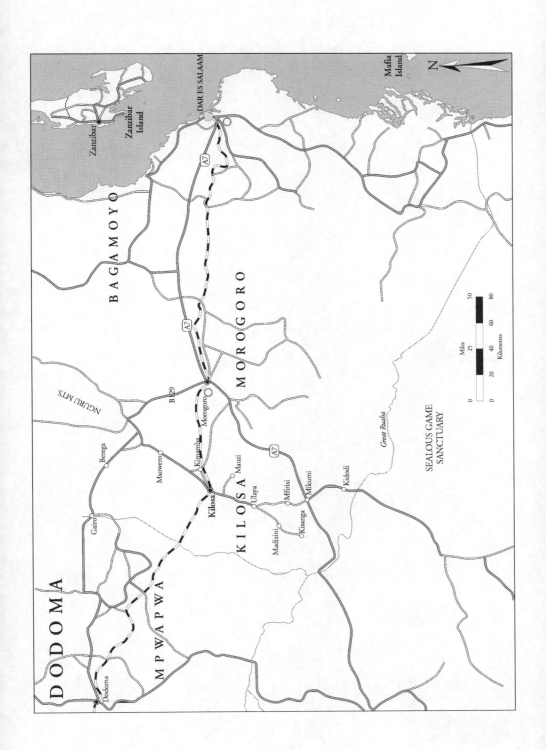

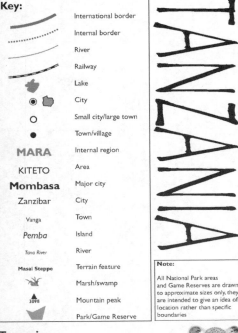

TANZANIA

Key:

———	International border
·········	Internal border
～～～	River
╫╫╫	Railway
(shape)	Lake
◉ ▣	City
○	Small city/large town
●	Town/village
MARA	Internal region
KITETO	Area
Mombasa	Major city
Zanzibar	City
Vanga	Town
Pemba	Island
Tana River	River
Masai Steppe	Terrain feature
🌿	Marsh/swamp
▲ 3098	Mountain peak
(shape)	Park/Game Reserve

Note:

All National Park areas and Game Reserves are drawn to approximate sizes only, they are intended to give an idea of location rather than specific boundaries

Tanzania:

Official name:	United Republic of Tanzania
Population (1990est.):	27 318 000
Area:	945 087 sq. K./364 900 sq. Mi.
Capital City:	Dodoma
Time zone:	GMT +3 hrs
Chief Religion:	Christianity (40%) Islam on Zanzibar
Official languages:	English, Swahili
Unit of Currency:	Tanzanian Shilling
Average Elevation:	1000m/3000ft
Highest peak:	Mt Kilimanjaro, 5895m/19340ft
Average Temperatures:	23°C (Jun-Sep), 27°C (Dec-Mar)
Average Rainfall:	over 1000m/40in
Exports/Economy:	Agriculture: maize, sorghum, coffee, sugar, sisal, cloves (most of the world market), coconuts, tobacco, cotton. Minerals: reserves of iron, coal, tin, gypsum, salt, phosphate, gold, diamonds, oil. Processing: Cotton, cement, cigarettes. Tourism: Mount Kilimanjaro, beaches and reefs, national parks and five game reserves.

East African Republic [largest] divided into 25 regions, includes the islands of Zanzibar, Pemba and Mafia. Population is mostly of Bantu origin.

Brief History:

Early link with Arab, Indian and Persian traders and merchants; Swahili culture develops between 10th to 15th centuries; Zanzibar capital of Omani Empire in 1840s; exploration, German Missionaries and British Explorers, of the interior in mid-19th C.; German East Africa Company in mainland Zanzibar 1885; 1891, Zanzibar a British Protectorate; 1891, German East Africa established; 1919, British mandate to administer Tanganyika; 1961, first east-African country to gain independence and join the Commonwealth; 1962, becomes Republic with Julius Nyerere as President; 1963, Zanzibar given independence as a constitutional monarchy with the Sultan as head of state; 1964, Sultan overthrown, Zanzibar and Tanganyika led to the United Republic of Tanzania; 1992, ruling party announced plans for a multi-party democracy; Governed by a President serving a 5-year term, a cabinet, a National Assembly of 244 members also serving a 5-year term.

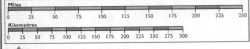

Miles
0   25   50   75   100   125   150   175   200   225   250

Kilometres
0   25   50   75   100   125   150   175   200   225   250   275   300

Map prepared by Mark Keating at Carnegie Publishing. © Carnegie Publishing 2001

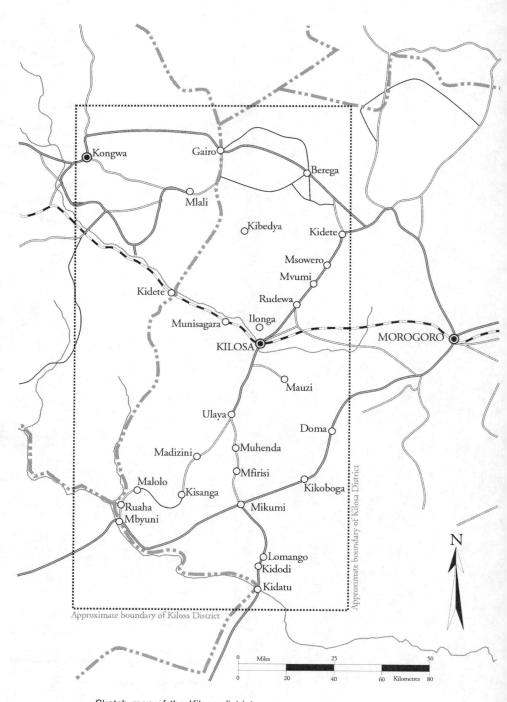

Sketch map of the Kilosa district

CHAPTER I

In The Beginning

I stared for a long time at the advertisement before me in the *Farmers Weekly* magazine. It said:

Wanted
Field Officers (Agriculture)
in Tanganyika Territory
- apply Crown Agents
4 Millbank, London SW1
Closing date xxxxxx 1958

Then I looked hard at it again. Its closing date was already past and gone. There was now no point in considering the possibilities of working in Africa any more, so I closed my magazine and returned it to its shelf.

I had completed a Diploma in Agriculture and Farm Management course at Harper Adams Agriculture College (now University College) in Shropshire in 1954. While there I had often seen overseas job vacancy advertisements posted on its noticeboards, but had never really studied them as I did not think it was 'me' to work overseas. I went on with milking the Friesian herd I was responsible for, as farm manager on Winchendon Hill farm, farmed by a fine Christian farmer, Stanley Clark. The farm was close to the beautiful Buckinghamshire village of Nether Winchendon in the Vale of Aylesbury roughly half way between Aylesbury and Thame in Oxfordshire. All the time I was doing the milking, my thoughts kept returning to that advertisement for a job in Tanganyika. I did at least know where Tanganyika was, as a good friend of mine, David Macdonald, had been managing a tea estate there before coming to college and he had often spoken affectionately and enthusiastically about what a wonderful country it was.

I just couldn't get the thought of working out there out of my mind. I had for a long time been looking for a better job in farm management in Britain, but without success, as I discovered that most of the best jobs going were already filled by the time the advertisements appeared in print.

Since leaving college. I had spent a year working on a large mixed farm which belonged to a good college friend of mine, Ian Sharples, near Ruthin in North Wales. Although happy there, I had left in order to get married to Dorothy, whom I had met when working on a dairy farm in Chaddesden, a suburb of Derby, where I worked on Ted Morten's farm to gain experience of lowland farming.

Before moving to Derby I had lived and worked for some years on a very progressive and well run hill farm, together with Lewis Armitstead, its owner, and Arthur Campbell, his experienced and hardworking farm hand, on Firbank Fell, near Sedbergh, in what is now Cumbria. We had evacuated to Sedbergh in the early part of the London blitz, having heard there was an excellent public school there, where I eventually spent four very happy years from 1944–48.

Deciding to work at Whinney Haw farm with Lewis Armitstead had been a good move on my part. Though still using only primitive traditional farming methods, it was an ideal place to learn all the basic rudiments, not only of agriculture, but also of life itself.

The only motive power on Whinney Haw was *Fanny*, a beautiful and highly intelligent Clydesdale farm horse and her now grown-up foal *Trigger* (so called because with one flick of the reins, she was off like a bullet!). All the field operations on this farm were either done by hand, or using one or both of these fine horses. I even learnt to plough with horses at Whinney Haw. I like to think that I am probably one of the last of a generation to have learnt to plough with horses before ever sitting on a tractor.

Back to milking my Friesians, my thoughts went back to Tanganyika. A good Christian friend of mine, Norman Good, a schoolmaster at Thame Grammar School, had gone abroad for a few years to teach at a British Army school in Wilhelmshaven in Germany, and had been most enthusiastic about the advantages of working abroad. As I continued to ponder over Tanganyika, remembering nevertheless that I was doubtless too late in any case, I vowed to myself that I would discuss the matter with Norman as soon as possible.

I had deemed it essential to look for another post, as on

Peter M Wilson
'Mr Agriculture'

Winchendon Hill farm I seemed to be working all the hours that God gave, to the extent that if ever I wanted any time off, it had to be between milking times, since we milked twice daily on this busy farm.

That evening I phoned Norman, who lived in the neighbouring village of Cuddington. 'Yes, of course I'll discuss it with you, come on over this evening and we'll talk about it!'.

Armed with my farming journal, Dorothy and I drove over that evening to Norman and his wife, Valerie.

I showed the advertisement to Norman, who without any hesitation, said, 'Well, I think you should go for it! I've never regretted going abroad to work, and I'm sure neither will you! Working abroad will either make you or break you. And knowing you as I do, I am confident it will make you!'

I discussed the matter of the past closing date with him.

'That doesn't need worry you!' he assured me.'If they want you enough, they'll still be interested in giving you a job!'.

The next day during my lunch break, I wasted no time in sending off my application to Crown Agents. Within a few days, I received an invitation from them to attend an interview and medical examination on 1 May 1958. I remember it was the first of May, because as I walked through the village to catch the bus, I passed the village school where the children were performing a Maypole dance.

Even though I felt I had not performed as well as I could at the formal interview, the first I had ever attended, I received a letter some ten days later advising me that I had been successful in my application and should be ready to fly to East Africa on 30 August 1958. A cheque for £50 was enclosed, being my outfit allowance.

I duly handed in my notice to Mr Clark who reluctantly accepted it, realizing that he really had no option.

Between milkings, Dorothy and I rushed about spending my £50, which all went, plus some more besides, in buying suitable strong, light suitcases for air travel.

After a day or two, I received another letter from Crown Agents advising me that I should not initially take Dorothy and the children with me, as I would, as soon as I reached Tanganyika, be attending a three month course 'under canvas' which would therefore be unsuitable for them. I was to travel alone from London Airport (not yet generally known as Heathrow) to Nairobi, where I would be met and driven south to Tanganyika.

Peter M Wilson
Bwana Shamba

On reading about Nairobi, I was reassured to know that the Mau Mau troubles in Kenya had at last come to an end, and that the country had stabilized.

By then, I already had two lovely daughters, Vanessa, born in 1955 in the Royal Bucks hospital in Aylesbury, and Yvonne, born two years later in our home in Winchendon.

By the time I left that August day, Yvonne was not yet able to walk. With mixed feelings, I waved goodbye to my mother, my wife, and my children, as on board a propeller-driven Argonaut airliner I taxied away from the primitive terminal buildings, then only rather tatty ex-army wooden huts, and took off for the 24-hour flight to Nairobi.

I found myself sitting next to a very friendly and cheerful young man, Mike Brownbridge. He was flying to Tanganyika in identical circumstances to mine, also to take up an appointment as a Field Officer. He proved to be a wonderful travelling companion, and he helped while away the twenty-four hours of the flight very pleasantly indeed.

We were due to land at Rome, Bengazi, Khartoum, and Entebbe on our way to Nairobi. The flight was pleasant and uneventful until we reached Entebbe. As at all our transit stops, Mike and I alighted to stretch our legs. Entebbe was a beautiful spot, overlooking as it did Lake Victoria, at that point exactly on the equator, the beautiful morning sunlight rendering it a deep blue colour. We thoroughly enjoyed the warm morning sun as we chatted, until we were summoned to resume our seats. All of sudden, just as we started to move towards our waiting aircraft, as if from nowhere, we were besieged by an enormous swarm of Lake Flies. There were millions of them buzzing about us as we vainly tried to shoo them away while running to our aircraft. Just before stepping aboard, we made a few last vain efforts to rid ourselves of them. It was only once safely aboard that at last we were rid of them. Once everyone was settled in their seats, a stewardess came down the aisle spraying insecticide to dispatch any lingering flies that had entered as stowaways.

As we took off, we were rewarded by a last exquisite view of Lake Victoria as we swung round to set course for Nairobi. Once well on our way, we were all presented with a smart certificate signed by our captain, to certify that we had joined that select band of travellers to have looked upon both hemispheres at once as we had crossed the equator on longitude 33 degrees East on

the 30th day of August 1958. It was exactly twelve noon by the
Nairobi Embakasi airport clock as the propellers of our aircraft
finally ceased spinning.

CHAPTER II

Into Tanganyika

M ike and I alighted and walked the short distance across the tarmac to the impressive terminal building.

We awaited the arrival of our cases, then proceeded to the exit door to be met by a tall good looking Scandinavian called Karl Johanesson.

He was obviously an 'old timer' in the country, judging from his deep, healthy tan. He greeted us warmly, then led us to his waiting GT, as all government vehicles were commonly known in Tanganyika since they all bore those registration letters. Karl's GT was an ageing long-wheelbase Landrover in which he would be driving us south to Arusha.

Our cases loaded into the back, we settled into the front hard seats and away we went. We had barely travelled more than two or three miles along a good tarmac road away from the airport, when we had to slow right down to avoid running into three full-grown giraffes which were crossing the road. They scarcely gave us a glance as they ambled across to the far side of the road, raising each of their long legs nonchalantly over a somewhat 'squashed' wire fence and into the '*bundu*'. Out came our cameras and there was a positive tirade of clicks as we took photo after photo of the spectacle through the, fortunately clean, windscreen, eager to capture the spectacle of our first African game shots. We were very impressed already to have seen big game such a short distance from a busy international airport!

We watched them amble off, heading towards a few *acacia* trees, then continued on our way.

After another mile or so, we left the good tarmac road which led to Mombasa, and took a right turn towards Arusha and Tanganyika. We now continued along a far from smooth murram road. A murram surface is one made up of what amounts to the natural soil type of the area, generally a sort of mixture of coarse sand and fine gravel, often with a red-brown colour.

This road was covered with the ubiquitous corrugations, which we were to discover was totally normal and to be expected on most murram roads.

These corrugations are an extraordinary phenomenon, with regular corrugated crests two to three feet apart, each with a trough of up to eight inches in depth in between. If negotiated with speed *in excess of* forty miles per hour, then all that is felt as one drives over them is an even vibration, but the moment the speed drops below 40 mph, then all hell breaks loose and it becomes almost impossible to control any forward movement at all as the rear end of the vehicle 'fish-tails' violently. At speeds below about 15 mph forward attempted movement becomes one violent contortion after another as the vehicle gets thrown in every possible direction, such is the intensity of the vibration as the wheels have time to drop into every depression. Consequently high speeds on such roads are commonplace. Corrugations taken at 80 mph are hardly felt, resulting in only a slight drumming noise. Nobody has ever been able to explain to me the extraordinary phenomenon of these corrugations. They can start to form on either or both sides of the road independently, but even if they do, they always match up *perfectly* in the middle!

We drove on for another half hour until we came to a collection of houses which formed the border village of Namanga near the base of a small mountain, which Karl told us was Longido, situated right on the border with Tanganyika. Karl swung off the road to the right and pulled up outside an hotel which had a long, wide veranda running the length of the building.

We emerged from the Landrover and each settled into a comfortable wicker armchair on the veranda. Almost immediately an African waiter came to take our orders. We were most impressed on hearing Karl's staccato Swahili instructions to the waiter who wore a long white ankle-length *kanzu*. On his head was a Tommy Cooper style red *fez* hat. He wore no shoes, so that he walked almost noiselessly on the red concrete veranda floor.

He soon returned with our ice cold drinks of Coca-cola and Fanta orange. I chose the latter which was deliciously cool and refreshing. More staccato Swahili from Karl followed as he instructed the waiter to give us each a separate receipt, as we would be able to claim back the cost as legitimate travelling expenses later.

Our drinks finished, and each of us armed with our individual receipts, we set off once more for Tanganyika.

Within half a mile as we progressed south along the now excellent tarmac road, we came upon a barrier pole across the road. As we approached it, I noticed a sentry box at the left hand side of this pole, and just outside it stood a very smart Kenyan policeman. He wore khaki uniform with shorts, and a tall blue *fez* type hat. As soon as we approached the pole, he swung it open for us, and as we passed through he gave us a very smart salute, his chest puffed proudly outwards.

We continued south and soon could make out a large grey triangular shadow ahead of us. Karl explained that it was Mount Meru, a 15,000 ft extinct volcano which dominated the town of Arusha, our destination for that night. Away over to the left, we could discern another enormous triangular mass with a flat top. That, Karl told us, was Mount Kilimanjaro, which, at just over 19,000 ft, is Africa's highest peak. Although from that range we could not see it all, Karl told us it had a perpetual snow cap despite being virtually on the equator.

Soon after, Karl stopped the Landrover to point out to us a massive herd on the horizon. His accustomed eyes could discern that it comprised a mixture of wildebeest and zebra which often co-existed on Africa's savannah. Although far too far away to photograph with ordinary lenses, we nevertheless piled out and snapped away. Such was my then dread of snakes, that before daring to set foot upon the tarmac, as I had at Namanga, I carefully had a good look around to ensure there were no snakes around before I dared place my foot upon *terra firma*. Needless to say there was none. In the course of the next few weeks, I was to get so accustomed to walking through thick bush, that I then never even gave snakes a thought! Another three quarters of an hour's driving saw us rounding Meru's eastern foot, as we encroached the Arusha bypass, now heading due east. We soon came upon a signpost directing us to take a right hand turn, still on tarmac, into Arusha itself. We soon found ourselves driving through a sort of shanty town, with houses of all shapes and sizes, mostly built of rusting corrugated iron, or opened out tin *debes*, a common square section tin container which has a capacity of four gallons. Africans both male and female were bustling about hither and thither, the women wearing very colourful *kangas*, a very light cotton cloth which they draped over their shoulders and let hang loosely down. Quite a few of the women we saw thus attired had wrapped a small baby in this *kanga* to hold it tightly against their backs, the baby bouncing up and down as they walked. I was struck by how many men, women and indeed children walked with elegant grace and poise, as they carried all manner of objects upon their heads with total confidence. I saw empty *coca cola* bottles, a rolled up umbrella, all shapes and sizes of earthenware cooking pots, tin handle-less saucepans called *sufuria*, and indeed *debes*, all being carried upon various heads with perfect balance.

Then the tarmac road dipped down slightly, we crossed a bridge and found ourselves in a much more modern part of Arusha, with large brick and concrete white buildings, on both sides of the street.

We climbed a slightly sloping street, at the top of which was a *kipulefti*, a roundabout, in the centre of which stood an attractive modern clock tower. To the right of this *kipulefti* stood our objective for our first night on the African continent, the New Arusha Hotel. It was a smart modern white building, the inside of which could have been anywhere in the world. To the right of the spacious reception area was an enormous dining room.

Karl saw us safely checked in, then left us, promising to collect us after breakfast next morning to go and meet the Regional Agriculture Officer, Fuggles Couchman, whose office was in Arusha. I was shown to my room by an African steward, wearing, as seemed normal, no shoes, a long white *kanzu* robe and a white skull cap on his head.

My room was a large square one, with a large bed, over which hung a knotted white mosquito net. The large windows, draped with lace curtains, gave out onto the street and the *kipulefti*. There was a washbasin in the room so I spent a little time washing off the red dust from the Nairobi road and generally freshening myself up before the evening meal.

I had just finished changing into clean clothing, when the dinner gong sounded. It seemed to be coming from much closer than the reception area, so I opened my door to see where it was coming from. An African steward, dressed once again in a white *kanzu* with red cummerbund, but this time wearing also a red *fez* hat, was marching up and down all the corridors, brandishing a hand-held gong in one hand and beating it with great gusto with a drum stick held in the other. He was beating it with a wonderful zestful rhythm which only an African can achieve.

I tidied myself up and went along to the vast dining room. There were only about six people in the dining room for dinner, but lined up against the wall were a dozen or so waiters, all dressed in white *kanzus*, red cummerbunds, red *fez* hats, and all without shoes.

I joined Mike who was already there and seated, and immediately two of the waiters came to bring me a menu. One waiter filled my water tumbler with fresh iced water whilst I perused the menu.

I opted for a steak and vegetables. Fortunately my waiter understood my order in English, and he disappeared to attend to our needs.

The beef steak turned out to be most delicious and succulent. For afters I opted for fresh pineapple, which was by far the most delicious and sweet pineapple, I had ever tasted. Kilimanjaro coffee rounded off the meal, then it was back to our rooms for our first night on the *Dark Continent*.

Whilst I had been enjoying my meal, my room steward had turned the bed down and lowered the mosquito net, which was now tucked in neatly all round the mattress. The top part hung tent-like from a hook directly above the bed.

It had been a long tiring day since I had last slept on a proper bed, so I gratefully climbed into my 'tent', retucked the mosquito net under the mattress as best I could, and let my heavy eyelids have their way at last as my head sank into the soft pillow.

CHAPTER III

Orientation

It was already broad daylight when my room steward knocked on the door and brought my early morning tea. I reached out under my mosquito net and gratefully drank down my cuppa. I pulled out the mosquito net, leapt out of bed, and after a quick wash, dressed suitably for a hot, sunny day, donning my khaki shorts and knee length stockings and sandals.

I then made my way to the dining table for a much needed breakfast. Mike was again already seated when I got there, so I joined him at our table, upon which a delicious looking melon slice, or so it seemed, awaited me. A slice of lemon was placed alongside the melon, which I thought strange as I had never thought of having lemon juice with melon before. I picked up my spoon and dug out a nice chunk of the orange/yellow flesh. No sooner had I put it in my mouth than, to Mike's great amusement, I screwed up my face as its unfamiliar taste and texture reached my taste buds.

It tasted awful.

Mike laughed out loud now.

'I bet you thought that it was melon!' he said, 'but it isn't. It's pawpaw! If you squeeze some lemon juice on it and add a little sugar, it really does taste rather nice.'

I was doubtful, after my first disappointing taste, but nevertheless followed his advice. To my pleasant and unexpected surprise, it did taste very nice indeed, and the lemon juice added a very nice flavour to it. I realized it had only been the *expectation* of it being a sweet melon that had disappointed me.

I devoured the rest of my pawpaw with relish, even to the point of scraping every last bit of its flesh from the thick green skin.

One of the many waiters then brought the next course, comprising a typically English breakfast of bacon and egg, with two eggs, sunny side up. Toast and marmalade completed the meal, washed down with Kilimanjaro coffee. We had only just retired to the reception area when Karl appeared, bright and breezy as usual to collect us in his GT.

It was only a short drive through the town to the Arusha *boma*. This is a Swahili word actually meaning a fort or fortress. But since many government offices were located in old forts, such as this one in Arusha, the word had also acquired the additional meaning of a government office block, even if not located in an old fort. The Arusha *boma* was in fact an old German built fort. It was surrounded by thick white painted walls, within which some offices had been set up.

Karl led us to a door marked *Kilimo* (Agriculture), and through this door to one marked R.A.O.

A knock on the door produced a friendly '*Karibu!*' from within, so Karl led us in, where we saw an amiable gentleman who immediately rose from his large desk to greet us affably, as we entered.

Karl introduced us.

'So, you're Wilson?' he asked as we shook hands. When I affirmed this, he immediately asked, 'So where is your wife and family? Why didn't you bring them with you?' When I explained to him that Crown Agents had specifically advised me to come out initially alone because of a course 'under canvas', he threw his hands in the air and uttered a few words I did not actually catch, apart from 'Typical!'

He then suggested that as soon as I was settled in to my eventual station, I should start wheels turning without delay for Dorothy and our daughters to join me forthwith. Fuggles then went on to explain that Mike and I were to be housed temporarily at a station called Tengeru, seven miles to the east of Arusha. There we would be joined by six new Agriculture Officers, therefore graduates, who included Mike Owen, Peter Myers, Barry Walker and Alistair Macdonald.

At Tengeru, far from being accommodated under canvas, we would be temporarily housed in Grade 'A' housing, sharing up to four per house, but taking our meals in a nearby 'tearoom' called Duluti tearooms, run by a Pole, Mr Czerny.

We were to learn later that Mr Czerny was one of many Polish people who had escaped the persecution in their homeland by crossing the Gobi desert on foot, thence across India to the coast and over the Indian Ocean to East Africa.

Many of these Poles had found their way inland and had

decided to settle down in the fertile area of Arusha. They had hewn out a large settlement at Tengeru, literally out of the bush. They had created a wonderful system of irrigation channels over its entire area. A few of the original buildings still stood, notably several *rondavel* thatched houses and a large thatched church. At least two other Poles still lived and worked on the Tengeru government station.

Fuggles told us that we would not only be taught Swahili on this course, but be given lectures by representatives from all the government departments and other businesses to give us an insight as to how Tanganyika 'ticked'. He told us that Tengeru was one of the best, if not *the* best station in the country and that our tutor was to be Horace Mason OBE. He had been awarded his OBE because of some very brave and tactful work he had quietly undertaken to pacify a potentially explosive situation within the nearby tribeland of the *Wameru*, who lived between Tengeru and Mount Meru to its north.

Fuggles then went on to tell us how fortunate we were to be started off with a Swahili course, as until we passed the Lower Standard government Swahili examination, we would not receive our first pay increment. There was to be no exam at the end of our course, after which we would be receiving our postings to wherever we were needed in the Territory.

We were told there was also a Higher Standard examination, designed for administrative grades, such as District Officers and District Commissioners. These grades would not receive further increments unless they passed the Higher Standard examination, written and oral. If we, however, as lowly grades, succeeded in passing the higher exam, both written and oral, even though not required of us in 'General Orders', we could expect a cash bonus of £20 for our trouble.

Mike and I looked at each other with raised eyebrows. I thought we would be lucky to earn our first increment with the Lower standard exam, never mind the Higher exam. Fuggles then went through a few of the basic government rules and regulations and took us on our way back to the hotel.

Karl drove us to Tengeru along a good tarmac road, which was in fact a continuation of the one we had followed down from Nairobi.

The road was flanked on its northern side by massive banana plantations, amongst which we could see, here and there, African houses made entirely of banana leaves. On the south side of the road, a mile or two out of Arusha, we saw endless well shaded coffee plantations on the south side of the road. After only a short distance, as we topped a slight rise in the road, we gasped as a huge, beautiful white-capped mountain came into view dead ahead of us.

'That's Kilimanjaro!' Karl explained, 'The flat topped snowy one is the main Kibo peak and the further one with the jagged top is its second peak at about 17,000 ft, called Mawenzi. There is also a third peak, not visible from here, which is insignificant compared to the others, but is the original volcanic core. It is called Shira and lies slightly to the northwest of Kibo.'

After a drive of only ten minutes or so, we turned right into a narrow tarmac road at the entrance to which a large wooden board announced:

Ministry of Agriculture Training Institute, Tengeru (M.A.T.I.T.)
Northern Regional Research Centre (N.R.C.)
Tanganyika Agriculture Machinery Testing Unit (T.A.M.T.U.)

Almost immediately the single track tarmac road rounded a left hand bend and led us down between two vast well shaded coffee estates. Numerous Africans, this time mostly men, were walking up and down this road, so that Karl had to hoot for many of them to move over to let us past.

Less than half a mile down this tarmac road we rounded a slight bend and approached a pole barrier across the road. As soon as we saw it, someone raised it to allow us to enter Tengeru station. We were now on a brown earth road.

Many young African men were milling about. We passed some neat red-tiled buildings on our left which a notice told us was the NRC.

Taking a left turn, we passed some more similar buildings on our right, which a notice announced as being MATIT.

Karl parked his GT near these buildings and led us along an open corridor to an office marked Principal.

After knocking on the door, and receiving a 'Karibu!' response, Karl led us in and introduced us to a tall European, Bill Snee, who shook our hands warmly in welcome.

He picked up a telephone to summon the bursar, Jim Dolphin-Rowland. He, too, greeted us warmly and bade us welcome to Tengeru. He advised us which house we were allocated for our brief stay, then accompanied us in Karl's GT to our temporary home. It was a lovely, furnished red-tiled bungalow with two bedrooms, a large lounge, dining room and kitchen. At the front, facing a large garden, somewhat overgrown and neglected, stood a large veranda reached by French windows from the lounge.

There were already two other new arrivals settled in, who would also be attending our Swahili course, so Mike and I carried our cases into the remaining vacant bedroom, which had two windows, one facing our garden, the other, Mount Meru, which dominated the scene directly to our north.

On our way back to the administrative building Jim showed us which was to be our Swahili classroom, a little way up the flowering tree lined drive. We then went on to be shown where we would be taking all our meals. We turned left immediately outside the barrier, and followed a track alongside a dense coffee plantation. After a couple of bends, the track led us over a sharp humpback bridge over one of the numerous irrigation channels that criss-crossed the area. As the bonnet of our vehicle dipped down over this bridge we gasped at the magnificent vista that confronted us. We saw a large blue lake which filled an old volcanic crater. The lake-filled crater was surrounded by a thickly wooded ridge which rose to a height of about five hundred feet above the lake. At the far side of this rim, we could see a beautiful large house, which we guessed must have had a magnificent panoramic view of the beautiful countryside in this area. Our track curved round to the right and followed the lake shore till we came across a grassy clearing. Facing the lake at the top end of this clearing stood a large thatched wooden building which a signboard told us was the Lake Duluti Tearooms.

This was to be where we would take all our meals, whilst at Tengeru. We could think of no finer a setting for us to feed in during the next few weeks. Karl told us that he had some gill nets in place in the lake, in which he caught many delicious *Tilapia* fish, but he warned us, on no account to enter the water either for a swim, or a paddle, inviting though it looked, as the lake was infested with the dreaded *Bilharzia* parasite. This terrible human parasite has a very similar life cycle and infestation in humans to that of the liver fluke in sheep, even to having a specific water snail as an intermediate host. Karl went on to tell us that he had once been infected by *Bilharzia*, and that the treatment for it, was, if anything, worse than the infestation.

We were then taken back 'home' where Mike and I met our house-mates, who, like ourselves, were newcomers to Tanganyika. We met a Scot, 'Mac' Macdonald, and Hall whom we immediately dubbed 'Henry' Hall. Henry was a most gifted artist and cartoonist, and it was not long before he had drawn the most wonderful caricatures of most of us, on our Swahili notebooks.

After spending the rest of the afternoon unpacking and settling in to our new surroundings, it was time to sample our first meal at Duluti Tearooms. As luck would have it, Henry had already managed to buy an old short wheelbase Landrover, so he was able to ferry Mike and me to Duluti, where we partook of an excellent meal. We had here the opportunity to meet the remainder of those who, like us, were newcomers and were to participate in 'our' Swahili course. Most were, unlike Mike and me, designated as Agriculture Officers and were therefore graduates and one grade above us Field Officers in seniority. Before coming to Tanganyika they had attended a course in tropical agriculture in Trinidad. Two of these had, like Henry, already bought themselves vehicles, but this time, new, small pick-up open back vans. We were very glad of this, as we who had only our legs with which to reach Duluti for our meals were frequently given lifts in these vehicles to and from our houses. Thus did our routine start for the next seven weeks.

On the course we had intensive Swahili tuition every morning until our eleven o'clock coffee break and in the afternoons we had revision and/or Swahili exercises. The second half of the morning, and also on an occasional afternoon, we had speakers from each other government department and from some of the local companies, to tell us how they worked and what they did. We also had occasional visits to local places of interest. Our weekends, however, were free, so various options were suggested to us as to how we could use this free time. These included visits to Amboseli National park just inside Kenya, the lake Manyara National Park or even an ascent up Mount Meru!

Dizzy Heights

Ever since the suggestion had been made that we could devote one weekend to climbing Meru, the idea had festered and developed in our minds, until we finally resolved that it would be an excellent feat to attempt. No sooner had we expressed our interest, than Horace Mason immediately mentioned it to his African assistant, Sam Magai, himself of the Meru tribe and a keen athlete. He was at Tengeru filling in time while waiting to go to the UK to attend a course at Sandhurst Military Academy.

In due course, he was to become the officer in charge of the Tanzania People's Defence Force (the TPDF). When he took over this appointment, he decided to make use of his formal family name and adopted the name Sam M. Sarakikya, by which time he had become a brigadier.

On the appointed Saturday we all piled into a convoy of Landrovers, to take us up as far as practicable up the western foot of Meru. We initially followed the tarmac Nairobi road right round to the western extremity of the mountain. Here we left the lovely, smooth tarmac road and turned right onto a rough stony track which wound its way up the lower slopes of the mountain, passing close the forestry school at Ol Motonyi.

After an hour's bumpy climb up this track we suddenly emerged from the rough forest to find ourselves on a large level plateau.

I was astonished to see all over this plateau numerous fields of small white, daisy type flowers. This was pyrethrum, a valuable cash crop grown for its excellent insecticidal properties.

This crop is grown widely in the highlands of both Kenya and Tanganyika, above 8,000 ft. There are some very strange facts about this crop, one of which is that though the plant can and does grow at virtually any altitude, it only produces sufficient quantities of pyrethrins (the active insecticidal ingredient, present in greatest concentration within the flower heads) to make its harvesting economically viable, at altitudes in excess of 8,000 ft. The plateau upon which we found ourselves therefore qualified with regard to altitude requirements. Another strange fact about this plant is that its chief pest are small sucking insects called thrips. The only truly successful insecticide effective against this pest is, oddly enough, pyrethrum itself. Yet the insect is totally unaffected by the plant's sap upon which it feeds.

We parked the Landrovers and left them ready for our return trip next day. Sam led us at a brisk pace across the plateau towards the edge of the indigenous forest which ringed the entire base of the mountain at about 8,000 ft.

We then were led up a very rough and stony path which led its circuitous and uncomfortable way up the lower Meru slopes.

We had only been following this rough track for some ten minutes or so, when Sam called a halt, pointing forward towards a Colobus monkey which was making its rapid way from branch to branch with graceful and comparative ease and confidence as it sprung from tree to tree to flee from us. As it 'flew' its beautiful, long black and white fur and tail billowed out just as if it had wings.

We watched it until it reached the lowest branches of the trees and made its way out of our sight. As luck would have it, I had had my cine camera 'at the ready' all loaded up and ready to go, so I did manage to capture most of the Colobus' antics on film. Many sub chiefs and tribal chiefs use this monkey's fur as a ceremonial head dress. I was also made to understand that many Africans consider its meat as a great delicacy, so that these beautiful animals' numbers were being decimated. It would be a tragedy indeed if it ever became extinct.

We continued on our way, forever climbing upwards along that very rough and circuitous track.

After another quarter of an hour, Sam again called an urgent halt, putting a finger to his lips. We had come across a herd of elephants. We fanned out as quietly as we could, to watch these giants casually gnawing away at tree branches and bushes, marvelling at the comparative ease with which they nonchalantly uprooted large bushes and ripped branches off trees. We stood in awe for about ten minutes, by which time they had wandered away from our path, so we continued on our way.

A further three quarters of an hour later we suddenly emerged from the forest and could see our ultimate objective, a massive forbidding grey ash heap towering some, 6,000 ft above us. The surface of this ash heap, or scree, as it is called, was perfectly smooth and rose at a constant angle of almost 50 degrees, occasionally interrupted by free standing rocks. Here and there, rising with the slope could be seen rock outcrops stretching their way upwards.

Sam followed the top edge of the tree line for bout ten to fifteen minutes, southwards, until we came across a wooden hut, built of tongue and groove boards. This was to be our official night stop.

Immediately below this hut was a heather lined depression, forming a neat hollow. In the very middle of this hollow, Sam started to lay out a fire with dried heather and other branches he asked us to collect. In no time, not long before dusk fell, he had a roaring fire going. We gathered round this fire, glad of its warmth, as at this altitude we could already feel the sharp cold night air. We ate our picnic supper courtesy of Mr Czerny, who had provided us with some magnificent sandwiches for the occasion. Sam told us that we could choose to sleep in our sleeping bags either inside the cramped hut, or make ourselves comfortable around the fire, which he assured us would be sufficient to keep away any lurking game such as leopards, or elephant. I was sure he knew about these things, so I opted to sleep outside under the vista of brilliant stars. I had never had the opportunity to see stars so clearly and brightly before, nor indeed have since. Every so often, and surprisingly frequently, a shooting star would fly across the sky. I noticed that the Southern Cross constellation was clearly visible, and easily recognizable.

Although it was not the most comfortable night's sleep I had ever experienced, I did nevertheless sleep quite well once I had removed numerous stones from under my sleeping bag.

About two hours before dawn, Sam roused us, and put some water to boil for tea on the still-burning fire. The intention was to reach the very summit in time to see the magnificent sunrise behind Kilimanjaro which lay fifty miles to the east.

I had fortunately had the foresight to bring out with me from England a good pair of light walking boots, in which I had accompanied my older brother as we walked around much of the Bernese Oberland a few years previously. These boots proved

Peter M Wilson
Bwana Shamba

Approaching mount Meru's peak with some scouts from Tengeru. The sheer 3,000ft drop is visible behind them.

invaluable on such an expedition, as were the bandage-type spats I was able to wind round and round over the tops of my boots, to keep out small stones, ash, and other uncomfortable bits and pieces which inevitably find their way into one's boots on such trips.

With a mug of hot tea inside us, Sam led us away up to the murderous scree. It was not until actually on this scree, which was literally a giant heap of fine volcanic ash, that I realized just what we had let ourselves in for.

We sank up to our ankles into the soft ash, and it became literally a case of three steps upwards and two down. As soon as we lifted one foot to raise it for the next step, the other foot would relentlessly slide down through the ash. It was exhausting work, as quite a lot of energy was required to drag out the foot which had embedded itself deep into the ash. The altitude, now in excess of 9,000 ft, also made a difference, and we were soon all gasping for breath as a result of our endeavours.

There was no respite. Wherever we went to try and find more firm footing, the scree was exactly the same. We therefore made frequent stops to try to get our breath back. Although it was still virtually dark, as we climbed higher, we could see over the top of the rain forest, that the plain, several thousand feet below us, was entirely covered by 'cottonwool' clouds way below us. In the brilliant starlight, we could clearly see our objective, still seemingly impossibly high above our heads.

We laboriously climbed on and on, with the top seemingly never getting an inch nearer as we progressed upwards. Sam kept on egging us on with assurances that the top was '*bado kidogo*' (or 'not quite yet'. I was to find out in due course that this was always the stock answer to the question 'How long?')

After about an hour of energy draining climbing we looked westwards, and since daylight was just beginning to make its presence felt, we were fascinated to see the large triangular shadow of Meru, on the clouds way below us.

At long last, gasping for breath, we reached the rock outcrop which heralded our arrival at the summit. It was sheer bliss at last to be off the murderous scree, but now we had a new problem. We found that we were having to take giant steps up from one rock level to another, as well as leap across gaps from one to another.

We kept relentlessly climbing higher and higher until, at last, we could go not further upwards. It was a frightening arrival

Peter M Wilson
Bwana Shamba

as we reached the very summit, as it was literally a case of 'one step too many' and we would have hurtled some 2,000 ft down a sheer rock face into the crater in the centre of the mountain.

The actual peak was marked by a crude cairn of stones, the top one of which had had an aluminium box affixed by the Sierra Club. Upon opening its wing-nut fastened lid, we found inside it a notebook in which we could inscribe our names as conquerors of the mountain.

I delayed this honour, as my eyes were by then firmly fixed on the magnificent spectacle that was unfolding some fifty miles to the east of us, as the sun rose majestically directly behind Kilimanjaro's enormous bulk. The space between us and Kilimanjaro was filled, as were the plains far below us, with cottonwool clouds. These had now taken on a beautiful pink hue as the sun's first rays caught them. Then I looked directly into the huge crater below. The actual volcanic cone right in the centre of this massive crater was clearly visible as the crater itself was totally devoid of cloud.

I had found out earlier that comparatively recently, geologically speaking, there had been a massive explosion in Meru, as it let out is last gasp of energy as it were, before dying forever. This massive explosion had ruptured its entire eastern side which was now a gaping void, and enormous chunks of rock which had once been bits of Meru were now littered all over the western foot of Kilimanjaro, fifty miles eastwards. Had it not been for that enormous explosion, it has been calculated, I was told, that Meru might in fact have been a close contender for the world's highest peak.

Having absorbed the unforgettable beauty of the spectacular sunrise to our east, I then signed the book, and let my eyes then refocus eastward. By then, the cloud base had retreated considerably, so that it was now possible to see clearly the Momella lakes, which lay a few miles just to the east of Meru's open side.

Such was the intensity of cold at the top, that we were all soon shivering. Despite the exquisite sunrise to our east, we decided not to linger too long at the summit and soon began our descent.

Once we were back on the scree, we soon found what a tremendous difference there was between climbing and descending! It was possible on the descent to take giant 'seven league' strides in the soft ash, and even every so often to leap into space ahead of us, only to land softly in the talc-like ash. This became great fun and in only a fraction of the time it had taken us to climb it, we soon found ourselves back at the bottom of the scree.

The corrugated iron roof of the hut had been a useful beacon to guide us back to where we had left our sleeping bags and other 'not wanted on voyage' belongings. We assembled in the hollow where most of us had spent the night, revived the fire and set some more water to boil for a welcome drink of tea.

The tea made, we settled down to eat our remaining sandwiches, and gulp down a welcome hot drink. Half an hour later we were ready for the final descent to the plateau. It was a very uncomfortable descent down the rugged path, full of protruding tree roots and boulders which all required a big stride to negotiate, but at last we reached the plateau and the very welcome sight of our Landrovers patiently awaiting our return. Totally devoid of all energy, we wearily climbed aboard, and mercifully each vehicle started up without a problem. We bounced and were thrown wearily about this way and that as we cautiously drove back down the rough, stony track until at last, joy of joys, we found ourselves back on heavenly smooth tarmac for the last leg of our expedition back to Tengeru.

We just had time to tidy ourselves up before making our way to the Duluti Tearooms for a hearty lunch. As we made our way up to Duluti, we gazed triumphantly at Meru's massive bulk towering above us, very content to know we had conquered its distant, bleak peak. It had been a very tough climb, but well worth the effort, though I am the first to admit that I never thought it would be, at the time we tackled that murderous scree! At that time, I also never for a moment imagined that I was destined in time to conquer its peak a dozen or so times more. Needless to say, the conversation throughout that very welcome and wholesome lunch was entirely concerning our recent expedition!

That afternoon found us all, without exception, having a long, deep sleep siesta on our respective beds. For that afternoon at any rate Swahili could be and was forgotten!

Peter M Wilson
Bwana Shamba

CHAPTER V

It's Those Hens

We had settled down to the routine of our interesting course comprising pure Swahili every morning and outside lecturers and visits every afternoon. This left the weekends clear to do our 'own thing'.

The following Sunday after the Meru ascent, I decided to sample a service at Tengeru's own church. The service was quite well attended by a mixture of European staff and African students.

After the service, conducted in English by the local Australian missionary, I met a very friendly Irish couple, John and Dorothy Russell. They in turn introduced me to a friend of theirs, Bill Carmichael, a forester. All three were keen Christians and they later invited me to accompany them on a picnic on the Tengeru estate down by the picturesque dam in the middle of the estate's natural forest. After that enjoyable picnic, I socialized with John and Dorothy on frequent occasions. Both John and Bill were on the Institute's staff.

Our course continued relentlessly on, and one afternoon, it was Bill Carmichael's turn to lecture to us about the activities of the Forestry Department in Tanganyika. He spoke for only a few minutes, then invited us to accompany him on a tour of the estate's own natural forest where he had undertaken an extensive replanting programme.

We duly followed him down to the forest and followed Bill as he picked his way through trees to a place where a sapling had been planted. We were following hard on his heels when he suddenly stopped, staring intensely at the ground. We followed his gaze and saw a shallow hollow where fresh mulch had been placed. Right in the middle, was a five inch miserable broken stem of a sapling.

Bill's face clouded over, 'Och! It's those hens!' he uttered loudly under his breath in his lilting accent. We all looked at each other in amazement at Bill's restraint from using bad language. Anybody else, on seeing the utter destruction of saplings lovingly planted out, caused by pecking and scratching hens, would have doubtless exploded into a string of four-letter expletives. But Bill, a practising Christian, knew better, and satisfied his extreme annoyance by uttering those memorable words.

Bill then made his way through the trees only to find an identical situation at each sapling he came to. He then moved on again and again, and each time the fate of the sapling was the same. After each discovery, poor Bill vented his rage with his new memorable phrase, 'Och! It's those hens!' I say memorable, because the restraint of using swear words rubbed off on all of us, and from then on, whenever any of us might have otherwise let fly with unprintable expletives over some annoyance or other, we satisfied our frustration by uttering Bill's words, 'Och! It's those hens!' no matter what our problem was, hens, or no hens.

Even now, all these years later, I still find myself in cases of extreme frustration looking for those immortal words, 'Och! It's those hens!'.

Peter M Wilson
Bwana Shamba

CHAPTER VI

Game

Arusha nowadays is the epicentre of the booming tourist trade in Tanzania. It ideally fits this bill since it is surrounded by easily reached wonderful national parks, notably Ngorongoro Crater, Amboseli National Park just north of Kilimanjaro, Lake Manyara National Park and, of course, the Serengeti Plains.

In 1958, no National Parks had yet been established, although, of course, the parks just mentioned were still marvellous areas in which one could go and see liberal quantities of big game.

On one of our free weekends during our course at Tengeru, Mike, 'Henry' Hall and I decided to pay a visit to Amboseli, which is actually in Kenya, just to the north of Kilimanjaro. We invited Henry along with us, partly because, as I have mentioned, he had already acquired a short wheelbase Landrover.

Not yet having been issued with our own officer's tents, we were kindly lent one. We duly loaded Henry's Landrover up with our tent and other camping equipment, a good supply of food and film for our cameras, and set off one Friday evening.

We drove back up the excellent tarmac Nairobi road to Namanga, where we made our way to the entrance to the Amboseli game park, as it was then known. Close to the gate into the park, we found a suitable level piece of ground upon which we decided to camp for the night.

We then enjoyed ourselves working out what was what on our tent and how to erect it. It comprised an enormous flysheet, inside which we erected the actual rectangular tent amply large enough for three or four *Hounsfield* camp beds we had brought with us. The area at the far end furthest from the entrance, we were later to find out was designed to be the 'bathroom' and could accommodate the folding bath with which we were eventually to be issued.

The tent was liberally supplied with long guy ropes, and once we had secured all these, our tent was ready to accommodate us for our first night out in the African bush.

We had not brought a safari boy with us, so we enjoyed ourselves warming up our own evening meal on a Primus stove we had brought with us.

Whilst we had been erecting our *hema*, many of the local children had gathered round to watch the entertainment. And now, since some of these still lingered around our tent, we offered them a few biscuits, which they readily accepted. I was shocked to notice that many of these children (as indeed I was to see repeatedly everywhere I went in the country) had grossly enlarged navels. Some of these navels stuck out at right angles to their tummies, and were often as large and as thick, in many cases, as an arm jutting forwards, often tapered slightly towards the rounded end.

We then opened out our campbeds and prepared them for the night. Our audience fortunately took the hint and disappeared. We settled down for the night and all slept well, and by the time we emerged next morning, it was already broad daylight and the sun was well up in the sky. We put some water on the Primus to make tea, and breakfasted on bread and marmalade or Marmite. We decided it might be wise to take the tent with us, so struck camp and folded it away in the back of Henry's Landrover.

We drove through the gate and followed a fairly smooth track into the park. After a mile or so we came across the totally dry Amboseli lake. This now comprised white parched and cracked clay across which a clearly defined track led us to the far side to pick up the track as it continued eastwards. Henry delighted in showing us as we crossed this totally smooth surface, how he could drive at up to 30 mph without touching the steering wheel!

As we crossed this dry lake, we had a superb view of Kilimanjaro which looked enormous, just a few miles to the south of us by now. Its profile was of course in reverse to that we had seen from its south side, so that Mawenzi peak now stood on the left of the main flat-topped Kibo peak. The latter looked truly magnificent with its large white snow-cap, which almost dazzled us as it caught the morning sun's rays.

Almost immediately on the far side of the lake we saw our first big game. A couple of elephants were reaching high into a 'sausage' tree (*mwegea* in Swahili). This extraordinary tree is aptly named as its fruit is in the form of giant sausages which are found hanging all over the tree from spindly fibrous stems.

Peter M Wilson
Bwana Shamba

Each of these fruit weights about six or seven kilos, so that should anyone happened to be standing underneath one as it fell, they could easily be knocked out and/or have a severe headache for some days to come! The fruit is of no use to man nor beast, even the elephants ignore them. We positioned ourselves so that Kilimanjaro formed a beautiful backdrop for our photos and clicked away.

We then drove this way and that on the white clay ground, seeing many examples of big game, including a magnificent white rhino lying down, also more giraffes, ostriches and countless gazelles and zebra. The whole of this area was alive with 'elegant starlings', a truly magnificent bird closely related and also of similar size to the starling commonly found in Europe. These birds could be seen everywhere proudly strutting this way and that as if anxious to show off their magnificent plumage afire with beautiful iridescent colours of every hue.

We also had the first opportunity to examine our first baobab tree (*mbuyu* in Swahili) at close quarters. This huge, grotesque tree is found throughout the dry savannas pretty well throughout the entire continent. Its enormous trunk, which can have a girth of twenty to thirty feet, is useless for anything, even firewood. It looks for all the world as if it is growing upside down, its branches and boughs very much resembling a root system. It bears pod-shaped fruit, about the size of a small coconut. This contains a soft pith which is reputed to taste, though I never had the nerve to sample one, like sherbet. It is much favoured by elephants. There is a legend concerning these weird trees, and that is that when Satan saw what a beautiful job God had done in creating the world, he was so annoyed that when he thought God was not looking, he went around uprooting certain trees and replanted them upside down. These were, of course, the baobab trees.

When we had exhausted our film supplies, we returned home by the same route, except that we stopped off at Namanga to have a good meal at the hotel there. This time, of course, we could not claim costs as legitimate travelling expenses.

In driving along the dry murram roads, we generated long, dense clouds of choking dust, as was usual on murram roads throughout the country. This makes overtaking on such roads a decidedly hazardous manoeuvre.

Another location where it was easy to see big game close to Tengeru, was the Ngurdoto crater. This is an old volcanic crater, situated between mounts Kilimanjaro and Meru. It is deep, with a diameter of about one mile, and is surrounded by an almost complete circle of tree-covered ridge rising some 1,500 ft above the crater floor. Karl very kindly showed us the way up onto the rim of this ridge, from where the view was breathtaking. We were, up there, very much closer to Kilimanjaro than we had been before and we were staggered by the enormity and majesty of this great mountain. To the west we could see right into Meru's gaping eastern side and indeed the actual original volcanic cone right in its centre. Through the gap in Ngurdoto crater's ridge we could see clearly the Momella lakes. These lakes incidentally feature in two feature films, *Sammy Going South*, with Edward G. Robinson and *Hatari*, with John Wayne, both splendid films.

I should like to digress here for a moment, if I may, to tell you what I consider a very amusing incident which was experienced by a missionary friend of mine, Earl Martin.

He was on safari with his car one day not far from Arusha, when it broke down. He had not long been stranded at the side of the road, when an enormous American Limousine glided past, then stopped a little way down the road. A veritable giant of a man emerged from the limousine, strode across to Earl and, extending a friendly arm said, 'Hi! I'm John Wayne, the actor!' Without pausing for breath, my friend replied, 'Hi! I'm Earl Martin, the missionary!'

As we stood on the edge of Ngurdoto, not yet a National Park, which it is now, we looked down into the crater and saw a whole, large herd of elephants enter into a vast area of tall elephant grass. We were astonished to see this whole big herd simply vanish into this extremely tall grass without trace, right before our very eyes!

Other game we saw in the crater, was the odd giraffe and a small cluster of buffalo. Unfortunately we were a good deal too high up above them to be able to see them clearly, or photograph them to any purpose, although we nevertheless did take numerous photographs of the crater as a whole, including , of course, the game it contained.

When later we expressed disappointment to Karl, that we had been so far away from the game to see or photograph it properly, he at once suggested we should spend the night in a tree close by a water hole where we would see plenty of big game at ultra close quarters. We thought at first he was joking, but in fact,

Peter M Wilson
Bwana Shamba

he was perfectly serious. He promised us that should we wish to take him up on his offer we would be guaranteed to see plenty of big game easily close enough to study and photograph. Three of our number enthusiastically took up the challenge, including young 'Mac'. Therefore the following Saturday Karl took these crazy volunteers to the Ngurdoto crater where they did indeed spend the night in a tree!

Much as I would have loved to see such game at close quarters, I certainly did not fancy spending an uncomfortable night up a tree, though I do admit to being somewhat envious when they returned next day highly enthusiastic, even if somewhat sleepy, about their night in a tree. They described with great excitement and detail everything they had seen, including huge elephants, buffalo, giraffe etc, coming to drink at the waterhole, but a few feet away in succession one after the other.

Given the opportunity again though, I very much doubt I would wish to give up a comfortable night's sleep in favour of a sleepless one up a tree, whatever the rewards!

CHAPTER VII

My First Posting

It so happened that both Mike and I had to go initially to Dar es Salaam after our course was over to meet the staff at the Ministry's head office in the capital. So once again Mike was my travelling companion. We had to go by train from Moshi, just to the south of Kilimanjaro, to Korogwe a few miles west of the seaport of Tanga. Our journey was now by railway then bus, due south to Morogoro. From there we would travel by train to the capital. There was not then, as there is now, a railway connection between those lines.

We were fortunate enough to have a sleeper as far as Korogwe, and as we pulled out of Moshi station, we gazed in awe at the spectacular sunset on Kilimanjaro towering above our heads, its snow cap now pink as it caught the setting sun's rays.

After it had disappeared from view, we settled down to get some sleep before our middle of the night arrival in Korogwe.

As luck would have it, our sleeping car was gently shunted into an empty siding in Korogwe when we arrived there, so that when we peeped out of our window after being roused from our sleep by the sleeping car attendant, we found ours was the only railway vehicle in an otherwise deserted station. We quickly got dressed and emerged into the morning sunshine to be directed to the station frontage, where a dark maroon railway bus, a Mercedes, was awaiting its load for Morogoro.

Unfortunately, in playing squash in the roofless court at Tengeru some days earlier, I had hit a ball out through the open roof, and in looking for it, had jumped onto some scrap metal hidden in long grass. In so doing I had badly sprained my right ankle. I had bandaged it up as best I could for the journey, but it still throbbed unmercifully as I hobbled onto the bus, with its leather covered seats. We patiently awaited departure time. We watched in fascination as packages of all shapes and sizes, as well as bicycles and chickens, their only restraint being their legs tied together in bundles, were hoisted onto the roof of our bus. Eventually we set off along the dusty corrugated road to Morogoro. I winced as the vibrations caused by the undulations and corrugations in the road set my poor ankle throbbing with renewed vigour.

The scenery was much the same all the way to Morogoro, namely thick bush scrub, comprising densely packed thorn trees and acacias. Every so often, in a clearing alongside the road, we would see a village made up of traditional mud and wattle houses. Thin columns of smoke often rose lazily through the thatched roofs of some of these houses. Incidentally, we had learnt always to refer to them as houses, no matter how flimsy they appeared, as we would have caused great offence had we referred to them as 'huts'.

Occasionally we would catch sight of women pounding maize in a large egg-timer shaped wooden container, using a long, heavy wooden pestle. Invariably, the woman would have a baby strapped to her back with a colourful *kanga*. After what seemed an interminable journey, we at last reached our destination, changing onto a good tarmac road for just the last half mile or so of our journey. My ankle was delighted with the serenity of the smooth tarmac at last.

The bus deposited us outside the main railway station, where we found we had a long wait for our train to Dar. I longed to walk about the town to explore it, but my poor throbbing ankle had other ideas, so we had to be satisfied with a hobble round the area in the immediate vicinity of the station. To the south of the town, we could clearly see the Uluguru mountains which stretched out westwards. They looked surprisingly attractive and at first I could not understand why, until I realized what made them so attractive. Unlike mounts Meru and Kilimanjaro, whose main peaks were merely grey ash heaps interspersed with rocks, totally devoid of any vegetation, apart from a ring of rain forest round their bases, the Ulugurus were covered in rough scrub all over. Here and there, as well, bare patches of red soil were visible, as if giving them a touch of make-up.

At long last our train arrived, hauled by a hissing giant in the form of a massive Beyer Garratt steam locomotive. We had, once more, sleeper reservations on this train, so with the aid of the attendant found our allotted places, and settled down for the remainder of our *safari*.

Incidentally, there is a myth that a safari is specifically a journey connected with wild life, shooting it either with a camera or a rifle. Nothing could be further from the truth. *Safari* in Swahili means any sort of journey made by any means for any purpose.

As we approached Dar es Salaam early the following morning, we passed through mile after mile of coconut plantations, until eventually we entered the built-up area, initially for a while composed of traditional houses, many roofed over with rusting 4-gallon *debe* tins hammered out to form a flat sheet. In due course these traditional houses gave way to more sturdy buildings of all shapes and sizes built of concrete blocks and often roofed with red tiles.

Whenever we caught sight of a street, traffic seemed very sparse, and the majority of the pedestrians appeared to be Indians, including Sikhs, wearing their traditional white turbans. Many of the Africans we saw were wearing the typical Muslim *kanzu* robes topped with a white or red fez hat; many, mostly the women, carried the usual endless variety of objects on their heads, all with perfect poise. At last we were conscious of our railway line having multiplied into a complexity of tracks as we wound our way into the terminus station of Dar es Salaam.

We wasted no time in alighting with our few possessions, and I hobbled painfully along the busy platform. After hobbling only a short distance we were met by a European who introduced himself as Alistair Gunn. He was wearing what turned out to be the traditional civil service garb for Europeans, smart spotless white shorts and shirt, with white knee length stockings.

He explained we were being accommodated for a couple of nights in the hotel Metropole right in the centre of town. He took us there in one of the ubiquitous grey government Landrovers, helped us check in to our hotel, then drove us straight to the ministry's head office. On the way there we reached the seafront overlooking the exquisitely beautiful, tranquil harbour.

Dar es Salaam means Haven of Peace, and I could not help thinking what an apt name it is. The small somewhat scruffy beach was lined on the landward side by numerous coconut palms each growing at a different angle. A narrow channel separated the harbour from the open sea, and immediately inside this channel was a collection of yachts of all shapes and sizes, riding on their moorings outside the Dar es Salaam Yacht Club. Away on the far side at the entrance to a continuing inlet we could see the actual docks where three or four cargo ships lay tied up at the quays unloading and loading their cargoes.

Right on the water's edge on the northern side of this fine view, stood a large white church with a tall spire at one end. This turned out to be the Lutheran church. We followed the tarmac road which hugged the inlet into the harbour, liberally lined with countless coconut palms, and soon found ourselves in a courtyard surrounded by low grass thatched buildings. These were our ministry's head offices.

We emerged from Alistair's GT and followed him at a hobble – how I cursed my rotten luck to have had a badly sprained ankle at a time like this. We were then introduced to a number of Europeans, including the Director himself, Derek Bryceson, destined to be the last remaining European government minister.

Although the outside air was very hot and humid, so that I could constantly feel rivulets of sweat running down my back, I found the interior of the offices surprisingly cool, fanned as they were by overhead electric fans. Another person we were introduced to was Dougy Dye, who was, as was pointed out, vital for the ministry's existence, since it was he who looked after its purse strings, and would also approve or not, as the case might be, all our respective claim forms. He was a charming man and immediately made us feel at ease and glad to be in the same ministry as he.

Alistair then made us welcome in his own cosy office, and told us a little about our futures. It transpired that in Kilosa I was to be seconded to the EPCC, the Eastern Province Cotton Committee, a branch of the Lint and Seed Marketing Board. It seemed that my services were urgently required in this predominantly cotton growing district, to help improve cotton culture and generally improve production. This alarmed me considerably, as at that time, I had no idea whatever what a cotton plant looked like, let alone how best to grow the crop, never having had cause to see a plant anywhere on earth!

I would, I was told, also assist in the general running and administration of the district's agriculture programme, assisting and advising local farmers 'in the field'. Much of my time there would be spent 'on safari', sleeping out either in my tent, or in rest houses in the local villages.

To this end, I was suddenly presented with an official *Issue voucher* to sign upon receipt of a whole range of items for my exclusive use. I was somewhat alarmed and amused to see, listed in amongst such mundane items as an officer's tent complete with flysheet, and a safari bath/washbasin set, a folding camp chair and table, one long wheelbase Landrover No. GT 4723, which was to be mine for exclusive use on duty only, although it later transpired I was to be allowed to use it for one shopping trip into Kilosa per week.

I had earlier set my heart on requesting a government loan with which to purchase a Peugeot 403 station wagon, which seemed an ideal family car for local conditions and which were to be seen everywhere in large quantities. Alas, my superiors were adamant that I could not have a loan, as such a car was 'too extravagant' for my salary scale and grade. I was bitterly disappointed, but had to be content with a brand new long wheelbase Landrover. As things turned out, it could not have been a more ideal situation vehicle-wise.

In Kilosa itself I was to live in an exclusive EPCC house, which was then already vacant for my possession.

Then routine Government procedures were explained, and I was introduced to the civil servants' 'Bible', known as *General Orders*. This laid down all the tiresome procedures to be followed for just about every conceivable situation. I was then issued with a book of Local Purchase Orders to enable me to buy petrol for my Landrover, and all the magical numbers or 'Vote' numbers as the various account numbers were called, to which every expense should be allocated.

My Landrover duly fuelled up, and my safari camping equipment stowed abroad, I set off three days after my arrival in Dar, and drove up the smooth tarmac road to Morogoro. There I stopped at an hotel for lunch, preserving my receipt for a legitimate claim of travelling expenses.

I now had two choices of route to reach Kilosa. I could either strike north along the Korogwe road, then turn left to Kilosa, along murram roads, or I could take the dry weather short cut across the Kimamba plains striking due west.

I decided to try the latter, and found myself for the majority of the route following a rough track across *mbuga*, black cotton soil, which when dry was fine, but when wet one could easily sink in up to the axles, I had been made to understand. I was unfortunately able to experience this phenomenon from personal experience in due course.

I saw quite a bit of game as I crossed these plains, mostly impala and Thompsons gazelle, usually called *Tommies*.

A year or two later an Italian friend and colleague, Attilio

Peter M Wilson
Bwana Shamba

The Kilosa boma or government office block. Note the profuse growth of golden shower climber on the roof. The central section was the local magistrate's courtroom. My office was in the extreme left hand corner of the boma (out of sight here).

Peter M Wilson
'Mr Agriculture'

Zappa, was driving along this route in his Volkswagen Beetle one night, when he unfortunately hit a lion. His immediate reaction was to stop, being concerned whether or not he had hurt the poor animal.

He therefore got out of his car, and had walked about fifty yards from it when he heard a lion roar! He froze as he realized only then what a stupid thing he was doing, and wasted no time in getting back to his car! He told us it was quite half an hour later before he had stopped shaking sufficiently to be able to drive on!

After about an hour I reached the small town of Kimamba, which boasted a station on the railway passing through it. From there, it was only a short drive due west along a badly corrugated murram road to Kilosa itself. As I passed the township sign, I sighed with relief on reaching a tarmac road. I followed the signs to the *Boma*, parked the Landrover and climbed up a few steps leading up onto a veranda which ran in a U-shape in front of all the offices spaced around the building. It was a single storey building in white painted concrete blocks, over which a beautiful creeping *golden shower* shrub had established itself, covering much of the roof, especially the two corners, its beautiful orange blossoms hanging down below gutter level.

I followed the veranda until I came across a suite of offices right in the corner marked *Kilimo*. I introduced myself to a smart African clerk, Michael Kitambi, who in turn took me to a neighbouring office to introduce me to my supervisor, a Scot called David Jack. David would soon be leaving to return home, once he had handed over to me the current projects in the district, for continuity's sake. He showed me a square, spacious office right in the corner of the building, which was allocated to me to be my own office. He then took me to an office in the opposite corner to meet the European District Commissioner, Major John Piper.

David then offered to take me back to his house to tidy up, as he was kindly going to put me up at his home until I was ready to move in to my own EPCC house. He suggested I leave my Landrover where it was, and he took me there in his smart white Holden pick-up.

Like most houses I could see as we climbed the deep-red soil murram road up the hill above Kilosa, David's was a bungalow type house with a mosquito-gauzed veranda and a corrugated iron roof painted green. Most of the houses I could see with iron roofs had them painted either green or maroon/red.

David gave me some tea, or rather his houseboy did, then showed me his spare room where I was to sleep. He then explained a bit of what was going on in his district.

It transpired that my first task would be to plot and build a 25-mile road through virgin bush between the villages of Kisanga and Mfirisi. For this task I was to be given two hundred or so labourers plus one or two supervisors, none of whom could speak English, so David was relieved that I had been put through a Swahili course. Unfortunately, I did not have the same relief, as I was anything but confident that I could oversee a road construction in a language I barely knew!

The next morning I awoke early and decided to get a few clothes on before I ventured out to the bathroom. My single bed was sited in one corner of my small bedroom, and the chair upon which I had left my clothes was situated in the opposite corner. I had slept stark naked due to the heat, and I swung my legs out of bed to walk across to the chair.

As I sat back on my bed having retrieved a few clothes to don, I noticed with shock a squashed scorpion on my bedside mat. It

Peter M Wilson
Bwana Shamba

could only have attained that state by my treading on it doubtless with the ball of my heel, before it had had time to sting me! I considered myself very lucky indeed not to have been welcomed to Kilosa with a scorpion sting my first day there.

When I told David, he said, 'Oh yes, you need to be on the lookout for scorpions here! Take my advice and always first knock your shoes or slippers on the floor to dislodge any scorpion that might be lurking inside!'

As it happened, I fortunately never saw a scorpion in my house during my subsequent stay in Kilosa.

After breakfast, David took me up the hill to see my allotted house. It was nearly new, and built of concrete blocks, painted white. Unlike any of the other houses I had seen, it had a white asbestos roof – much cooler therefore than corrugated iron, I was pleased to note.

It had two bedrooms, but a third large square one was in the process of being added to its left hand end. The house was perched right on the edge of Kilosa hill, having therefore a fabulous view out towards the south-west. All the plain I could see was covered in sisal plantations. In the distance stood a flat topped mountain, Pala-ulanga. Immediately below the house, down a steep slope, I could see the main east-west railway line skirting the bank of a river, the Mkondoa.

Just as I turned away, I heard a train hooter as a steam hauled freight train hove into view, continuing alongside the river until, amidst much hooting, it disappeared round a corner to the left, heading for Kilosa station. Just before this final curve, a fairly large lattice ironwork bridge crossed the river, carrying the road I could see heading south west across the sisal planted plain.

Since there was another steep slope down to the left of the house, a terraced road had been carved out of the hillside to give access to a corrugated-iron roofed carport, complete with inspection pit.

My house was already furnished with standard government issue furniture, so David went through the inventory with me, then asked me to sign for it all, then the house was 'mine'. He suggested we return to the *boma* to allow me to bring my Landrover up and unpack my meagre belongings. Just as we were heading for his car, an African appeared from nowhere wielding some very dog-eared pieces of yellowing paper. He was a house-boy/cook seeking work, and the scruffy pieces of paper he wielded were his references of work from his previous employers.

I read through them, most of which seemed contradictory, but reading between the lines, Juma seemed as promising a young man I could hope to have around the place. I asked David's opinion, and as luck would have it he knew well one of the referees, so since he had a good reference from him, I decided to take Juma on. We then agreed his wages, with David advising what I should offer, and I then had my first ever employee.

As we returned down the hill, David pointed out to me that Kilosa had no electricity, and that therefore I would need paraffin lamps and a paraffin refrigerator. He took me into the town to show me where were the best shops, all owned and run by Indians. Almost all the shops had verandas on their frontages and upon many of these could be seen a young African boy, treadling furiously at a treadle sewing machine. David explained that some of these seamsters were experts at copying shirts and shorts. If I wanted more of either garment, I only had to leave them with an example of one, and they would recreate a similar garment in whatever materials I chose. I was advised to use a pale khaki twill called *Amerikani*, with which to have some shorts and shirts made. I followed his advice.

A week or so later, having left an example of a shirt and shorts of my size, I collected some very smart new shirts and shorts which fitted me perfectly.

I was introduced to Mr Patel, a charming man who ran a well stocked hardware shop and Dharamsi Stores the town grocers. Back at the *boma*, David showed me where I could draw some Tanganyika shillings; at that time the exchange rate was twenty shilling to the pound sterling. The country's coinage comprised 100 cents to the shilling. I was intrigued to see that the copper coins, of 10, 5 and 1 cent had a hole in the centre. This hole enabled the Africans, who had neither pockets nor purses, to thread either a piece of string, or a corner of their *kanzu*, through the holes to keep these coins safe. Oddly enough, neither the nickel shilling, nor the fifty cent coins had holes.

I then bought a large paraffin fridge, a Primus stove, a *debe* of paraffin, and a simple paraffin pump with which to extract the paraffin from the *debe*.

One of my important purchases that day was a water filter. It was necessary to boil and filter all drinking water. The filter comprised a sort of aluminium tower in two halves, one resting on the other. At the bottom of the top half of this tower was a sort of clay 'candle'. Boiled water was poured into the top half,

Peter M Wilson
Bwana Shamba

which was fitted with a lid. The water then seeped through this candle and into the bottom half of the tower, which was fitted with a tap. The boiled and filtered water was then generally stored in empty bottles, and kept in the fridge, to provide nice cool drinking water as required. I then bought a Petromax pressure lamp and some spare mantles for it, and a few candles.

My last port of call was the grocers, where I stocked up with all manner of tinned foods, and other edibles.

It was always the practice, especially with Indian traders, to haggle over prices, I think any Indian trader would have collapsed in a dead faint had any European agreed to pay the asking price for any goods sold! I had therefore to haggle over what prices I paid for all my purchases, and managed to save myself up to 20% of the cost as a result. It was more usual, however to pay the asking price for groceries, so although I did not haggle at Dharamsi Stores, of his own volition he did give me a good discount. As I made my way home, I was surprised to see a very large and ornate cinema overlooking the market square, complete with elephant statues on its front roof. Upon enquiry how an electricity free town could muster a cinema, I learnt that they had their own generator. I drove back up the hill and Juma helped me unpack and stow my groceries. I had been kindly lent one of each type of eating utensil, including a cup, saucer, plate, knife, fork etc., so I then sat down and sampled Juma's first afternoon tea which he brought me in great style.

I dragged an easy chair out onto the small veranda overlooking my superb view, and felt like a millionaire as I relaxed in such exquisite surroundings, complete with a servant to answer my every whim.

I gave Juma the sheets I had mercifully brought with me, and left him to prepare a bed for me.

Near the front door just outside the house was situated a ubiquitous Tanganyika boiler. This comprised a 44-gallon oil drum set in a concrete tower complete with chimney, beneath which was located a wood-burning fireplace. A veritable array of plumbing led cold water in and hot water out of this contraption and into the house. Juma had already established a good fire in this boiler, so I already had piping hot water on tap. Since there was no risk of freezing, it was perfectly sensible to have bare water pipes out of doors.

After my afternoon tea, I roamed around my estate, comprising a very rough 'lawn' set in shallow terraces because of the slope. There were numerous bushes of *frangipane* and *bougain-villaea*, some of which had grown over the servants' quarters situated above my house's kitchen area. One or two rather weedy looking pawpaw trees completed the contents of my garden.

It was plain I would need to employ a garden boy to tidy up my estate. David Jack also told me I should also employ a safari boy/cook as I would be doing a lot of safari around the district.

As it happened, although the road I was to build was urgently needed, my first duties in Kilosa district were totally non-related to agriculture.

Some local elections were coming up, for which my assistance was urgently required by the District Commissioner, as an officer in charge of polling stations scattered around the northern end of the district.

As far as the supervision of the actual voters and voting process were concerned, there was little difference in the system to that found in Britain. Where the main difference arose, however, since most of the voters were illiterate, was in the manner of nominating candidates. Since nobody would have been able to read names, candidates had, therefore, to choose a symbol with which to be represented. These symbols were taken from common animals, such as a lion, a giraffe, or an elephant. Since, in everybody's mind, by far the most successful animal from the list was the lion, it turned out that regardless of whom it represented, it was always the lion that won the election!

Once the penny dropped with regard to animal symbols, everyday objects were put up instead of animals. The objects chosen included a *jembe* or hoe, a *panga* or machete, a spade and an axe. Once more, however, amongst the objects selected, there was no doubt which was the most useful, so it was always the *jembe* which won the election!

Although the problem was appreciated, by the time the election was over, no satisfactory alternative had been found, so that it was all the shrewd candidates quick enough to chose either the lion or the *jembe* as their symbol who had won. It was an interesting experience from which many lessons could be learnt!

Peter M Wilson
Bwana Shamba

CHAPTER VIII

Kilosa District

My first agricultural working days in Kilosa were spent with David, as he took me round every corner of the district in my Landrover GT.

Before we left, however, I sent a formal letter to my head office in Dar es Salaam, asking for Dorothy and my daughters to join me in Kilosa, sending the letter u.f.s. the regional agriculture officer, as well as the Agriculture Officer, Kilosa, who, of course, was David Jack. The u.f.s., which stood for "under flying seal", system was an antiquated though nevertheless very efficient system of sending letters from 'lowlies' such as myself, through senior officers on its way to the addressee, enabling them to add their comments and countersign the letter as a means of showing they knew its contents and therefore what was going on. All replies had to go through the reverse procedure.

We took our safari camp beds and other camping equipment, plus a good supply of food. We were going to be staying in either government or EPCC rest houses which had been built in all the key villages throughout the district. All the rest houses were of similar pattern and comprised two large bare, square rooms, each of which had a door giving out onto a veranda of similar proportions. Nearby stood a separate kitchen and cook's quarters. A little distance away in the opposite direction generally, stood the *choo* or toilet, pronounced 'cho'. This was of the 'Asian' variety and comprised a concrete-block square building, supplied with a thick concrete floor, in the centre of which was a six–inch square hole, over which it was necessary to squat to perform what was necessary. Beneath this structure was a deep well-like pit, more often than not teeming with large cockroaches.

We also took with us David's safari boy/cook to prepare all our meals for us. Kilosa district measures one hundred miles

Peter M Wilson
'Mr Agriculture'

from north to south, and fifty miles from east to west, Kilosa township itself being situated more or less right in the middle of its district.

Throughout the district were scattered the agriculture department's African 'agriculture instructors', who were stationed one to each of the district's key villages. They were housed in government or EPCC-built concrete-block houses, and issued with a khaki uniform comprising shorts and bush jacket, no hat being issued. Each wore either a brass DA (Department of Agriculture) monogram, or EPCC, as appropriate, on his tunic lapel.

They were our local representatives and as such were to relay our latest policies and procedures to the farmers in their village, as well as to offer advice as required in agricultural matters, reporting back to us in the event of any specific problems they encountered in the course of their duties. On the whole, they proved to be all most pleasant and reliable, performing their duties ably and cheerfully.

With regard to the agriculture in the district, by far the most obvious cash crop was sisal, exclusively grown by Europeans (mostly Greeks) on estates of several hundred acres. Only a year or two previously, sisal fibre had commanded a price of £200 per ton, so that these estate owners had expanded their sisal fields to be able to produce the optimum possible at that time. But with the advent of synthetic fibres, the bottom had by then dropped right out of the market, so that only a few estates now produced minimal quantities of fibre, it being barely economic to do so.

Most estates had their own narrow gauge railway, made up of portable lengths of track, which could be taken up and relaid throughout the estate as required to transport the heavy, bulky leaves to the central decorticating plant, where the green fleshy part of the leaves was combed out, leaving only the pure fibre, which was then washed, dried and sun-bleached before being hessian-baled ready for export. The stench from the rotting sisal flesh on all these sisal estates took much getting used to, as it permeated round every corner of each estate.

It was reputed that many such an estate had changed hands over a gambling table, the Greeks reputedly being compulsive gamblers. It was also alleged that many a wife also changed ownership in like manner.

Amongst African farmers, undoubtedly the main cash crop in the district was cotton, mostly grown in hand-cultivated fields of one or two acres.

Peter M Wilson
Bwana Shamba

The next most common crop was cereals, of which maize had the greatest acreage, this being, for most, the staple diet. It was generally consumed in the form of *ugali*, a stodgy form of dough. The other cereals encountered were sorghum, finger millet, and in the lowland swamp areas, rice. Most of the latter three cereals were consumed by being poured down throats in the form of *pombe*, the locally brewed African beer. Rice, in particular, I was assured, made a particularly potent drink, akin I was told to whisky, though I never personally sampled it.

Around many homesteads grew a small quantity of cassava, as well as a few plants of castor oil. This produces quite a large and attractive bush which profusely bears pods very similar to small conkers, complete with many blunt spines on the outer shell. Inside these pods are to be found at least one large richly oil-bearing seed, resembling very much a large, engorged cattle tick. I never did discover why these plants were to be found in so many homesteads. I suspect they were purely for ornamental purposes, I never did find anyone growing them commercially. The last time I saw these plants growing, curiously enough, and very healthily indeed at that, was in the front garden of the royal palace right in the centre of Brussels, of all places.

The main east-west railway line bisects Kilosa district, and four stations are to be found in this length, Kimamba to the east, then Kilosa, just east of centre, Munisagara in the centre, and Kidete to the west. The latter was totally devoid of any buildings or even a passing loop or sidings, it was merely an official stopping place for passenger trains. No station in the country, other than Dar es Salaam, had any platforms, since all passengers coaches were fitted with adequate steps to allow relatively easy boarding and egress at ground level. The whole east African system was to metre-gauge track, laid on steel sleepers to combat termite damage. All lines were single track, each principal station having passing loops to enable opposing trains to pass.

Two principal rivers are found in the district, the Mkondoa which passes close to Kilosa itself, and the Great Ruaha, which flows from west to east in the southern end of the district.

A good murram road (if any murram road can be good!) runs from north to south passing through Kilosa itself. The rest of the district is supplied with a liberal network of secondary murram roads. For the greater part, the district is basically flat plains, but in the north are found the Rubeho mountains, mostly

Peter M Wilson
'Mr Agriculture'

devoid of any forest. They rise to some five thousand feet above sea level. In the south are found the Usagara mountains, these rising to only two or three thousand feet.

The vast majority of farmers in the district were very receptive to new ideas and farming practices, but a small minority were decidedly not so. David gave me an example of their rare cussedness.

Whilst famine is rare in Tanzania, it is not unknown. The powers-that-be in Dar, therefore, decreed that every farmer in the country should grow a small area of cassava. Now cassava, from which, incidentally, tapioca is derived, suffers from hardly any pests or diseases, and is quite drought resistant. Despite the fact that it has virtually no nutritional value, it is therefore eminently suitable as a famine crop, as it is nevertheless very useful for filling empty tummies.

All instructors in Kilosa district were therefore sent a supply of the cassava woody stem cuttings for distribution around the district. Whilst many farmers readily accepted these and planted them out as shown, others were decidedly contrary.

The evening after these cuttings had been planted out by the instructor, these obstinate farmers uprooted them all and deliberately replanted them badly, doubtless hoping they would die off as a result. When they were seen, nevertheless, to be still thriving, these wayward farmers uprooted them again and this time replanted them upside down. But when, despite this abuse, they still thrived, the farmers accepted defeat and let them grow in peace.

David decided to take me round the northern half of the district first, so we struck out of town on what turned out to be a diabolically corrugated murram road. Within a couple of miles, we passed the Ilonga agriculture research station, to which Alistair Macdonald, from 'my' Swahili course, had been posted as an agronomist. We did not actually enter the station on this occasion as David was anxious to press on with our safari.

We continued northwards, eventually coming to the next village on this main road, Msowero. We went straight to the rest house which happened to be situated close to a river which was blood red, due to all the red soil it carried, as a result of bad erosion caused by recent heavy rains. We needed more drinking water so we set about boiling and filtering water from this river. It took ages to accumulate a reasonable amount, as, due to the high content of silt in the water, the filter candle

Peter M Wilson
Bwana Shamba

My Landrover stuck
up to its axles in
mbuga mud.

kept clogging up, necessitating our having to scrub it clean of
silt at frequent intervals. David then took me round the village
to meet the local *Mkuu*, our instructor, Suleiman Sapira, and a
number of the local notable farmers, *wakulima stadi.*

Having done what we had set out to achieve in Msowero, we
continued northwards the next morning, heading for the village
of Gairo. We did not linger here, it being in a predominantly
livestock area. Instead we took another small road, and headed
more or less due south up into the Rubeho mountains, the road
meandering back and forth as we gained altitude.

After about a half hour's drive up into these smooth tree-less
mountains at this point, we stopped to admire the vast panorama
we suddenly came across over to the north. This was the vast
Kongwa plain, where the infamous ground-nut scheme *should*
have been. We were now looking into the Mpwapwa district
which neighbours Kilosa district on its western side. As far as
we could see, a vast level plain unfolded itself way down below
us, reaching out of sight.

This is the sad tale as it was told me concerning this shameful
saga, and its disastrous failure.

First, it might be helpful to describe the unique botanical
features of the groundnut plant. It belongs to the Leguminosae
family, that is the pea and bean family. Once its small yellow
flowers have been pollinated/fertilized, the flower stems elong-
ate. This results in the flowers burying themselves in the soil
where they then develop their familiar seed pods, hence the name

Peter M Wilson
'Mr Agriculture'

*ground*nuts, which are in fact the probably familiar 'monkey-nuts' pods so-called because they were frequently sold in Britain in this form in zoos with which to feed monkeys. Due to this strange phenomenon of burying themselves in the ground, they are best suited to sandy soils. Kongwa plain is predominantly sandy, so in that respect at least, the Kongwa plain was well suited to the crop.

When the idea of using the Kongwa plain for a groundnut scheme was first mooted, it was learnt that a certain European farmer who had a vegetable small-holding farm way up in the mountains kept rainfall records. Despite the fact that he was several miles away, as well as being way up in the mountains, well away from the plain, he was asked if he would kindly supply his rainfall figures.

At this point, it is alleged, seeing an ideal European market for his vegetables almost on his doorstep, should the scheme go ahead, he allegedly 'cooked' the figures to make them more attractive.

As far is known, I was told, not one trial plot of groundnuts was ever planted out to test the suitability of the area before the scheme was launched.

Thus, Mr Strachey and his Whitehall advisers, it was alleged, decreed that a groundnut scheme should be established on the Kongwa plain. To this end, a completely new town, Kongwa, was built on the plain, comprising numerous grade 'A' houses, a school, hospital and even an airport. A branch railway line was also built to serve the new town which was built around some good tarmac roads.

Once this work was completed to house the scheme's staff, bulldozers and other heavy plant were brought in with which to cultivate a vast acreage of the plain, preparatory to planting out the actual groundnut seed.

In due course, the vast area was all planted out with groundnuts, and everybody sat back to await the onset of the vital rains.

They waited and waited, to no avail.

'Oh well!' they eventually said, 'we've hit a bad year. The rains have failed! Never mind, we'll try again next year!' So the whole process was repeated the following year with identical results, and again the following year. Eventually, after several failed crops and not so much as a single groundnut having been harvested, the penny finally floated gently to the ground that

Peter M Wilson
Bwana Shamba

the Kongwa plain was not after all, suited to groundnut production.

Kongwa town is now a ghost town, its brand new tarmac roads liberally covered with sand drifts blown in off the surrounding plain.

After gazing for a few moments at the vast plain spread out below us, we continued on our way up into the mountains. After another few minutes, we entered an area where parts of the mountains were covered with indigenous forest. A further half hour's drive brought us into a sort of courtyard, at the top end of which stood a long, low bungalow dwelling.

No sooner had we pulled up near this dwelling, than a pleasant genial European introduced himself. He introduced himself as John Bond (yes, I did say *John* Bond), the forester responsible for the indigenous forest in the Rubeho mountains. He kindly invited us into his house for a cup of tea. No sooner had David told him of our purpose in visiting him, than John immediately invited us to stay in his house for a couple of nights. We naturally accepted, so that we found ourselves being generously given dinner bed and breakfast for those two days.

John Bond's *choo* is worthy of mention. It stood about fifty yards from the house. It was, in fact, quite famous, a governor of Tanganyika having once used it and commented much upon it in a report he published at the time.

It comprised a wooden hut or shed about eight feet square, glazed on one side by an enormous window facing a wide swathe of cleared forest as a 'fire break'. Right in the middle of this shed, stood the 'throne'. I use the word throne advisedly, for that was exactly what it resembled. It stood on a plinth so that anyone seated upon it had an uninterrupted view down this wide clearing, which would enable the person upon the throne a clear sighting of any wild life that might venture across the clearing. There was also a considerable library in this *choo*, but I could not envisage anyone wishing to while away their time on the throne with their nose in a book, lest they miss sighting any wild life which might venture across.

We spent much time chatting with John and catching up on all the local *habari* (news and gossip) of the area, which was very beneficial for us to know, particularly if appertaining to agricultural matters.

Having left John and showered him with our profuse thanks

for his generous hospitality, we made our way back down to Gairo, and from here, we headed more or less due east to reach a CMS mission hospital at Berega. Here we met a charming doctor, Juliet Backhouse. She made us most welcome in her rooms and over tea and biscuits, we again discussed all the local *habari*.

David then took me to meet the local *jumbe* and a few of the *wakulima stadi*. Then we set off southbound to return to Kilosa more or less the way we had come northwards.

Back in our respective offices, we spent a couple of days in Kilosa catching up on our paperwork, then we set off again, this time striking southwards.

We followed the murram road I could see heading south, from my house. It, too, turned out to be abominably corrugated. For the first few miles we passed through acre after acre of sisal plantations, these all being Greek owned. Just over half an hour later, we reached the large village of Ulaya. Oddly enough, Ulaya is the Swahili word for Europe, but I never did discover any connection between the two.

Prominent in the village was the *Mkuu's baraza*, meeting room/courthouse. It was a pleasant concrete building comprising a large concrete floored hall, with large openings in the side walls instead of windows. It stood right in the apex of a Y-shaped crossroads. Further back from this junction, but still situated between the two roads, stood a mountain of sizeable proportions, Pala-ulanga, which I could clearly see from my house in Kilosa.

David bade me drive up the road to the left, and after a climb up a short gradual hill, we came to Ulaya's rest house, where I was destined to stay many a night in the future. No sooner had we stopped there, than the local *Mkuu* turned up with the local instructor, Seif Rukemo.

They welcomed us to Ulaya, then Seif and David led us on a walking tour of the village to meet in particular the *wakulima stadi*. Amongst these were two notable characters, Ismael Chande and Shomari Mjomba. I was to see a great deal of these two wonderful farmers in the future, and Ismael in particular who was to become a very close friend. He had a wonderful sense of humour and was a very charismatic person. I grew to love him dearly in the course of my many safaris to Ulaya in the future. Both these farmers turned out to be as keen as mustard to learn and try out for themselves every bit of advice that was put to them.

The next morning, David took me up the right hand road from the *baraza* junction. This road, though murram, was exceptionally smooth, albeit somewhat circuitous. It was, as it happened, the old Morogoro-Iringa road, now replaced by a fast murram road across the southern end of the district.

After a few minutes driving down this road, we saw a small river following the road on our right. After a short distance we then noticed a neatly tended *Robusta* coffee plantation on the far bank. Five minutes later, we came across a most precarious looking bridge. It comprised two sturdy tree trunks spanning the actual river, supported at each end by a concrete pier.

Resting across these two tree trunks were numerous giant bamboo poles creating its deck. A crude sign nearby informed us that this was Juani coffee estate.

David bade me cross this flimsy looking bridge. At first I thought he was joking, but he was perfectly serious, assuring me the bridge was easily capable of supporting the weight of my Landrover.

I therefore gingerly drove onto the bridge. The bamboo poles creaked and clacked abominably as I drove slowly across, but I was never in any doubt, once on the actual bridge, about its ability to withstand our weight. Then I was safely across. I followed the dirt track round a sharp corner to the right, and almost immediately came across a well-built bungalow dwelling. No sooner had I stopped outside it, than a European appeared, smiling broadly, exposing several gold teeth as he did so. He introduced himself as Bjorn Graae, the Danish owner of Juani estate. He was soon followed by his tall, good-looking, also-smiling wife, Daphne, a Swiss-born lady. They showed us into their house for tea and biscuits, during which time Bjorn told us how he came to settle in Madizini, the village in which we now found ourselves. Our tea finished, he invited us to come on a brief tour of his coffee plantation and to see the processing 'factory' he himself had built. We eagerly followed him as he led us out to his factory.

Now the coffee bush grows to a height of between six and seven feet. Its fruit, which is borne in clusters at each leaf node, is approximately the size of a rose hip. To begin with they are green in colour. They develop from small white flowers which grow in a cluster round each leaf node all the way up the stems of the bush. Bjorn grew the *Robusta* type of coffee, which is well suited to lowland farming, and which mostly goes into producing

The somewhat precarious looking bamboo bridge leading onto the Juani estate.

instant coffees. The other, better type of coffee is called *Arabica* and is chiefly grown at higher altitudes, such as on the lower slopes of Kilimanjaro and Meru within Tanzania.

As the coffee fruit mature, they eventually turn pink, then red, at which stage they are generally called 'cherries'. Inside each cherry are found two of the familiar coffee 'beans' lying flat side to flat side. At this stage they are a pale ochre in colour and thickly coated with a transparent slime. Their familiar

Author and his wife with Daphne and Bjorn Graae (on left).

Peter M Wilson
Bwana Shamba

chocolate colour only comes later after being roasted, usually within the importing country.

The first process for the harvested cherries is to pass them through a sort of rotary crusher, which forces the two beans out of their skin, the latter being discarded. The beans are then collected in a heap within a concrete trough, where they are left for approximately 48 hours to ferment off their slime coating.

This operation completed, the beans are then washed thoroughly in copious quantities of clean water while they are being swept along by this water in a series of concrete troughs which erode the last vestiges of the slime. The beans are then collected in a wire mesh tray where they are left to drain off, dry, then sun bleach to a pale ochre colour. At this stage they rustle loudly when disturbed, at which stage they can be bagged up, ready for sale and export.

Bjorn now showed us the neat concrete troughs and fermenting containers in which he would process his harvested coffee beans. Before we returned to the house, he insisted on processing a few beans for us to demonstrate how it all worked.

After further tea in their house, Bjorn disappeared for a moment, returning shortly with two enormous pineapples for us both. When I eventually ate mine, it was decidedly the most succulent, sweet and delicious pineapple I had ever tasted, or indeed since. It transpired that Bjorn grew a half-acre plot of these, mostly for home consumption. After extracting a promise from us to be sure to call in again whenever we passed in the area, we returned once more to Ulaya rest house.

After another night there, David took me the next day to Kisanga to show me where a start was to be made on the road I was to build. To reach there, we had to retrace our steps from the previous day, passing through Madizini and the Graae's coffee estate. The road continued to be the smoothest murram or dirt road I had yet encountered in Tanzania, as it wound its way and that up the Kisanga valley.

We reached the village of Kisanga at the head of the valley where the old Iringa road had been truncated. We could clearly see the course of the old road zig-zagging its tortuous way up the Usagara mountains as it headed for Malolo in the next valley beyond the mountains.

David directed me up a small road to the left in the village which wound its spiral way up a small hill. At the very apex of this hill, the Kisanga rest house had been built. The view from the top of this hill was exquisite. We could admire the beauty of the Kisanga valley up which we had just driven. In the opposite direction we could clearly see the old road's zig-zagging course.

The last task David wished to do while we were at Kisanga was to show me the starting point of the road I was to build. He took me through the village, then turned left to follow an old road, still in reasonable condition, for about half a mile. We then came to a river which was known to have crocodiles resident within its waters. The presence of this small river unfortunately meant that I would only be able to reach the site workings on foot as there was no way of crossing the river with my GT until a bridge was completed. As Mfirisi, the ultimate destination of this road was 25 miles away from here, I could see I was in for a lot of walking before the road was finished. Having completed our business in Kisanga, David wanted to press on to the next objective which was Malolo and its valley. Had we been able to follow the old Iringa road, it would have been a simple journey, since the village of Malolo lay at the other end of the now defunct mountain pass.

So instead we had to retrace our way all the way back to Ulaya, and, taking the left fork at the *baraza*, follow the badly corrugated road south to the village of Mikumi, a small village situated right on the crossroads between our road south and the new, busy murram Morogoro-Iringa road, along which a succession of lorries plied in both directions, creating an almost constant thick cloud of dust as they sped through. Consequently everything; houses, trees, and other vegetation throughout the village was cloaked in a thick layer of dust.

Dominant to the scene as we descended the slight hill towards the Mikumi cross-roads, was a weird collection of leafless palm tree trunks. They were completely devoid of branches, and their trunks stood erect and straight apart from a slight bulge towards the top. I found out later that they were the dead trunks of a palm tree, called *Mkoche* in Swahili, being *hyphaene coriacea* or dwarf palms, though from where I stood there did not seem to be anything dwarfish about them.

David introduced me to the Mikumi instructor, a charming young man called Yonah Michael. Yonah then explained these mysterious palm trunks. It transpired that the sap from these palms makes a very tasty and potent form of *pombe*. To bleed the palms of their sap, the growing point at the very apex has to be cut off, along with all the leaves. The sap is then collected in a container strapped to the top. Unfortunately, this treatment kills off the palm, hence the forest of dead palm trunks. Unfortunately, Yonah went on to say, it was not only the palm tree that died as a result of this operation, but several of the inhabitants of Mikumi had also died resulting from this treatment.

It seemed that, having got well and truly intoxicated from this *pombe*, more than one drinker had got it into his head to climb the smooth trunk in order to collect some more of this sap. A state of intoxication is not the ideal state in which to perform such a daring feat, especially when it comes to negotiating the inverted part of the bulge near the top, at which point more than one climber had fallen to his death.

We continued along our way to Malolo. We followed the new Iringa road, which after a few miles followed the Great Ruaha valley, climbing, in due course, quite high up on the northern side of the attractive valley. Then the road dropped right down to just above river level which it followed for a few miles until we came to a substantial steel and concrete bridge taking the road across the river.

Just at this point, I noticed the fuel gauge on my Landrover was alarmingly low. When I pointed this out to David, he merely pointed to a filling station which lay a hundred or two yards up a track to our right, off the main road. I turned up this road, just before the bridge, which happened to be another fragment of the old Iringa road, stemming from Ulaya.

I am being somewhat generous in calling our objective a 'filling station', as all it was, was a corrugated iron shack in front of which was a collection of 44 gallon oil drums full of petrol. A hand operated pump, such as used to be common on petrol pumps in Britain before the advent of electric pumps, was used to pump the petrol gallon by slow gallon into the thirsty tank of my Landrover until at last it was full. I gave the attendant one of my purchase vouchers, which did not please him at all. But neither David nor I had sufficient cash to pay the total due for the petrol, and with the petrol now safely in my tank, it was Hobson's choice for the hapless attendant who had no alternative but to accept the purchase voucher.

We then continued along this sandy track towards Malolo. As we had done on the main Iringa road, we kept disturbing troop after troop of both baboons and vervet monkeys which ran in panic across the road ahead of us. I noticed that within each troop, there appeared to be a high proportion of mothers carrying their young, which clung for dear life to their mothers' bellies as they scampered across the road. The vervet monkeys looked like and acted in exactly the same way as the baboons, except that they were only a fraction of the size. We also disturbed many a guinea fowl, causing them to hasten out of our way, half running, half panic flying, uttering their strange 'clicking' call.

The bush at this point was much more open than I had seen it anywhere else up till there, and there were wide empty spaces between the scattered umbrella thorns. About half an hour later, we reached the small village of Malolo, with its scattered mud and wattle houses.

An EPCC rest house was being built here, and David had hoped that it would be sufficiently completed for us to be able to stay in, but when we spoke to the *Mkuu*, it transpired that although the walls and veranda were all finished, it had yet to have its roof added.

We therefore held a 'council of war' to discuss the option of sleeping in a roofless building. As it was a cloudless evening and there seemed no prospect of rain, we decided to settle in it despite the absence of the roof.

As it happened, I thoroughly enjoyed sleeping under the brilliant starlit sky, punctuated as it was, by surprisingly frequent and brilliant shooting stars. As I fell asleep, I was conscious of an almost constant flashing of a violent electrical storm way over on one horizon. The storm was totally devoid of thunder and not a trace of sound came from this storm. Next morning, David told me that such storms were quite usual in heralding the approach of the rainy season.

The following morning the local instructor lead us on a walking tour of the village, introducing us as usual to the *wakulima stadi.*

Almost without exception, they all had the same complaint. It seemed that both monkeys and baboons which abounded in the area were a major pest. These serious pests persisted in targeting the maize fields. Had they helped themselves to just the odd maize cob and completely consumed it, then that would not have been too much of a problem.

But unfortunately, this was not their style. Instead, these vandals persisted in going down the rows of maize, row by row, tearing off the cob from one maize plant, taking just one bite out of it, then discarding it disdainfully, before moving on to

Peter M Wilson
Bwana Shamba

the next plant down the row and repeating the same procedure all the way down each row. Clearly, maize being their staple diet, this was totally unacceptable to the poor farmers of Malolo. We promised to look into the problem and see if we could come up with a practical solution to the problem.

The Malolo valley is a real sun trap, and even in the shade of trees, it was by far the hottest temperatures I had experienced since arriving in the country. We were both desperately thirsty, so bade our farewells to the instructor and *Mkuu*, then went back to the rest house, where, after a long, refreshing soft drink, we packed our belongings and retraced our steps to Kilosa the way we had come.

We did make one stop on our way back, and that was at Mfirisi, situated about 5 or 6 miles north of Mikumi on the Kilosa road. There David showed me the eastern extremity of my road, which unfortunately, like Kisanga, required a bridge to cross a small river. The only difference with this river being that there were no known crocodiles in it.

Back in Kilosa we spent a day clearing up our paper work, then David took me out to Ilonga to introduce me to the staff there.

The senior staff were almost exclusively European. I met the chief research officer there, 'Van' Van Rensburg, a thoroughly pleasant and cheerful South African. I also met the agronomy team who were busy working on the latest and improved cotton variety, which was dubbed 'Ilonga 58'.

Most of the Ilonga staff with some wives.

Peter M Wilson
'Mr Agriculture'

Back in Kilosa I spent several days in the office reading through relevant files and generally getting myself familiar with all the office routine and so on, then came the time that David Jack had to leave on terminal leave.

I as a mere Field Officer, was not senior enough to take charge of a district, traditionally a post requiring an Agriculture Officer, most of whom were graduates. Accordingly, a wonderfully friendly Tanganyikan African turned up in Kilosa to take over. He was Carmichael Mpupua, a graduate from Kampala's Makerere university in Uganda. I therefore had to repeat the whole Kilosa Cook's tour once again, but this time, myself as guide. Soon after his arrival, Carmichael got married in a local catholic mission, and kindly inviting me to his wedding.

As things turned out, Carmichael did not stay for more than a year or so in Kilosa. His place was eventually taken by Dickie Brown, a veritable giant of a man, who towered at about six foot four inches or so. He came down on transfer from Mwanza district, close to Lake Victoria. Once he was settled in, I again had to tour the district to show him round.

By the time I had completed these three Cook's tours, I was pretty well conversant with the whole of Kilosa district and its inhabitants. I certainly grew to love and appreciate, not only the district itself, but also and especially its inhabitants, who were all so friendly and cheerful.

CHAPTER IX

Wadudu – Insects and Creepy-Crawlies

W hilst living and working in Africa I developed a deep fascination for African entomology.

Many people associate life in Africa with having to contend with numerous insects and other nasty creepy-crawlies.

Certainly it is true that there is a profusion of insects in Africa and I could write a whole book on just insects in Africa. Yet despite the undeniable profusion of insects on that continent, it is strange to relate that if ever we had a picnic outside in the garden, we never experienced any insect there to compare with the menace of an English wasp. Certainly we had a few flies and in the evenings things such as midges and mosquitoes, but no insect ever drove us running into the house or frantically swotting with a newspaper such as do wasps in England.

Many insects have an incredible fascination of their own, such as the *Praying Mantis* or *Mantid*, whose female proceeds to devour its copulating mate whilst in the very act of mating, starting with its head and working towards its tail. I shall restrict the bulk of this chapter to my personal experiences and observations concerning *wadudu.*

Many species of insect in Africa live and feed in extremely large colonies, and undoubtedly the most notorious species of this kind is the *Driver ant*, locally almost affectionately called *the Safari ant*. These foraging ants live and work in massive colonies bigger than one can imagine. These colonies comprise very small worker ants which form the greater part of the colony's inhabitants, and also the soldiers which have massive outsized heads with equally massive outsized calliper jaws. Incidentally, the Masai tribesmen have discovered a very useful and ingenious use for these soldier ant heads. They use them as sutures to help heal wounds. They achieve this by getting the soldier ant to bite each side of the cut or wound, then simply snap its head off! Bingo! There they have a perfect suture to keep the wound closed until it heals.

These ants are truly fascinating to watch in action. The use of the term *Safari ant* is totally appropriate when one observes their method of mass transit. Always being on the move, they quickly build up a complete network of roads' guarded on each side by soldier ants to keep the traffic flowing without outside interference. I have even seen them create roundabouts or *kipu-lefti* on some sections of their extensive road network. They also show their skill as bridge engineers, and can span a small stream or watercourse by creating a living bridge of ants, their soldiers forming the main supporting arches, whilst the small workers swarm across the bridge.

If one is unfortunate enough to stand in the midst of such a colony unawares, these creatures deftly and stealthily swarm all over you without creating any awareness whatsoever of their presence. Then, seemingly at the given command 'Bite!'They all bite in unison. The effect of such an attack can produce some spectacularly amusing entertainment, providing, of course, that you yourself are not the victim! For it is not an uncommon sight when out in rural Tanzania to see a person suddenly start to scratch frantically all over the body, then after a short period of such an activity, the unfortunate victim is generally observed to undress in spectacular record time totally oblivious of any onlookers, in their frantic efforts to rid themselves of their unwelcome immigrants!

If ever such a colony invades a home, which we did experience once or twice in our own home, they bring good news and bad. The good news is that they certainly clean up the house and rid it of anything organic, such as bat excreta in the loft and even any dead bats which might be lurking up there, thus ridding the loft of all those nasty fusty smells which bats create. They will also get rid of any *sisimisi* (tiny 'sugar' ants often found in the kitchen) or any other infestation one might have in the house, such as cockroaches. Trouble is, that they will also devour anything else organic they can find. I once had half a large bathroom sponge almost entirely eaten during one night.

Stories were rife of human babies being completely eaten overnight leaving only the skeleton, but I strongly suspect these were pure fable aided by a strong imagination rather than fact,

Peter M Wilson
Bwana Shamba

and I certainly never had conclusive proof or evidence of this presumably far fetched claim.

We were once rudely disturbed in the middle of the night. Vanessa was screaming her head off. When Dorothy and I rushed into her bedroom fearful as to what we would find. We found little Vanessa standing stark naked and covered in *Safari ants*. She had got out of bed to use her potty only to be instantly invaded by these ants, unaware of their presence all over the floor. Mercifully, their bite causes no stings or inflammation of any sort, so that no sooner had we brushed them all off, than Vanessa quietened down and was able to resume her sleep, the ants mercifully being apparently unable to negotiate the casters to climb onto the bed.

One other story I heard from several sources concerning these ants and which does appear to be possibly true, and that was that Safari ants are the only creature in Africa, apart from man, capable of killing an elephant. This they achieve, the story explains, by getting into the elephant's trunk then biting it inside. This irritates the unfortunate elephant so much that it bangs its trunk hard against some tree in an attempt to dislodge the ants. This action makes the poor elephant's trunk so sore and tender that it can't use it to feed with and thus starves to death.

There is another species of ant which, however, does bite and leave an extremely painful sting. These were commonly called '*Boiling water ants*' for the very simple reason that when disturbed, they scatter in all directions and emit a loud sort of hissing sound just like that of boiling water. If one of these large black ants measuring up to about one and a half centimetres in length wants to bite, it bends itself double so as to inject a dose of concentrated formalin into the bite, resulting in an extremely painful burning sensation. These ants travel in a dense column of up to just over a meter in length as they make their way to the nearest termite colony, which they invade and take 'prisoners'. A minute or two after being seen heading for the termite colony, they are generally to be seen returning whence they came, each ant carrying one or more termites in its jaws. Fortunately one only normally encounters these ants when out in the '*bundu*' and I certainly never found any in our house.

African bees have in recent years become somewhat legendary for their vicious swarming attacks upon humans, and apart from occasionally seeing a poor African running for dear life whilst frantically waving his arms above his head in an attempt to rid himself of an attacking swarm, I am glad to say that I never did personally experience such an attack, neither did anyone else in my family.

Stories are legion of some poor victims being stung to death by these vicious bees. Yet, curiously, many Africans nurture these very bees for their honey. They achieve this by hanging *mzinga* high up in large trees such as baobabs to act as a beehive. Yet despite undoubtedly being repeatedly stung many times, they appear to show an immunity to the sting of these bees.

The word *mzinga* actually means a cannon as well as a beehive, since all it comprises is a large hollowed out log just over a metre in length, therefore resembling a cannon, hence the name.

Another colonized insect with which I had experience, is the *Army worm.* In truth it is not a worm at all, but the caterpillar larva of a pale brown moth. In certain weather conditions, these moths lay millions of eggs which, if favourable conditions still continue, then hatch out into millions of black wriggling caterpillars. This seething army then advances across the countryside devouring all vegetation in its path, completely denuding all before them as they devour their voracious way forward. There are even stories of such an army stopping railway trains by crossing over the rails in such numbers that any passing locomotives crushes so many caterpillars as to create a slippery, slimy surface on top of the running rails. This causes the driving wheels to spin uselessly at high speed, unable to get traction grip on the rails!

One colonized insect I mercifully never personally experienced was the dreaded *locust,* a species of swarming grasshopper, though other parts of Africa, and indeed occasionally Kenya, are certainly plagued by these voracious feeders which are capable of denuding vast acreage of all types of vegetation in seconds.

I have already mentioned the swarming Lake flies which seemingly only exist by Lake Victoria insofar as Tanzania is concerned, so I move on now to mention another Tanzanian insect noted for its curiosity and behaviour.

It is the *dung beetle* to use its polite name. This extraordinary insect is just a largish looking black beetle with a round body. But here its 'ordinariness' ends, for this beetle lays its eggs in cow dung. It does not, however, just lay its eggs in any old cow dung it might find. The dung must be located in precisely the right environment and conditions. In order to ensure the selected cow dung is located in precisely the right spot, this enterprising beetle, working almost always entirely alone, rolls a clump of still moist dung into a perfect sphere sometimes almost as big as a table tennis ball. In order to get this to its ideal location, this energetic beetle then proceeds to roll its prize to the chosen location. This she achieves by rolling her ball forward with her hind legs whilst getting purchase on the ground with her front legs so that, in effect, she does the rolling whilst in an inverted position, pushing on the ground with her front legs. She energetically pushes her ball seemingly haphazardly this way and that until at last she seems satisfied she has found the perfect location. She then lays her eggs within the ball and just leaves it.

I cannot leave colonized insects without mentioning *the termite* or *white ant*. These wood eating ants are extremely common throughout Tanzania. They can devour wood at an alarming rate, and for this reason, railway track sleepers throughout East Africa are made of steel not wood. Another surprising fact concerning this small ant is that, despite being a tropical insect, they detest strong sunlight, and, in fact, soon die if exposed to it even for only a short time. For this reason, they only travel along carefully constructed tunnels made from the local soil mixed with their saliva which sets incredibly hard. Furthermore, before starting to feed on any wood, living or dead, they cover the whole feeding site with a coating of soil, mixed with saliva, allowing them to feed at leisure securely shaded from the sun. They actually live in a huge *termitarium*, or large termite mound also built of local soil and saliva. *Termitaria* are commonly found throughout the Tanzanian savanna. Sometimes there are situated at the base of a tree or perhaps, more commonly, are built free standing in the savanna.

Termitaria vary enormously in size, some towering to as much as ten feet high, often built with a large tubular 'chimney' at the apex. Inside a *termitarium*, is to be found a real labyrinth of tunnels and corridors, creating, in effect, a perfect air conditioning system. Inside they also carry out a sort of farming system where they cultivate a fungus garden. Almost in the middle of each termite mound, is found the royal chamber where the massive queen termite lives, whose sole purpose in life is to lay eggs. As fast as she lays them, the workers carry them off to the nursery chambers. Also to be found in the queen's chamber, is the 'king' termite, a dark brown ant about one inch long, whose purpose in life is to tend the queen as well as to fertilize her eggs.

The queen ant herself, is of grotesque and massive proportions, totally dwarfing all others ants in the colony. She can measure up to some eight or nine centimetres in length with a positively obese width of up to some two centimetres. She is in reality nothing more than an egg producing factory laying eggs as fast as her attendant worker ants can carry them away. Just so long as she is present, her colony faithfully remains with her, but should she die or disappear for any reason, then her colony will desert the mound and move elsewhere.

The termite eggs hatch out eventually either into workers or soldiers or winged potential kings or queens. When weather conditions are just right, generally following rain, at which time there is, of course, no direct sun, these winged termites leave their colony in huge droves on what is called their *nuptial* flight. It is only flight they will ever make. They fly off on their one and only short flight in their thousands. Africans, incidentally, love to catch and eat these flying termites, eating them raw as fast as they can catch them, stuffing them into their mouths then spitting out the wings. Such ants are regarded as a great delicacy. And, no, before you ask, I did *not* ever taste one!

As soon as these flying ants land, they have to find a mate as soon as possible, some being male and other female. As soon as a male finds a landed female he mates with her, shedding his lacy wings as he does so, as does the female. Having mated, they then go off together to look for a suitable site where to build their own, brand new *termitarium*. And thus they cycle starts all over again.

I cannot leave insects, without mentioning the *cicada*. These are large insects measuring on average about two centimetres long. They belong to the *Hemiptera*, or bug, family. A day spent in the African bush would just not be the same without the noise generated by these insects. They are extremely difficult, if not impossible to find. They live a solo life on tree leaves, generally high up towards the top. Once settled there they emit a very loud, almost deafening at times, hissing or screeching noise, giving the African bush its familiar 'alive' sound. Although one would think that by emitting such a loud noise, they would give the game away as to their position, it is impossible to trace the source of the sound they make.

Now moving away from insects to other creepy-crawlies, I

Peter M Wilson
Bwana Shamba

feel this chapter would not be complete without mentioning the famous *Tanganyika Train* millipede. It is a fat shiny millipede which has a black segmented cylindrical body measuring up to 10 centimetres in length and a diameter of about 15mm, and a mass of red/orange legs. Its head is permanently bowed down and it has a slowly tapering blunt tail end. It is entirely harmless to anything but plant life. It gets its name by virtue of the fact that it makes its slow way along the ground, meandering this way and that just like, in fact, a Tanganyikan train. My children kept one as a 'pet' for many months and loved to watch its tiny orange coloured legs busily propelling it slowly forward as it meandered about in every direction.

Another creature Yvonne, my second daughter, found and kept for a while as a 'pet' was a *Strawberry mite*. As the name suggests, it resembled a tiny red strawberry. Being a true mite, it feeds by sucking sap from vegetation. But alas, Yvonne's new pet never being given any vegetation in its little box, it soon died, and poor Yvonne cried and cried over its loss. It is, of course, totally harmless to humans.

To close this chapter, I shall mention the chief and most hated and dreaded creep-crawly of all creepy-crawlies in Tanzania, the *African hunting spider*, an enormously fat, brown, hairy spider by any standards, complete with large and hairy legs. Many people assume it to be a *tarantula* spider, but *tarantulas* do not exist in East Africa, being a south European species. They are mostly ground living, living a solo existence. They are often to be found patiently waiting for an unsuspecting prey to emerge from a hole in the ground, ready to pounce on it. As far as I know, they are harmless, though they may possibly inflict a harmless 'bite' if handled, and no, I certainly did not handle one, though saw many, mostly on my lawn.

Fun and Games

The epicentre of all the social life at Kilosa was undoubtedly the gymkhana club. It boasted a pleasant club house, which had a large hall. The front of the building had a large, wide veranda across its length, at one end of which stood a well-stocked bar. In visiting the club for the first time, I couldn't help noticing footprints in coloured paints of all shades, all over the extensive ceiling.

Upon enquiring how they got there, it was explained to me that it had become the custom that whenever a member had to resign from the club because he was leaving the district for whatever reason, he would be divested of his socks, the soles of his feet painted in some brightly coloured paint, then he was unceremoniously hoisted upside down to the ceiling to plant his footprints thereupon as a lasting memento of his membership at Kilosa. I was to see many a retiring member hoisted up this way, in an inverted position. As it happened, I got away without having to experience this treatment, as, mercifully, the practice had been abandoned before I left.

Outside were half a dozen hard tennis courts and opposite the clubhouse was a large undulating grass field kept mown with a tractor mower.

The majority of the European population of Kilosa faithfully attended all the special 'dos' held in the club approximately once every two or three weeks. These generally took the form of a dance, music being supplied by a good gramophone system. These evenings generally comprised traditional 'sensible' dances such as waltzes, quicksteps and the like, with plenty of 'smooching' music. Occasionally, an eightsome reel was thrown in as a digression. A great deal of fun was had by one and all, especially on fancy dress nights and so on. On 'normal' evenings, dress was always formal, gentlemen wearing 'penguin' suits, which were most uncomfortable on warm, humid evenings. The ladies also wore formal evening dress. The ladies made the most of their ornate evening dresses, which, for them, were nice and cool, since the smarter the dress, the greater the expanse of bare flesh on arms and back, and legs.

The bar always did a roaring business in bottled beers and spirits. Fortunately at that time, I did not much care for the taste of beer, nor had I acquired a taste for whisky, so I was never tempted to go too much 'on the bottle'. Instead, I always stuck to Coca-Cola, and drank gallons of the stuff. Everyone mocked me from drinking such stuff, assuring me that my teeth would rot away. I am glad to say, however, that I still have all my teeth.

Christmas was especially a time for celebration, and usually on the Saturday nearest Christmas day, Father Christmas would put in a personal appearance, arriving with a sack full of toys for all the children, though, alas, only for the European children, there being no African members of the club at that time, membership sadly only being open to Europeans in those days.

On one occasion we held a simple sports day for the (European) children which they thoroughly enjoyed.

Although there were some excellent tennis courts there ready for use, surprisingly little tennis was ever played on them. One very regular activity which did take place, sportswise, was rugger, even though there was no suitable pitch at the gymkhana

The Kilosa rugby team.

Peter M Wilson
'Mr Agriculture'

club. For this purpose, the town's football pitch was adopted for dual-purpose use, by the simple expedient of substituting the goalposts with rugger H-posts, the bottom half adequately serving as soccer goal posts.

There were just fifteen of us 'young blood' Europeans on the station, so we could just muster a rugby team. I never saw any African playing rugger, as either they were not interested, or were not 'eligible', regrettably.

More as an excuse for socializing than for the actual sport, we used to play away matches against many distant town teams, such as Dodoma or Iringa for example. We all went in a convoy of cars, generally taking our respective wives with us. We tended to think of these matches as being 2 or 3 hours' driving away, rather than so many hundreds of miles.

On one occasion, when we had gone to Iringa to play a match, we had gone with Pat Kelly and his wife, Joan, who both worked on the large EASP sisal estate just outside Kilosa. They had a black Ford Consul saloon car which accommodated us very comfortably.

We were on our way back from Iringa along the main murram Morogoro road, when we caught up with an African cyclist, riding his bike, as was common, on the wrong side of the road, in search for corrugation free murram. As we approached him, Pat gave him a hoot to warn him of our approach, and at the very last moment, to our utter horror and astonishment, the African suddenly took it upon himself to come across to his correct side on the left.

I can even now, recall vividly seeing the windscreen filled with the image of a cyclist but a few feet in front of us.

Fortunately, Pat was alert, and after a quick assessment of the situation, swerved sharply to the left, jumping a wide storm ditch at the side of the road. As luck would have it, this trench had gently sloping sides, so Pat, still using the forward momentum we had, was able to drive back up the slope to finish up on the road. We had had a nasty shock, and had also had a severe bump as we jumped the ditch. This had filled the car with choking dust, having disturbed, no doubt, years of accumulated road dust. Of the African we saw not a trace. He had abandoned his bike and run off into the bush.

Pat then picked up the abandoned bike and secured it firmly by means of a rope he had with him, to the back of his car, reasoning that we were doing him a favour by taking the bike

Peter M Wilson
Bwana Shamba

away before he killed himself on it. When we were ready to continue on our way, Pat called out in Swahili to the African we could still not see, that he would be able to reclaim his bike back at Kilosa police station.

We never won any of our rugby matches.

On one occasion, just before a Christmas day, we were, unusually, practising rugger on our field in Kilosa, when I was approached by a young European gentleman. It turned out that this young man I knew very well indeed. It was Timothy Bain-Smith, the younger son of the bursar at my old school at Sedbergh. It turned out that he was the naval lieutenant in charge of a rugby team the British navy had sent to Kilosa for a Christmas rugger match, Kilosa being easily attainable, being on the direct railway line from Dar es Salaam, where their ship had called in on a goodwill Christmas visit. When Timothy told me he had yet to check into an hotel, I was glad to be able to offer him accommodation at our house for the duration of his stay in Kilosa. During the course of subsequent conversation, we realized it had been just six years since I had been at his house in Sedbergh for Christmas day.

I forget who won the match. Undoubtedly it was the Royal Navy. It was bound to have been, as I am sure I would remember such a momentous occasion as Kilosa actually winning a rugby match.

On another occasion, I was practising place kicks, wearing only my plimsolls, as was our habit on the concrete hard ground, where proper studded boots would have been very uncomfortable.

The ground being so hard and concrete-like, it was impossible to make an indentation in the soil in which to stand the ball for a place kick. I therefore had to lean it up against the side of a shallow small trench that had been ploughed out to mark the twenty-five yard line from the goalposts.

In trying to get my toes under the ball to lift it into the air, I unfortunately kicked, very hard, the rock-hard far side of the furrow, the ball then merely trickling pathetically a few yards forward.

My foot ached abominably after that, so that I had to hobble painfully home on it. As the throbbing continued painfully all night, I figured it might be as well to have it looked at the following day. I duly turned up at the Kilosa hospital next day, where a doctor suggested my foot by X-rayed if only to eliminate a cause for the pain in my foot. To both our astonishments, it turned out I did indeed have a fracture. I had cracked a metatarsal bone in my right foot. It was therefore bound up to the knee in plaster of Paris, and as I hobbled around Kilosa for the next few weeks, I felt really stupid having to admit I had broken it, not playing a rugger match, which would have been an 'honourable' injury, but merely in practising place kicks.

Some months later, well after my foot was normal again, I had my opportunity of glory, by being offered the chance to try and convert a 'try' our team had miraculously scored during a match.

The ball was duly placed on a small heap of sand for the kick. I had never before taken such a kick in a real match situation, so was totally unprepared for what happened next. Although I had become quite proficient at kicking the ball over the goal bar in practice, I had completely forgotten that the opposing team can charge the kicker as soon as he makes a move to try to 'convert' a try.

I was therefore totally caught off guard when, no sooner had I started my short run towards the ball, I suddenly saw fifteen burly men charging towards me. Not surprisingly, I took my eyes off the ball. It was now or never time to kick the ball, so I stupidly kicked the ball with the last fragments of impetus from my short run. So, instead of the ball sailing through the air between the goal posts, as it had indeed done many times in practice before, it stupidly and pathetically dribbled towards the charging opponents. I felt a complete fool, and very disgusted with myself at having 'blown' my chance of actually being able to score points for the Kilosa rugby team.

The other annual event the gymkhana club organized was a car rally. This was a simple affair involving simple map reading, driving a set distance at a particular average speed, the speedos having been hidden beneath masking tape, a braking and acceleration test and so on. I always enjoyed this event and generally performed quite favourably in it.

The Standard Vanguard van I had bought, as being all I could afford, had entirely lost its brakes. In fact I had driven all over the district with it totally devoid of all brakes, hand and foot varieties. The method I had developed for slowing down and braking, depended solely on the engine and gearbox. For emergency stops, I had become expert at crashing the column gear change into a low gear, then letting in the clutch with the engine switched off. Such was the engine's compression, that on occasion, I could even skid the wheels in stopping by this method, when on tarmac.

It was with my car in this condition that one year I entered in the annual rally. I was a little apprehensive as to whether or not I could perform my emergency braking technique under rally conditions. To my, and everybody else's astonishment, however, I won the rally that year. Not only that, but put up the fastest timing in the braking and acceleration event too.

In addition to all the sporting activities which were organized, the annual Queen's Day was always an excuse for something different.

On such days, unfortunately for us menfolk, we were all expected to wear our formal 'penguin' suits, which, in view of the intense heat, meant of course having to endure fastened neck buttons and ties, which I totally detested in such circumstances. The women of the station, however, delighted in the excuse to show off all their finery with square yards of exposed bare flesh on their backs, legs and arms. The District Commissioner, on these occasions, always turned up in all his finery, complete with white feathered ceremonial hat and sword.

A parade was generally held on the football field, at which the entire police contingent was on parade, supplemented by girl guides and boy scouts from local African schools. The DC, on these occasions, took the opportunity to present any medals won by any of Kilosa's police officers.

The ceremonial occasion climaxed with the DC taking the formal salute as the contingents of police, girl guides and boy scouts marched past, without any music, alas.

CHAPTER XI

Reunification and Multiplication

Soon after my first Christmas in Kilosa which regrettably I had to spend alone without my family, I received a wonderful Christmas present in the form of a letter from Dar es Salaam informing me that at last Dorothy and our two daughters would be rejoining me early in the new year.

I was overjoyed as I hated living alone in my huge EPCC house and missed my family abominably. Dorothy had written to tell me that since my departure from Britain, Yvonne had not only learnt to walk, but was almost running as well. I longed to see them all again and have them share my life in Africa.

As the day of their flight out drew near, I was able to arrange a couple of days leave to go down to Dar to meet them.

I booked a sleeper on the mail train to Dar, and on the eve of their arrival, caught the 1 a. m. mail train from Kilosa. After being aroused by the sleeper steward as we approached our destination, I washed as best I could in the folding wash basin in my cabin, then dressed and made my way to the dining car to have 'civilized' breakfast.

I caught a taxi to the New Africa Hotel which I thought better for the occasion than the Metropole which was of doubtful reputation at that time.

Dorothy and the girls were scheduled to arrive at Dar es Salaam airport, a little way out of the city inland, on the first scheduled BOAC Britannia aircraft (The *Whispering Giant*) to Dar es Salaam. As the hour of her scheduled arrival drew near, I took a taxi out to the airport, climbed up to the waving base on the terminal building roof and leant on the rail overlooking the airfield. I was then astonished beyond words, to find myself standing beside a former master from my old school, Mr Pentney. Like myself, he was there to meet his wife arriving from London to join him on the same *Whispering Giant* flight.

After we had had a lengthy chat, it was announced that the

Peter M Wilson
Bwana Shamba

Page: 71

flight we awaited was due to arrive an hour late due to technical trouble at Nairobi. So much for the *Whispering Giant!*

Mr Pentney therefore kindly took me back to his house for some tea to kill time. We duly arrived back in good time for the rescheduled e.t.a. We resumed our positions on the waving base and saw history in the making as the Britannia suddenly appeared stage right to make a perfect landing on the main runway, the first such aircraft ever to arrive there.

It made a turn at the end of the runway then taxied to the apron, very considerately parking itself neatly right in front of us. With excitement mounting, we watched as the mobile stairway was wheeled into place at the exit doorway and the passengers started to emerge. Yes! There she was! There stood Dorothy at the top of the steps, waving as she spotted me on the waving base! A steward then appeared carrying Yvonne in his arms, whom I had expected to see walking under her own steam. They descended the steps with Vanessa between them, and then made their way towards us, waving and blowing kisses as they came, Vanessa following her mother's example. Then they disappeared from view beneath us as they entered a door directly below where we stood into the customs hall.

Mr Pentney had also spotted his wife alighting, so we made our way downstairs to greet them as they emerged from the customs hall. Once down there, I only had a couple of minutes wait before Dorothy and the girls appeared through the exit door.

Then, of course, it was kisses and hugs all round as we greeted each other after an absence of nearly five long months.

Dorothy greeted me with the words, 'You are lucky we have Vanessa here, as she might quite easily be in Johannesburg right now!'

Upon further enquiry it transpired that because of some technical fault on the Britannia, the passengers had been invited to wait in a comfortable transit lounge at Nairobi airport, until the trouble was sorted out.

Whilst they sat there, Dorothy had barely heard an announcement for passengers to Johannesburg to proceed to their aircraft now. Accordingly, there had been a general evacuation of passengers to an aircraft, and Vanessa, unable to see her mother, assumed that she should be going too. So she simply joined the crowd right onto an aircraft. The doors of the aircraft had actually been closed and secured, when the cabin staff made a last minute head count. Upon finding one head too many, they re-counted and re-counted, but each time they were one head too many. They therefore re-opened the doors and held up the aircraft until they had sorted the problem. When, totally baffled by the extra head, they had just started a ticket check, a passenger said to a passing stewardess, 'This little girl does not seem to be with anyone!'

Problem solved. Vanessa had somehow walked her way through ticket and passport checks unobserved.

She was then led back to the transit lounge to an astonished Dorothy who had not even noticed Vanessa's absence in the meleé.

At last reunited, we bade Mr Pentney farewell and took a taxi into the city. Next day, having settled into our hotel rooms, the receptionist rang up to say we had a visitor in reception. I went down to see whoever it might be, and was surprised to see a smart European gentleman dressed in immaculate white shorts, shirt and white knee-length stockings. He introduced himself as my cousin, Jack Cooper.

My uncle Harold in England, upon hearing I was headed for Dar es Salaam, had told me he had another nephew working in Dar as Director of the Audit Department. My uncle, having heard Dorothy was due in Dar to join up with me, contacted Jack, and here he was to meet us.

He invited us all back to his house which was situated in the Oyster Bay area of the capital. So I went back up to collect Dorothy and the girls. We were then driven to my cousin Jack's beautiful house overlooking Oyster Bay.

They were fortunate to have a large balcony on the top floor of their house that overlooked the exquisite view of Oyster Bay itself, the sea in the sunlight having taken on a deep blue colour which looked most inviting. Almost opposite their house, slightly to the left, stood H.H. the Aga Khan's house in Dar, in a prime position right by the shore.

The sea looked so inviting that our hosts suggested that before eating we should repair to the beach. We were therefore driven to the exquisite beach, with its perfect soft, white sand, fringed by an array of coconut palms, each growing at a different angle.

We all had a quick dip in the amazingly warm Indian ocean, then the girls were allowed to play to their hearts' content in the beautiful soft, clean sand. Three quarters of an hour later we returned to the house to be given a feast fit for a king. Our host eventually drove us back to the New Africa.

Peter M Wilson
Bwana Shamba

Next day, we took a taxi to Dar station to catch the mail train back to Kilosa. It was not a great distance to Kilosa, but because trains in Tanganyika at that time rarely travelled at more than fifteen miles per hours, instead of arriving at a sensible hour, like, say, teatime, we arrived at just after 1 a. m.

Fortunately David Jack had very kindly arranged to meet us off the train, so he whisked us up to our house. I could see Dorothy was much impressed by our new home, having feared much worse conditions, despite my having enthused about it. We both put our excited children to bed, allotting them both to the second bedroom conveniently opposite the bathroom.

To the children, of course, it was all a huge adventure to be able to go to bed in 'tents', as they considered the mosquito nets, draped over their beds.

Next morning there were more 'oohs' and 'aahs' in profusion from Dorothy as I showed her round our estate, especially when it came to admiring our fantastic view. Dorothy could not resist the temptation, so we asked Juma to serve us breakfast on our veranda, and were thus able to eat while admiring our view.

At last, we settled into and resumed family life. I took Dorothy into Kilosa in my GT to do some urgent shopping and stocking up of essentials.

Before Dorothy's arrival, I had been jokingly asked if I was ready for a third child, as it seemed all new couples arriving in Kilosa had a child almost exactly nine months after arrival. It had been reckoned that this was due, to a large extent, to the fact that at 1 a. m. three times a week the mail train arrived in Kilosa station amidst a positive cacophony of whistles and hoots, thereby waking everybody up.

It would appear that we kept up tradition to the letter, as after a few weeks, Dorothy was pronounced pregnant again, being due exactly nine months after her arrival. There was one snag, however, to this pregnancy, and that was that Kilosa hospital was not geared up to accommodating Europeans, and therefore it was advised that we should move over to Morogoro in time for the birth to take place there, where the hospital was well able to cater for Europeans.

Dorothy's pregnancy posed no problems at all throughout her time. In fact she accompanied me on several safaris, as by then I had started fully to take over my responsibilities in the district. Then, one evening, a few weeks before our planned temporary exodus to Morogoro, Dorothy had a hot bath. It seemed 'Philip' as we had dubbed our unborn child, had objected to being 'cooked' in his abode, so decided enough was enough and began to announce his arrival.

There was, at that time in Kilosa, a charming and efficient German nurse on the station, Sister Elizabeth. We thought it prudent to advise her of Philip's impending arrival, so I sped down in the GT to fetch her. Upon greeting her at the door of her house and explaining the situation to her, she said in her thick German accent, 'Vot for, you are haffing babies in Kilosa? You should be in Morogoro!'

I was not very encouraged by her words, but then she suggested that I take Dorothy immediately to Kilosa hospital where she would be ready for us. As I turned to go and fetch Dorothy, I heard her muttering once more to herself, picking out the word 'Morogoro' yet again. I sped back up the hill to collect Dorothy. Fortunately, we were able to leave the girls at home with Juma who promised to take good care of them.

I drove Dorothy to the hospital in my GT and, true to her word, there we found Sister Elizabeth waiting for us on the hospital veranda. Dorothy was taken straight away to a small private ward which had a window looking out on the veranda. As luck would have it, there was a convenient chair right by this window, so I sat outside Dorothy's ward window, able to hear in detail everything that took place and what was being said. Sister Elizabeth herself attended to the birth, which fortunately went without a hitch. I then heard the proclamation, 'It's a girl!'

We had both set out hearts on a son, so I easily detected disappointment in Dorothy's voice as she verified this statement.

Then I heard Dorothy excitedly proclaim, 'It's a boy!' Only to be assured it was not. Dorothy had caught sight of the navel cord and jumped to the wrong conclusion as to what she had seen.

We therefore had to settle on our reserve name, and called our new daughter Diane. A few days later, we decided to give Diane a second name, and settled on Elizabeth after the sister who had brought her into the world.

When subsequently Sister Elizabeth learnt we had named Diane after her, she was overjoyed. After all her admonishments for having dared to have a baby in Kilosa instead of Morogoro, it was quite a relief for us. Kilosa hospital, as I have said was not geared to accommodate Europeans. This was principally

Peter M Wilson
Bwana Shamba

because they just did not have the resources to provide for European-type catering. This problem, however, was easily resolved by my being told I should bring all Dorothy's meals to her, ready prepared at home. This made a wonderful excuse, as if I needed it, to visit Dorothy and Diane Elizabeth three times a day for the next ten days, until they were allowed home.

What a homecoming it was too, with Vanessa and Yvonne chuffed beyond words at having a brand new sister to play with. Juma too participated in the admiration ceremonies and genuinely seemed delighted with the newcomer to the household. We have certainly never for a moment regretted Diane not being Philip.

Triple Christening

A few weeks after Diane came to us, we decided to have her Christened, as her two sisters had been before her.

It so happened that two other babies had added themselves to Kilosa's population at about the same time as Diane. Barbara and Richard Norman from the neighbouring EASP sisal estate had a little girl, Gillian, and David and Pamela Jenkins had a little boy named Peter. David Jenkins was the district's labour officer.

We therefore put our heads together and decided to have a triple Christening ceremony in the Kilosa church, followed by a joint party at, as it turned out, Dickie and Joyce Brown's house.

In the absence of Dorothy's brother, whom we wanted to be Diane's godfather, we asked Dickie Brown to be her proxy godfather, along with Jane Holmes, the wife of the PWD officer, Peter Holmes, to be her proxy godmother in lieu of Dorothy's sister, Barbara.

We therefore contacted the local CMS missionary, Ted

The interior of Kilosa's church during a rehearsal for the christenings with the local CMS pastor officiating.

Peter M Wilson
Bwana Shamba

Arblaster, an Australasian, who was based at Morogoro, 81 miles away and who regularly came across to Kilosa on Sundays in order to conduct the services in Kilosa's church.

The chosen day came, and we all waited in the pleasant little church which had open spaces for windows, to keep the place pleasantly cool. Most of Kilosa's European population was present, which nicely filled the church. We waited and waited, and while we continued to wait, Mrs Dorothy de Lucy, one of the regular parishioners, kindly led us through an adaptation of morning worship while we awaited Ted Arblaster's arrival. At last, the District Commissioner arrived with the news that, due to the rains, Ted Arblaster could not get through from Morogoro, as the roads were impassable.

We were now in a quandary, as all the arrangements had been made for the reception afterwards etc. etc. So we held an urgent 'council of war' and decided ask the resident African pastor, the Rev. Dan Seng'unda, who lived in a house just by the church, if he would kindly step in and conduct the ceremonies for us.

He immediately concurred, so quickly robed up and entered the church. He walked up the aisle of the church to his desk, picked up a prayer book and started to read from it in Swahili.

It wasn't until that moment that I realised that pastor Seng'unda, who knew no English, had of course no option but to conduct the ceremonies in Swahili. Although as yet I could not understand every word that was being said, I found it immensely moving, as did Dorothy, to be having our daughter christened in Swahili. It certainly made no difference to Diane, who of course could not have understood a word, even in English.

Then came the moment of the actual baptism, when Diane was taken up into the arms of the ageing African pastor and he lovingly and tenderly carried her across to the font. The look of sheer joy and pride on his wizened face as he baptized her was a joy to behold. Diane was the first European baby he had ever baptized. He managed well to get his tongue round the names Diane Elizabeth, then handed Diane back to Jane Holmes. He then repeated the ceremony for the other two new members of the church, then it was all over.

We invited the pastor to join us at the party afterwards, for which a huge and beautifully iced cake had been prepared, upon which the initials, D, G and P were prominent. The pastor was delighted to come to our party, even though he only stayed a very short time alas.

Our mammoth party was held on Dickie's veranda and over-flowed into his garden, the rain mercifully not having reached Kilosa. The three babies' heads were well and truly wetted, besides the holy water that had by then in any case already evaporated. Numerous photographs and cine shots were of course taken, of the three babies in their godmother's arms, in their mothers' arms, in their fathers' arms etc. etc., one of these photographs eventually finding its way into the *Tanganyika Standard* newspaper a few days later.

The three proud mothers with their newly christened babies. Left to right: Pamela Jenkins with Peter; Barbara Norman with Gillian, Dorothy with Diane.

Then it was time to cut the iced cake, and we all sampled its delicious flavour, except, of course, the three guests of honour, the three babies. Throughout the day, all three behaved perfectly and we never heard so much as the slightest murmur from either of them, not even when receiving the holy water upon their foreheads.

The afternoon passed all too quickly, and the sun was already dipping towards the horizon when we all dispersed to our respective homes, well pleased that the day had passed so per-fectly despite the initial set-back.

Personally speaking, and certainly meaning no offence to Ted Arblaster, I would not have wished anything to have turned

Peter M Wilson
Bwana Shamba

out differently, and even found myself glad that the rains had prevented Ted's arrival, by blocking the Morogoro road for him.

CHAPTER XIII

Tea Break in the Southern Highlands

A good Christian friend of mine, David Macdonald, from Harper Adams, was still in Mufindi in the southern highlands of Tanganyika at that time, managing one of the Brooke Bond tea estates which flourished in the area. I was able to make contact with him to try to arrange to meet up sometime. In response, he kindly invited me and the family to spend Christmas with him on his tea estate.

We were delighted to accept, doubly so, having heard David, whilst at college, often talk so lovingly of the Mufindi district, that I had been very keen to visit the area myself and sample its pleasantness and European-type climate.

There was just one problem, though, and that was getting ourselves to Mufindi. I could not use my GT for such a private journey, and public transport there was virtually non existent. There was no railway, and the rare buses which might or might not reach Mufindi did not have much appeal for travelling long distances with three young children.

The only option left open to us therefore, was to use the old Standard Vanguard I had bought secondhand from the Ilonga research station entomologist, Valentine. Although I had become very proficient at driving this ageing vehicle with no brakes whatever, I was somewhat apprehensive about driving it all the way to Mufindi, never before having had cause to drive it on such a long run, Dar es Salaam having been the furthest I had dared drive it. But it was a question of Hobson's choice. Either we entrust our journey to the van, or Christmas in Mufindi was a non-starter.

We therefore loaded our blue Vanguard with all our suitcases and other safari equipment, also taking a few tools and a rope in case of mechanical problems. A few days before Christmas, therefore, we climbed aboard our laden van and set off for Mufindi, setting off south to go via Ulaya and Mikumi.

It seemed strange to be driving my Vanguard along the familiar corrugated road, instead of my reliable GT.

I had just joined the new Morogoro-Iringa road at Mikumi, when I had a puncture. I did at least feel confident that I could repair a puncture, so, jacked the van up and changed the wheel, fortunately having a spare on board.

Since I felt the likelihood of a further puncture a distinct possibility, I decided there and then to repair the puncture as I had all the necessary gear with me. I drove the front wheel of the van onto the deflated punctured tyre, to force it off the tight rim, then, using my good tyre levers managed to extract the inner tube in which I quickly located the puncture. It was possible, in those days, to buy what were known as 'hot patches' to repair punctures with a vulcanized patch, even in the middle of nowhere.

These patches were fastened onto a small tin tray in which a pad of some inflammable compound was kept. This patch was held firmly in position onto the puncture by means of an efficient little clamp designed for just that purpose. A smouldering match was then applied to the patch's inflammable pad which then smouldered at a very high temperature, thereby vulcanizing the patch firmly in place as well as could be done in any garage.

The puncture repaired and the tyre replaced and inflated, we continued on our way towards Iringa.

It was not long after we had sighted the Great Ruaha river, that mechanical trouble raised its ugly head. The engine started making very unfriendly noises, which alas, became louder and louder by the minute. I thought it prudent to stop at the side of the road, overlooking the river. I switched off the engine, lifted the bonnet and peered at the engine. Not being any sort of mechanic, there could have been an atomic pile under the bonnet for all the difference it made to me. But everything seemed much as it had always looked to me, except that I did notice an ominous drip, drip, drip of black oil making a small puddle beneath the engine sump.

I decided to see if I could detect any other clues as to the trouble whilst the engine was running, so I went back to my seat and applied the starter. Not a glimmer of life. I tried and tried until the starter motor began to show unmistakable signs of weariness as it started only just to turn the engine. My battery now exhausted, and clearly with a major problem deep within the engine, there was nothing further I could do. It now began to look as if we would be spending Christmas in the Great Ruaha gorge, and not in Mufindi after all. I closed the bonnet, and took out our two folding camp chairs and set them up at the edge of the road behind the van, facing the pretty view of the river down in the gorge. At this point, poor Vanessa started to cry, fearing we were stuck here for eternity. Before long Yvonne, then Diane joined the vociferous choir. We spent the next few minutes reassuring them that all would be well and that we would, I hoped, get a tow at least to Iringa. Diane was quickly pacified with a quick feed. Since there was nothing to be done except wait for some kind passing motorist to offer us a tow, we settled ourselves down comfortably in our chairs at the side of the road, and tucked into a few of the sandwiches Dorothy had thoughtfully brought along. Cans of Coke were also produced and drunk.

We received a few peculiar looks from some of the passing motorists, especially the African and Asian lorry drivers, who efficiently enveloped us in clouds of choking dust every time they passed.

After we had been thus relaxing for what initially seemed to us to have been like half a day, but in reality was probably not more than an hour, a kindly Indian gentleman driving a Landrover stopped and asked us if we needed any assistance.

I could have kissed him! Upon asking him if he could kindly give us a tow as far as Iringa, he readily assented and went to his Landrover to produce an even better rope than mine. He immediately dived under my van to fasten the rope securely to the front axle, then fastened the other end to the towhook at the back of the Landrover.

Then we were off, fortunately at a safe, steady pace. Inevitably, of course, we were constantly having to follow in his dust, which was profuse and choking, but at least we were on the move. There was nothing we could do about the dust. We could either open the windows to gain some fresh air and choke in the dust, or keep the windows shut and fry in the heat.

After what seemed an age, we reached Iringa's tarmac, the silence and smoothness of the road was serene after the noisy rattles and vibrations of the relentless corrugations of the murram road.

Our good Samaritan stopped to discuss our next move. As luck would have it, he had a friend who ran a good garage, so he kindly towed us there. Things could not have turned out better. The mechanics were able to make an instant diagnosis,

Peter M Wilson
Bwana Shamba

which sounded all Greek to me anyway, but more importantly, they promised to make the necessary repairs over Christmas, so that we would be able to collect our repaired van on our return to Kilosa after Christmas.

Even better, it turned out that our good Samaritan was actually on his way to Mbeya close to the Zambian border, which meant he would be driving through Mufindi. He very kindly offered to take us there, so we loaded our cases into his Land-rover, and away we went, striking south to the southern highlands after all.

After about an hour's steady progress, we reached the first of the many Brooke Bond tea estates, heralded by large sign-boards. Then at last, we reached David's estate, and our Samaritan drove up the long drive up through the tea plantation. The closely packed tea bushes on each side were all perfectly flat on the top, creating a vast expanse of level bushes, like a giant billiard table, called the plucking table. Regularly spaced throughout the tea plantation were attractive shade trees, such as we had seen on Bjorn's Juani coffee estate.

We pulled up in a sort of courtyard outside David's house, whereupon almost immediately David came out to greet us, shortly followed by his mother. We, together with our Samaritan, were invited in and offered tea, though not necessarily home-grown.

After our superb Samaritan had left to continue on his way south, David showed us our rooms, where we changed after washing off the considerable accumulation of rusty red road dust. After another chatting session, to catch up on our news since leaving our college and to put to rights all Tanganyika's problems, David took us out into the pleasant sunshine to show us round the estate.

He showed us the actual part of the tea bush which is plucked at harvest, being the top three leaves of each twig, including the growing point. Then he took us to see the processing machinery housed in open wall-less out buildings.

A few cattle were also kept on the estate, so we watched them reluctantly going through the plunge-dip, a necessarily evil the poor cattle had to endure at regular intervals to rid them of ticks and other *wadudu*, many of which were able to transmit diseases fatal to cattle.

The last call we made with David was to his elderly neighbour, a European by the name of Alistair Watermeyer, affectionately known by one and all as 'Watermelon'. He was an incredibly knowledgeable amateur botanist, who specialized in orchids, which he even collected for Kew Gardens in London.

He was also an artist of exceptional talent. He used to draw orchids with crayon, so that the finished drawing looked every bit as real and delicate as the original. He used to add crayon to crayon to crayon until the petals looked three dimensional. Having shown us many of his drawings as well as his collected specimens, he invited us to meet him the next day when he would take us out into the nearby indigenous wood to go orchid spotting.

So the next day, we did just that, old 'Watermelon' leading us at a brisk pace through the indigenous forest, stopping every so often to point out all manner of orchids, some on the ground, some high up in the trees, none of which we would have ever noticed had he not pointed them out. It was a fascinating walk.

That evening, David showed us a small natural lake near his house, upon which he kept a canoe. I took the children one at a time out on this, each in turn, but not, of course Diane.

The next day was Christmas day itself, and the day started with the local Africans, most of whom worked on the estate, treating us to a special rendering of some of their tribal dances, *ngoma*, in which they danced happily round in a circle to a very infectious and rhythmic drum beat. Then *zawadis* (presents) were exchanged with them, and it was time to prepare for Christmas lunch.

The rest of the day was spent quietly relaxing and watching our children playing with their new toys and games.

Like all good things, our stay there rapidly came to an end, and David very kindly offered to take us back to Iringa to collect our, hopefully by now, repaired van to return to Kilosa. He drove us in his treasured Morris traveller car to Iringa where thankfully we found our van ready and awaiting us. We transferred our belongings from David's car to our own, settled the fortunately not too expensive account, then set off back to Kilosa.

Our journey home was thankfully totally uneventful, not even getting a puncture. It had been an action-packed Christmas, but all thoroughly enjoyable and even Vanessa and Yvonne had enjoyed it, despite their passionate tears when we broke down on the way south, and we were most grateful to David for his kind and generous hospitality.

Peter M Wilson
Bwana Shamba

CHAPTER XIV

A Shilling a Tail

One day when I was at the gymkhana club, a friend of mine, jokingly, or so I thought, asked me if I wanted to buy a 0.22 calibre rifle.

I immediately declined as I had never thought about, nor even dreamt about possessing any sort of firearm. But nevertheless I just could not get the idea out of my head. I kept on day dreaming about bringing home countless prizes to supplement our meatsafe.

Then at last, after discussing the matter with Dorothy and numerous friends and colleagues, I decided to go for it, so contacted my friend to tell him of my decision. I asked him also to set the wheels in motion for my getting an official firearm licence, to get the whole deal formalized and legal.

Thus I became the legal owner of a firearm which was, as it happened, a 0.22 calibre hornet rifle, and therefore a potentially very powerful gun. It was a beautiful weapon with a small 5-round magazine and a comfortable butt.

I therefore went down to Mr Patel's hardware shop and bought a couple of boxes of ammunition for it. I had been recommended to use dumdum rounds which have a small hole in the tip of the actual bullet. This makes it spread on contact with its target and therefore gives a better chance of killing an animal rather than the bullet passing straight through it and only injuring it. Clearly I did not wish to go around injuring animals in this way, which is why I stocked up on dumdums.

From that day on, I always took my rifle with me on safari. A friend of mine in the local *hazina* (Local council administration) told me that the *hazina* paid out a shilling for every monkey or baboon tail brought in as proof of destruction of these pests. This was to encourage the destruction of these vandals of maize plantations.

On my next safari to Malolo, I found my new acquisition really came into its own.

To begin with, there were countless guinea-fowl in the area, and I also sighted several dik-dik there, these being a very small type of antelope about the size of a Jack Russell terrier dog.

I had barely unpacked my Landrover at the by-now roofed rest house, when a small deputation of Africans arrived, together with the local *Jumbe*, headman.

Daudi Lucas, whom I had brought along with me, had seemingly wasted no time in telling the local *wakulima* that the *Bwana Shamba* had a *bunduki*.

It transpired that there was a large troop of monkeys near the village which were decimating their maize crops.

They pleaded with me to bring my rifle and accompany them to see what they meant. I therefore left Dorothy to get on with unpacking our gear into the rest house. They led the way towards the far edge of the village, and on the way we passed a good looking field of maize when they suddenly stopped and said, '*Tazama, Bwana!*' 'Look, Bwana!' I followed their pointing chins and saw countless damaged cobs of maize lying on the ground, just as if some vandal had come deliberately to damage the field.

Clearly this meant a great loss to the farmers, who would not be able to tolerate this sort of loss to their main food crop for too long. Something needed doing, and just then, some young lads came running up to explain excitedly that they had chased a whole troop of monkeys up an umbrella thorn tree only a short distance away, where they could be easily shot down and slaughtered. They bid me follow them urgently.

I followed them and we soon came across a tree in which there must have been about a hundred vervet monkeys chattering excitedly upon the tree's canopy.

I loaded up my rifle, filling its magazine. I hoped my aim would be good, so that I would not make a fool of myself.

I walked under the tree and selected a particularly large specimen looking all round him, his head bobbing up and down as he did so. I took a bead on him and squeezed the trigger. I had clearly hit him, as he stopped his bobbing motion and all but fell, clinging desperately to a branch to stop himself falling. My considerable audience cheered as they watched the monkey's grip weaken, till he fell with a thud on the ground, stone dead. Only then did I remember the shilling per tail, so I asked Daudi

Peter M Wilson
Bwana Shamba

to rescue its tail for me, which was done with great relish by one of the young lads in my audience.

I carried on, shooting one monkey after another, each time a massive cheer going up as each one hit the ground stone dead. They were quickly deprived of their tails, so that soon I had built up quite a good collection of severed tails.

I was not altogether happy at the thought of decimating such a lively troop of monkeys, all chattering away to each other at the top of this tree, then I remembered the utter destruction in the maize field I had seen, so that I felt better about the carnage. It became all too easy a routine, select a monkey, take aim and fire, then watch as the eager young lads deprived the creature of its tail.

By the time I had reduced the seething troop of monkeys in the tree to only a handful, I decided enough was enough and called it a day, telling Daudi so. I asked him to retrieve all the tails, which he did. The tails were carried in a *kikapu*, basket, and counted. I was astonished to hear that there were 65 in all. The 65 shillings I was due to be paid for them would more than cover the cost of my ammunition.

It was extremely hot in the Malolo valley, and by then I was desperately thirsty, so decided to return to the rest house for a drink.

As I left the scene of the carnage, the farmers were jubilant, and for a moment, I quite thought they were going to carry me shoulder high back into the village. Fortunately this was not the case, but as I walked purposefully back to the rest house, I was closely surrounded by a happy chatting crowd of jubilant farmers.

As I neared the rest house more and more of my entourage disappeared, so that by the time I reached it, totally parched and desperate for a drink, I was almost on my own. When I reached it , I saw that someone else had arrived in another GT and was busy unloading his gear onto the veranda and into the other room, Dorothy fortunately having occupied only one of the two rooms.

As soon as I arrived, the newcomer, on seeing my state said, 'Would you like a drink of squash, or something?' I replied, 'Oh, yes! Please! I am totally parched!'

Whereupon he delved into one of his boxes on the veranda and produced a pint beer mug wrapped in newspaper. He quickly unwrapped it, and after some more delving in boxes, produced a bottle of Rose's lime juice, also wrapped in newspaper. He opened it and poured about an inch worth of it into the mug. Further delving produced another bottle filled with clear liquid, we both assumed was water. It went glug, glug, glug as he filled the mug three quarters full, then handed it to me. I noticed that, strangely, the lime juice had not seemed to mix in with the water, but stayed separate at the bottom of the mug.

I was too thirsty to worry about such detail, however, and ravenously gulped down a couple of mouthfuls. I had just filled my mouth with a third, when I stopped abruptly and sprayed the contents of my mouth out over the edge of the parapet. The newcomer looked in astonishment at my behaviour, treating his drink with such disdain.

'Ugh, paraffin!' I uttered in disgust, desperately trying to spit out every trace of the foul taste in my mouth.

The poor newcomer was beside himself with remorse, 'Oh, I'm terribly sorry,' he said, 'I must have pulled out a bottle of paraffin instead of water from my box!' Fortunately, Dorothy was quickly able to produce a can of coke from somewhere, with which I quickly slaked my desperate thirst, swilling my mouth out with it in an attempt to rid myself of the foul taste in my mouth.

At long last I was able to quench my desperate thirst with the coke, but getting rid of the foul taste of paraffin was something else, and for the next several weeks, at least, everything I ate and drank tasted of paraffin!

In the cool of the same evening, I decided to try my hand at bagging a guinea fowl or two. I still had just over half a box of ammunition, so after supper went off towards the Ruaha in search of guinea fowl in my GT.

They were not hard to find, as they stupidly called out to me with their strange and unique chirping type of call. Before long, I spotted one roosting up a tall tree. I took aim and fired. He fell like a stone, twitching slightly as he lay dead on the ground. I picked him up, slung him in the back of the Landrover and headed on towards the Ruaha. I had not gone very far, when I spotted a dik-dik lurking in the undergrowth. So I stopped and approached carefully and took aim. He too fell over, stone dead. So I went over to pick him up and he joined the guinea fowl in the back. I pressed on towards the river, having heard more guinea fowl summoning me.

Right at the top of a large tree on the bank of the swollen

Peter M Wilson
Bwana Shamba

river, I spotted another guinea fowl. I went underneath him and fired. Missed! I aimed again and missed again. I could see his head bobbing up and down. He must have thought the midges very noisy and active as the bullets whistled past his head as I fired several more times, missing each time, it being difficult, in the gathering dusk, to set my sights accurately on him. I decided to try one more shot. Bingo! At last I got him. He fell like a stone, hit a branch half way down the tree and bounced neatly into the swollen river, landing with a splash. I could only watch helplessly as the strong current swept him away downstream.

I decided enough was enough and headed back to the rest house. Back there, I passed on my prizes to Mohammed, our safari boy, to gut and pluck.

Having done what I had set out to do in Malolo, we packed up and left the next morning. I had barely gone five hundred yards down the road, when I spotted a maize cob up in a large tree. Realising that maize cobs don't grow in trees, I surmised that a monkey must be holding it up there. So I stopped my Landrover, grabbed my rifle and went to investigate. I could see the cob moving slightly, so took aim and fired. I was astonished to see, not one monkey fall, but two. I had hit and killed a mother vervet and as she fell, her baby fell with her. I went to collect the baby which still clung pathetically to its dead mother. It was a male baby, and presumably because his mother did not flee my approach, he must have thought there was no danger. He let me pick him up with no objection. I cradled him in my arms as I went back to the Landrover. He was a sweet little thing, and seemed to appreciate being cradled in my arms. I passed him to Vanessa in the cab, and he settled straight away in her arms. He seemed to have oversized ears for his head, so he was immediately dubbed Bigears. Then I remembered the shilling a tail, so went back to collect the mother's tail, making my total haul 66 tails in all.

Bigears travelled very contentedly in Vanessa's arms all the way back to Kilosa, where we released him in our house. We put our foot down, however, when Vanessa wanted to have him in her room that night.

There was a second veranda at the side of our house, which happened to be totally caged in with steel mesh, which made an ideal cage for Bigears, so, from then on, he slept every night in this cage, quite happily.

The next day, I took my 66 tails to claim my prize, causing

a great deal of open mouth astonishment that I had 'bagged' so many. I was complimented and called 'hodari sana' (very able) for my efforts.

Back home, I decided to let Bigears out of his cage to see what he did. Juma had just brought in the tea on a tray, which lay on the low coffee table. Bigears was very curious about these strange objects on the tray, so picked up one of our Poole china cups. He then spotted the large wooden box-pelmet above the window. He leapt for it, then found that he needed both hands to grab hold of the pelmet. So he let go of the cup to grab the pelmet. He made it safely onto the pelmet, but of course the cup smashed to smithereens as it hit the concrete floor. It all happened so quickly that Bigears repeated the same trick twice more before we woke up to the fact that we should remove the tea tray!

We managed to catch him and shut him in his cage. He looked so pathetic in there, that I took pity on him and offered him a banana. He took it from me, but didn't have a clue what to do with it, so let it drop disdainfully on the floor. I went into the cage picked it up and peeled it for him. This time he was in no doubts as to what to do with it and gobbled it down greedily.

The next afternoon, there being no tea tray in sight, we let him out again. This time, however, our black cat *was* out. From the very first moment of meeting Bigears and Felix our cat hit it off famously. They chased each other everywhere round and round the garden having a great time. Then, as cats often do, Felix would suddenly decide, in mid flight, that it was washing time. He would stop dead in his tracks and start methodically to wash his face. Bigears invariably cannoned into him, so also stopped and immediately took Felix in his arms and started to comb his fur for fleas, every so often either finding one, or pretending to, and putting it to his mouth to chew it. Felix just loved this sort of attention and sat there purring his heart out. This ritual was repeated frequently from that day on whenever we let cat and monkey romp freely throughout the garden. They even chased each other high up into some of our trees, the de-fleaing even being carried out up in the tree.

Thus Bigears became a family pet giving us all much pleasure as he romped around, perfectly at home with new friend, Felix.

Peter M Wilson
Bwana Shamba

CHAPTER XV

Stop Thief!

On the whole, there was very little thieving and dishonesty in Tanganyika in those days, apart from the odd case of 'pole fishing'. In these cases, the thief stole whatever he could retrieve by means of a pole, fitted with a hook on the end, stuck through the gap of an open window, or through burglar-proof bars. Thefts of this kind were mostly limited to clothing, or bed linen etc.

I did, however, have just two experiences of thieving in my thirteen years in the country.

The first one occurred in Dar es Salaam, where we had driven in my old Standard Vanguard van. It had no fuel gauge on it, so I always carried spare petrol in a can, plus a piece of hose pipe with which to siphon the petrol.

We were just entering the city on this occasion, and had just reached a *kipulefti*, on the outskirts, when I ran out of petrol. Knowing exactly why my engine had died, I immediately got out my jerry can of spare petrol and put it on the roof above the filler cap, in preparation for siphoning the petrol into the tank. Taking my length of hose pipe, I tried to get the siphon going, but in so doing, I was afraid I would dislodge the can off the roof. So I called to Dorothy, who was seated in the front passenger seat to come to my assistance and hold the can till I got the siphoning going. She came at once and held the can. A couple of good sucks, and in no time, I had a good flow of petrol into my tank.

I thanked Dorothy, who returned to her front seat. Then I heard a sort of muffled scream 'My handbag!' she shouted.

'What about it?' I dimly asked, still concentrating on the siphon.

'It's gone!'

'How do you mean gone?' I stupidly asked, the penny not yet having dropped as to what had happened.

Peter M Wilson
'Mr Agriculture'

Page: 92

Only then did it occur to me that her handbag had been taken from her seat, whilst she helped me with the siphon.

Of course, I had no clue as to who could have taken her bag, but I looked around the area just in case I might see anyone or anything suspicious. Just then, I spotted a group of street urchins pointing excitedly down one of the side streets off the *kipulefti*. They were beckoning frantically to me to come over.

I therefore left the can on the roof and ran across to them. They pointed excitedly down the narrow street, shouting and pointing '*Huyu!*' (Him!) As I looked, sure enough, there was a young African looking at something he held in his hands. As soon as he spotted me looking at him, he suddenly hid the object of his scrutiny under his loose shirt, and ran off fast.

I immediately gave chase and rapidly caught up with him. We ran up and down all manner of side streets and alleys, I knew not where. After a time, as we ran down a narrow alley, I was almost on top of him. As he looked around and saw how close I was to him, he threw the bag down, clearly hoping that it would satisfy me and would give up the chase. In true rugger player style, I bent down and scooped up the bag as I ran, not even causing a 'knock-on' . Such was the level of adrenaline in my blood by then, that I continued the chase. He emerged from the alley with me still hot on his heels.

He turned up a narrow alley which led into a courtyard. I was still in hot pursuit. There was an outdoor *choo* in one corner of this yard, so my quarry went straight into it. Then I heard him bolt the door on the inside. There happened to be a bolt on the outside as well, so I bolted this one too.

So here I was with a thief inside the *choo*, with the door bolted on both sides. By now half the population of Dar es Salaam was in the courtyard with me, eager to see why this *Mzungu* (European) was chasing an African.

I hoped that out of this vast throng, someone would give me a hand in seizing this thief. Some hope! not one person at any stage of this fracas lifted a finger to offer the slightest assistance. There was now an *impasse*. I had no idea what to do next, I could not get in to him, and he could not get out.

As I was wondering what to do next, my quarry made the next move. There was a ten inch gap between the top of the door and the roof. Through this gap, the thief started to make his escape. He was climbing through this gap, and trying to reach the top of the wall separating this yard and the next one.

Peter M Wilson
Bwana Shamba

He was just too high to be able to push him back, so I figured the best way to stop him climbing into the next yard, which would be the end of the chase, was to wait till he was half way across to the wall, then jump up and pull him down. This is, in fact, just what I did. At the crucial moment, I leapt up and with all the strength and weight I could command, I pulled him down on top of me. He was a nasty piece of work, and he fought savagely, head butting me severely. His head came into sharp contact with my large nose, which immediately started profusely to bleed. There was soon blood everywhere, my white shirt and shorts were soon covered in it. We fought hard as I tried to get a good grip on his arm to twist it behind him, but what with his sweat and my blood, his arm was too greasy and slippery to be able to get a firm hold. Still not one person in that vast throng, offered me the slightest assistance. It was entirely up to me to restrain him. After a long, slippery and vicious struggle, I, at last, managed to get a good hold on his arm, twisting it behind his back, I endeavoured to frog march him out of the yard. Because of the tight throng around me and especially in the narrow alley out of it, this was easier said than done.

At last, however, I did manage to get him back out and into the street. I was astonished to see that in the street, the other half of Dar es Salaam's population was there to see what all the commotion was all about. My captive was still trying to head butt me all the time. It was just at this moment, that, at last, someone in the vast crowd offered assistance. An Indian gentleman, very kindly offered me the use of his van, conveniently parked by the kerb nearby, in which to hold him prisoner. Between us we managed to bundle him in through the back doors, whereupon the crazed prisoner began to destroy the poor Indian's van. He tore off all the panel linings, and even broke one of the windows.

About five minutes later, the police arrived to see why the city's traffic had come to a complete grid-lock.

They soon found the epicentre of the problem – the *Mzungu*, and the thief in the van. After a quick explanation, the police dragged out the hapless thief, handcuffed him and led him away. The police extracted a promise from me to come as soon as possible to the police station to make a statement. Having had my name and address taken, I was left on my own.

I now had a major problem, I needed to get back to Dorothy

and the van, guessing that poor Dorothy was by now, frantic with worry.

The trouble was, I had not the slightest idea where I was, nor however to find my van again.

Mercifully, the street urchins came to my rescue again, and led me through countless narrow streets and alleys back to the *kipulefti* where the whole adventure had started. There was the van, precisely where I had left it, the petrol can still sitting forlornly on the roof. Dorothy was standing beside it, and, upon seeing my clothes crimson with blood, was not too reassured by my triumphant return.

That was not all, however. Dorothy's voluminous bag also served as a shopping bag. As luck would have it, or not, as the case might be, we had bought a few eggs before this incident, to have later for our supper. The mess, when we later opened the bag, had to be seen to be believed. Fortunately, we saw the funny side of the incident, and had a good laugh as we extricated all Dorothy's make-up items, keys and other handbag paraphernalia from the gooey omelette inside.

The thief would have been bitterly disappointed in his haul, had he had the chance properly to examine it, for there was not so much as one cent in cash in the bag, nor indeed anything else of any value whatsoever.

Later on, after tidying myself up as best I could in some hotel's cloakroom, I presented myself at the main police station, still crimson with blood from my nose, to make my statement. I did not press charges against my quarry, figuring he had already paid for his misdemeanour.

I was especially glad I had not pressed charges, when I later learnt that the poor unfortunate had only been released from a prison term for just such an offence, but a few days earlier. I felt sure he had learnt his lesson by now.

The second experience we had with a thief, was nothing like as spectacular. In Dar es Salaam, we lived in a ground floor flat, fitted with louvre windows at ground floor level. Due to the incessant heat, and despite an air conditioner in our bedroom, we had formed the habit of always sleeping with the louvre windows open to catch what sea breeze there might be.

One Sunday morning, we were lingering in bed trying to summon up energy to get up. Suddenly, I was rudely woken right up by a scream from Dorothy next to me. I wondered whatever had happened, and as I sat up sharply, I was just in time to see black hand round Dorothy's handbag as it disappeared through the open louvre window.

Without thinking about the open louvres, Dorothy, as had always been her habit had left her handbag on the chair by her bed. An opportunist thief had obviously spotted it as he walked past, unable to resist his chance encounter. As with the previous experience, I had not the slightest clue who the thief was, nor where he had gone.

Again due to incessant heat, I had developed the habit of always sleeping stark naked. I clearly could not go running outside to give chase, stark naked. So as quickly as I could, I pulled on some clothes, but inevitably, as always happens when trying to get dressed in a panic, I found myself trying to put both my legs down the same hole in my shorts, and my neck through the armhole of my shirt.

At last, I was properly dressed, so ran outside in the optimistic hope of finding the thief and retrieving Dorothy's handbag. I vainly ran round the building, and down our access road, but saw no-one, nor anything suspicious. On this occasion, there were no street urchins to direct me. Thus, this time, Dorothy's bag had gone once and for all, or rather twice and for all.

CHAPTER XVI

Railway Construction

There were, at the time I was in Tanganyika, three railway lines, all to metre gauge. They were all run by the East African Railways and Harbours administration. The principal line, ran east-west from Dar es Salaam on the coast, through Morogoro, Kilosa and Dodoma and on westwards through Kigoma to Tabora on the eastern shore on Lake Tanganyika which formed the border with Belgian Congo (now Democratic Republic of Congo). A branch from Kigoma took a line northwards to Mwanza on the southern shore of Lake Victoria.

A second line, quite separate from the others, ran from Arusha eastwards through Moshi, at the southern foot of Kilimanjaro, on through Korogwe, then eastwards to Tanga, a seaport on the Indian ocean.

There is now, which there was not when I was there, a connecting line between these two principal east-west lines, it follows a parallel course with the coast, though a few miles inland from it.

The third line in existence in those days was right down in the south eastern corner of the country. It started at the seaport of Mtwara, and went westwards a short distance inland. This fragmented system left many of the country's principal towns and districts totally devoid of any rail link. The railway administration did run regular passenger bus services to link up some of these towns, and also ran a considerable fleet of lorries to carry freight between these outlying towns, but neither the buses nor lorries could hope to make up adequately for the lack of rail link.

All these lines were single track, each principal station having passing loops for opposing trains to pass.

One of the main areas devoid of a railway, where the need was greatest, was the southern highlands, Mufindi, on the way south to Mbeya, close to the border with Zambia (in those days

Northern Rhodesia), and indeed on into Zambia and Lusaka its capital ...

To this end, the EAR&H administration decided to build a branch line south from Kilosa on the main central line. This resulted in a sizeable influx of Wazungu in Kilosa, more than doubling its European population. They built their own accommodation in the form of a sort of suburb of prefabricated buildings.

Before they could strike south from Kilosa, it was necessary to take the line across the Mkondoa river right on Kilosa's south-western border. There was already a substantial road bridge across the river in this area, which we could clearly see from our house terrace. It was a lattice girder bridge, and therefore there was no way the engineers could get across it, even with a temporary track upon which to take rolling stock across the river. It was neither strong enough for the task, nor was there adequate headroom beneath its girders. The engineers, had therefore no alternative but to build their own bridge in order to get their rolling stock and heavy plant the other side of the river.

I was able to watch the goings on for this operation from the vantage point of my house. I could scarcely believe what I saw. First they built up piers of stacked steel sleepers in the water directly on the sandy river bed. Upon these seemingly flimsy structures, they laid lightweight girders, directly upon which the track was laid, only a few inches above the river's water level, to the extent that the water frequently lapped the underside of the girders and rails. A few sidings were laid out on the south side of the river and these were connected up to the precarious track upon the temporary 'bridge'.

Whilst I held my breath in disbelief, they then shunted across this structure some loaded flat trucks, being pushed by an old steam engine. Even from my house, I could hear the frightening creaks and groans as this flimsy structure took the weight of its train, especially when the locomotive ventured onto it. I could even see the water lapping on the bottom of the locomotive's wheels as it reached the middle. Miraculously, and if I had not seen it all happening, I would never have believed it possible, the locomotive made it safely to the far bank and it pushed its train into one of the prepared sidings.

Now that they had most of the heavy plant they needed for the job, work proceeded apace with building the line south through the sisal estates we could see from our house.

I was astonished at the rapidity with which they levelled the trackbed, and built up embankments or dug out cuttings as necessary, then laid the track out upon it. It only took a few days before the building work was out of sight from my veranda and terrace.

Meanwhile, life in Kilosa continued as ever, the gymkhana club's activities considerably livened up by its swollen membership.

A few weeks later, the engineers had completed a proper bridge to carry the line over the river. Well out of sight from my house, however, the work of building the trackbed continued at great speed, until another river was reached. But that is another story.

Peter M Wilson
Bwana Shamba

Road Construction

My first duty as *Bwana Shamba* at Kilosa, after I had done my share of helping the District Commissioner to organize the local election, was to get on with constructing the road from Kisanga to Mfirisi, a distance of twenty five miles through virgin bush and scrub.

Two hundred labourers plus a few overseers had been assembled at Kisanga. None of these was able to speak more than the odd word of English, so that I would soon be able to gauge how much Swahili I had learnt.

Daudi (pronounced Da-oo-di) Lukas was to be my local agriculture instructor, but then he knew virtually no English either. I duly turned up at Kisanga with my Landrover, and brought along my new safari boy/cook, Frank.

I had just got to the rest house at the top of the hill, and parked by the veranda for ease of unloading, and Frank was half way walking across the short distance to the kitchen unit, when lightning struck the tree growing just behind the kitchen unit. The bang was terrific, and poor Frank was knocked to the ground. It was a long time before our ears stopped singing after that deafening crash.

Then a short time later, the heavens opened up. I had never seen the like of it before, nor indeed since. To liken the rain as falling like stair rods, was totally untrue. It fell like scaffolding poles. In no time at all, the dry red soil was a quagmire of mud, and rivulets appeared everywhere already eroding miniature gullies all over the place. It was therefore some considerable time before Frank was able to appear with the tea I was craving for.

When he did at last appear, I thought at first he was wearing some different shoes, but he was still barefooted, it was merely the thick caked red mud clinging to his feet. I was just settling down to drink my tea, when I heard a great commotion over by the kitchen area. I got up and peered around the end of the veranda. I could scarcely believe my eyes. There was Frank, along with another two Africans, frantically trying to grab as many flying termites as they could as they emerged from their underground nests in their thousands. The rain had triggered off a mass migration and the Africans were cramming as many of these as they could into their mouths, later spitting out their large wings. I hoped that Frank would not decide later to serve me with termites on toast or something similar for my supper.

My tea finished, I decided that I should go back down into the village to pay my respects to the local *Jumbe* (headman). I got into my GT and slithered across to the spiral track leading down the hill. It was very difficult to steer the Landrover due to the sticky consistency of the mud. Once on the spiral road downhill, in only that short time, the heavy rain had already eroded many deep rivulets, making the road extremely bumpy and hazardous. As luck would have it, Daudi was already with the *Jumbe*, so I was able to kill two birds with one stone as it were.

The next morning I collected Daudi and we drove the short distance to the starting point of my road.

Unlike the railway engineers I had observed, I did not envisage having to build a flimsy temporary bridge to get across the river, which was inconveniently sited just where the road should begin. I certainly needed to get across. I did not fancy wading it, as it was known that crocodiles lived in it.

As luck would have it, a substantial tree had fallen across this small river some time before, and this had become established as a useful footbridge across. Its boughs and branches provided many useful handholds, so we were easily and safely able to negotiated it to reach the far side of the river. Daudi had organized half a dozen of the labourers plus a couple of the overseers to meet us, so that we could get started on road building. As luck would have it, one of the overseers was a local man, coming from a hamlet more or less on the direct line between Kisanga and Mfirisi. He was therefore well acquainted with the lie of the land.

I asked him to walk in as direct a straight line as he knew how from our starting point towards Mfirisi. Every thirty or forty yards, he was to stop, hack out a stout stake with his *panga* (machete), and drive it into the ground as a marker. In this way, we were able to sight up these stakes in as straight a line as possible between Kisanga and Mfirisi. Once we had erected a dozen or so of these stakes, I got the labourers, using only their *jembes*, heavy duty drag hoes, and their axes, *shoka*, to start on road building. I explained how I wanted them to clear a twenty-five-foot swathe along the alignment, chopping down any trees in the way, and to create a shallow camber, to help drain water to the sides of the actual road. No wheelbarrows were available to help move soil from one place to another. Instead, they used *karai*, a sort of heavy duty wok-like container which the labourers carried on their heads.

Daudi and I supervised the work for the first few hundred yards or so of the road, preparing it to my liking, then we staked out a further mile or so of the line through the bush, then retraced our way back to Kisanga, leaving our workers to get on with the road building alone. I dropped Daudi off in Kisanga and returned to the rest house, having to engage four-wheel drive to get to it up the slope. Even so, it was not easy to get to the top, due to the slippery mud.

Next morning, as arranged, I again collected Daudi and we went back to the construction site. As luck would have it, following the previous day's heavy downpour, we had had mostly good sunshine in the daylight hours ever since the storm. This meant that much of the gooey mud had already dried up considerably, and even the vegetation had dried out too.

I was pleasantly impressed by how well and efficiently the road gang had progressed since we had left them the day before and they had reached the stage when more marker stakes were needed ahead. Daudi and I went forward into the bush to help with the staking out. It was at this time that I was introduced to the dreaded *upupu*. This is a type of wild 'buffalo' bean, also called cow-itch or mucuna bean. Its pod is roughly the size of a broad bean pod. But here the likeness ends. It is covered with the finest down imaginable, almost like velvet, comprising countless minute short hairs. The slightest vibration or breeze dislodges this down when ripe, so that the tiny hairs get scattered far and wide. These hairs must surely rank as the world's most efficient itching powder.

Once airborne, the wretched down hair easily sticks everywhere to sweaty skin, and if ever such pods were disturbed for any reason, everybody started scratching everywhere as the diabolical hairs worked their relentless way to all parts of the body, even beneath clothing. I very quickly learnt to recognize the plant and to avoid it like the plague. This was, more often than not, easier said than done. It is a climbing plant, so that often its wretched pods, generally growing in pairs, could be found up to ten feet up in other trees and bushes. I did not envy the labourers who were having to hack down all the under-growth, and therefore having to disturb the *upupu*. I made sure I gave these workers a wide berth while they worked. It was dreadful stuff and virtually impossible to rid oneself of it once infested, to the extent that one could scratch till the skin became raw, and it would still itch. It still makes me itch now in writing about it, it is such dreadful stuff!

The work of digging out the road carried on apace, and the labour gangs very quickly got the hang of what was required of them. I practised my Swahili as much as I could in supervising this job, and quickly learnt many stock phrases, such as 'Nenda moja kwa moja' (go straight on).

One evening as we were returning to Kisanga in my GT just as dusk was falling fast, I had Daudi in the cab with me, when we disturbed a beautiful full-grown porcupine. It ran down the road ahead of us, caught in the glare of my headlights. It ran on and on for several hundred yards. Daudi pleaded with me to run it down. I asked him why, and he replied 'nyama nzuri kabisa!' (excellent meat!). Needless to say I did not run it down, much preferring to watch in fascination as it ran quite fast down the middle of the road ahead of us. Seeing it from the rear, its large black and white quills were all fanned out wide open, which made it look very beautiful, and very much larger than it probably was. Daudi kept urging me to kill it, but eventually he got the message that I intended to spare its life. After a while, I noticed one of its quills work loose and eventually drop out. I went back next day, and managed to find it. I still have it at home somewhere.

Once a fortnight, once I had established the road building routine on site, it was necessary for me to pay the labourers. A few days before pay day, Daudi would bring in the pay and attendance sheet, listing the hours worked by each labourer. We would give this to Michael Kitambi in the office to check and calculate the total payment due for that fortnight. The following Monday, I would draw the necessary cash in the appropriate proportions of bank notes and coinage from the cash office, then go to Kisanga, keeping the cash in a stout strong box designed for the purpose. The other vital item I took with me was an ink pad.

It speaks much for the general honesty of the population, that nobody had the slightest qualms about my roving unarmed in the district with that amount of cash. Even at the remote spot where I paid out, there was never the slightest qualm about my safety or that of the cash.

At the appointed time, I turned up at the Kisanga end of 'my' road near the river crossing, and using the tailgate of the Landrover as a table, called each man forward by name to collect his wages.

This was where the vital ink pad came in. Since most of these men were illiterate, there was no question of their writing their names, let alone producing a signature. So as each man took his pay, he was asked to '*Tia kidole!*' (put the finger). I would then get hold of his hand, extend his grubby thumb, press it on the ink pad, then press it onto the pay sheet opposite his name. The thumbs were generally so caked in mud, that I often wondered what legal standing such 'signatures' would hold if ever it came to it.

At the end of paying out, I was left with a filthy paysheet covered with purple thumb prints.

The labourers, having received their pay, spent considerable time secreting the cash about their person in all manner of hiding places. The coins with holes generally having a corner of a shirt or *kanga* squeezed through, then knotted for security.

The strong box now virtually empty. I used to lock it in my cab, then walk with Daudi up the road works to examine progress. I was always very impressed by the weekly progress, and pleasantly surprised how much had been done since my last visit. Only very occasionally would I suggest that the alignment be modified slightly to avoid an unnecessary obstacle such as knoll or small hill, or even something like a baobab tree which would have needed a bulldozer or elephant to shift, neither of which we had at our disposal.

Mercifully never again, on any of these trips, did I ever again come into contact with the dreaded *upupu*.

Then came the time when it was necessary to make a start on bridging the small river at the Kisanga end. I went to consult the *hazina* (native administration) engineer, one Bill Shenton, whose office was in a compound just below the Kilosa *boma* and who happened also to be my next door neighbour up on the hill. He was most helpful and amiable, and explained patiently just how I should build the bridge.

I was first to get two sturdy piers built the full width of the bridge, one each side of the river, using cement and local stone, which was present in abundance on site. He explained what height these should be built up to.

He advised me what type and size of girders to order to carry the main deck across, even offering to order them for me, when I told him the length required.

I made a special trip the next day to Kisanga to get the work on the piers started, having first ordered the cement and arranged for our own ancient Austin EPCC lorry to collect it and deliver it to Kisanga on site.

Some weeks later, upon returning from my pay safari at Kisanga, I found an urgent note waiting for me on my desk. It was from Kilosa railway goods yard, advising me that a pair of steel girders had arrived for me, and should be collected forthwith, lest I incur demurrage charges. This was a sort of compensatory charge made by the railway, to compensate for their not being able to use the railway wagon upon which my load was resting until collected.

I went straight down to the station to examine my girders. I was staggered by their size. They were huge, and clearly far too big and heavy for our Austin lorry to be able to carry all that way on bad roads.

I had precisely twenty-four hours left to remove them from the goods yard before hefty demurrage charges were inflicted on me.

I was at a loss, initially, as to how to deal with the problem, then I remembered seeing a substantial articulated low loader lorry the railway construction people had used to carry lengths of railway lines and other girders to their construction sites. Just what I needed! But how to get hold of it?

I went straight away to see one of the railway engineers I had befriended and got to know quite well. I explained my predicament and asked if I could hire his articulated low loader. He emphatically said I could not, then before I could even register disappointment on my face, he said he would *give* me the use of his lorry to get the girders to Kisanga for me. When I explained the problem of the threatened demurrage charges, he promised to have the girders collected from the goods yard that very afternoon. He would then see about getting them to Kisanga on the morrow. This was as classic a case of the

The completed bridge at Kisanga.

advantages of using the 'old boy' network as anyone could wish for.

True to his word, my engineer friend came up trumps, and when I next went to Kisanga, the girders lay at the side of the road right there in Kisanga village, the lorry driver not having dared to venture upon the track road as far as the actual bridge site. I then, of course, had the problem of getting the girders down the half mile or so to the bridge site. I had brought some chain with me with the intention of towing them down there with my GT, but the moment I tried to do this, the leading edge of the girder immediately dug its way into the dirt road and became immovable. So then I thought I could try lifting the leading end onto the Landrover. The problem was lifting their dead weight up onto the Landrover. I was not sure what they each weighed, but clearly it would take many strong hands to lift it up those four feet or so. So I went down to the road site to collect a dozen strong men. They all chanted together in a sort of 'heave ho' chant as they lifted the end up. It was a struggle to raise adequately, but they just could not drag it the few feet to rest their end on the back of the Landrover. I solved this problem by getting them to lift it the necessary height, then reversing the Landrover under it. This done, we secured it in place with the chain I had brought, then dragged it along the road to the bridge site. The trailing end scored two deep ruts in the murram road, but this was not serious and did not particularly matter. I got the first girder down to the site, then returned with the labourers to repeat the process for the second one.

Back at the bridge site, I was now faced with the problem of getting them across a crocodile infested river from one pier to the other.

I had had a temporary deck of local timber put across to facilitate this part of the operation, using pieces of trees which had been cut down in clearing the path for the road. It was not exactly a masterpiece of engineering, but everyone seemed to consider it adequate for the job in hand.

I rounded up to twenty labourers, and amidst more *heave ho* choruses the girders were raised one at a time and carried across the temporary decking. At this point, I decided spontaneously to take a leaf out of EAR&H's book. I got the labourers to lay the I-shaped girders flat way down rather up on edge as they would eventually lie.

The second girder was ceremoniously carried in like manner, then I got the girders spaced apart to coincide with the wheel track of the Landrover and got the labourers to build up an earth bank up to the girders at each end, and carefully drove up onto the girders. I was confident that they were strong enough to take the weight of the Landrover sideways on rather than edgeways, and through there was marginal sagging when I reached the centre, it was nothing to worry about. At last I had my GT on *terra firma* on the Mfirisi side of the river. I invited Daudi into the cab with me and set off up 'my' road, the first ever to drive along it.

The reactions of the local residents was most interesting. Whenever we approached any of the scattered hamlets along the alignment, the womenfolk took to their heels and ran deep into the bush for dear life. The children, on the other hand, did precisely the opposite. Amidst whoops of delight, they ran towards us, and began running alongside, clinging dangerously to the side of the Landrover whilst shouting with glee. I was worried lest one fall beneath my wheels even though I was not going very fast. So I stopped and invited them aboard. They needed no second invitation and leaped aboard in record time amidst further whoops of joy and excitement.

I drove as far as the end of the road that had been completed. I would have liked to go on forward as far as the river crossing at Mfirisi, but dared not go 'bush-bashing' through the *bundu*, on account of my precious cargo. I knew that the children would not willingly dismount, and even if they did, there would be the danger that they would run into my path, and not be seen due

Peter M Wilson
Bwana Shamba

to the thick undergrowth. So I turned round and drove back to Kisanga.

I dropped off the children where they had come from, and they departed amidst choruses of '*Asante sana*', which was nice to hear.

I stayed one more night in Kisanga, then spent a few days in Kilosa to catch up on office work. A few days later I went to Mfirisi to get work started on the bridge at that end. The bridge was to be similar in design to that at Kisanga. The only difference to building it lying in the fact that there were no known crocodiles in the river. Bill Shenton again ordered the girders for me. Since these were considerably smaller than those at Kisanga, it was possible for my EPCC lorry to transport them down to the Mfirisi site without problem.

My next job at Kisanga involved getting the bridge decking built in accordance with Bill Shenton's advice. In due course my GT was the first ever vehicle to cross this completed bridge.

My tour in Kilosa was just long enough to see the completion of 'my' road, and to be able to drive along it from end to end. It had been a very enjoyable and satisfying project. In later years it was used for the purpose for which it was built, to transport cotton out of the valley. I later learnt that a bus route was established along it, and that when an oil pipeline was built from Dar es Salaam to Zambia, some years later, the construction lorries also made use of it. I feel sure that by now, unless it has been properly looked after by the PWD, it has probably reverted back to natural bush and disappeared without trace, which is what tends to happen out there. The maxim generally being 'use it, or lose it!'.

CHAPTER XVIII

Bridge of Sighs?

Work progressed at staggering speed in clearing and preparing the track bed for the railway branch line from Kilosa. The work included many large embankments and cuttings which were completed in miraculously short time.

After a few weeks, the engineers came to an obstacle that called for careful attention. It was a dry, sandy river bed, for a 'flash flood' river. This meant that, whilst it remained totally dry for most of the year, it was capable of becoming a raging torrent within seconds, should there be heavy rain in its catchment area upstream.

To allow for just such an eventuality, a full size bridge had to be built over the dry river bed. The engineers had already built up a sizeable embankment to and from each river bank in preparation for a bridge to go up between them. This then, was the situation for the start of this somewhat spectacular episode. The budget for the railway was somewhat thin and the engineers had been given the directive to economize wherever possible.

The engineer responsible for building this bridge therefore sought a way of keeping the costs down for building it, right out in the middle of nowhere. By rights he should have had the use of large, cumbersome cranes on site to hoist the heavy girders into position. But the trouble was, that to get such large cranes on site, then remove them afterward, would have cost quite a large sum of money. He therefore decided upon an alternative, crafty plan to do away with the need for any crane at all.

The three substantial piers had already been built in readiness for the girders. One pier on each bank, and a third one right in the middle of the river bed. First he had some railway track laid out directly upon the sandy river bed of the river below the bridge piers. This was then connected to the actual main track already permanently laid as far as the bridge site. It only needed slewing slightly on one side to make the temporary connection.

Peter M Wilson
Bwana Shamba

The flat wagons loaded with the bridge girders were then brought down from Kilosa and shunted onto the temporary track on the river bed. With the aid of bulldozers already on site, the engineer had a huge sand ramp bulldozed up from the river bed, between the girder wagons and the tops of the piers. Similarly he had a further ramp pushed up to the level of the flat wagons. By means of his bulldozers, the girders were simply pushed up the sand ramp and up onto the tops of the piers. Bingo! There the heavy girders were permanently secured to the pier crowns, and, with the sun setting fast over the horizon, everybody went home well satisfied with the day's work. What they did not notice, however, was that a violent electrical storm was continually lighting up the far horizon over to the north.

As I am sure you have already guessed by now, yes, it did rain very heavily that night high in the catchment area of that river. Down came the water at thunderous speed, torrents of it. All was well until it came to an immovable object in the form of a large sand dam right across its path. Up till then the natural river banks had easily been able to contain the tremendous forces of the raging torrent as it followed its natural course. The water built up and built up against the sand ramp, as if wondering what to do next, until a sizeable lake had formed. Water then spilt round each side of this lake, held up by the huge sand ramp level with the pier crowns. The deluge flowed round the corners until it came to another obstacle, the railways embankments.

Now neither the embankments, nor the sand dam in the middle of the river, had been built to withstand the sort of tremendous pressure of water that was fast building up upstream of these obstacles. The level of the new lake built up and up until, such was the tremendous pressure, something had to give way.

All at once the water found its way through and over the obstacles and surged through the ruptures with such force that hundreds of tons of river sand were carried along with it.

No sooner had the water broken through both embankments as well as the central sand ramp, than it spread out sideways, flooding hundreds of acres of prime agriculture land which had already been cleared, cultivated and planted out with maize and cotton. As the raging torrent of sand-laden water spread out, it slowed down, and deposited its load of sand on this prime farm land, resulting in a deposit of up to ten or twelve inches all over this vast area.

Some of the devastation caused by the disastrous flash flood.

When the engineer returned to his site next day, he could not believe the devastation that confronted him. Gone were huge sections of the completed embankments each side of the river, as well as the bulk of his huge sand ramp on the river bed. Each side of the river, as far as the eye could see, was total devastation, with deep sand covering every square inch of the ground, right in amongst all the scrub trees, many of which had been uprooted by the brute force of the deluge, and lay either fallen or leaning at a crazy angle.

A deputation of angry farmers was waiting for him to vent their anger and frustration at their *shambas* being ruined beyond redemption. They demanded compensation for their ruined land, and wasted efforts in time spent in cultivating and planting out the seed, plus the cost of the wasted seed.

The result of this catastrophe was that the hapless engineer had to come to our office, cap in hand, to ask us to assess the damage and compensation payments due to pacify the angry farmers.

When the news of this episode reached the EAR&H head office in Dar es Salaam, I could visualize the sighs that must have resounded around the board room, especially when they received the bill for all the compensation.

I got to know all about the extent of the permanent damage to this prime farm land in the area of the bridge of devastation because I was the poor *Bwana Shamba* who had to go out on

Peter M Wilson
Bwana Shamba

site to assess and measure it all up for the compensation payments, which I am sure far exceeded the cost of bringing in and setting up a crane to build the bridge – oh well!

CHAPTER XIX

Witchcraft

The building of the Kisanga-Mfirisi road now virtually complete, I had time to divert my attentions to other matters in the district. With David Jack having gone and Carmichael Mpupua having taken his place, I had spent some time showing him round and help him settle in to the district's work.

I now spent most of my safari time at Ulaya, where not only the *Mkuu*, but many of the *wakulima stadi* (progressive farmers) were as keen as mustard to get on and improve their husbandry methods. Cotton was the principal cash crop grown in Ulaya, but there was much room for improving its quality and husbandry.

Whilst staying in Ulaya rest house, I often used to wander out in the evenings just to chat to people and generally get to know everything and everyone in the locality. This included Bjorn Graae, who was always very well informed about all the local *habari* which it was important for me to know.

It was on one of these evening visits that Bjorn told me about his experience with local witchcraft.

He was certain that the yields he was getting from his coffee estate were well below what he could reasonably expect from his acreage, particularly bearing in mind the healthy state of his coffee bushes.

After some careful investigation, he concluded that considerable quantities of his coffee harvest were being stolen from the bushes. He therefore went to see his local *Mkuu* who agreed to alert the local witchdoctor. A day or two later the witchdoctor came to see Bjorn to size up the situation, promising to come back later.

A week later, true to his word, he turned up at Juani estate bringing a *kikapu* (basket) full of various types of *dawa* ('medicines') in little bottles. He spent the morning following the perimeter of the estate and hanging one of these little bottles of *dawa* every few yards whilst muttering all sorts of *mumbo-jumbo*. His job completed, he went to see Bjorn to get paid for his services. Bjorn wondered if it would be worth the expense, but had no alternative but to pay up and see if the proof of the pudding would be in the harvesting.

From that day, Bjorn immediately noticed a substantial increase in the yields from his estate, suggesting that the *dawa* was serving its purpose to keep thieves away. Certainly, the news had got around the whole of Ulaya and Madizini areas that Juani estate was now strictly 'off limits' due to the *dawa* which had been put in place by the *Mchawi* (witchdoctor).

In spite of this, however, two people, for some reason, *did* one night venture onto Juani, and helped themselves to some of Bjorn's coffee beans. It just so happened that a few days later both these particular gentlemen were involved in separate road accidents and were killed.

As far as the local inhabitants were concerned, because they knew for certain that these two victims *had* stolen from Juani, these deaths were without a doubt due to their having defied the *Mchawi's dawa*, and was proof enough that Juani estate was strictly off limits.

Bjorn had no trouble with thieves from then on, and even started leaving his store room doors unlocked at night with perfect impunity, and with never any thefts. Early the following season, when Bjorn was in amongst his coffee bushes pruning them, he came across a large heap of rotting coffee berries hidden beneath a pile of twigs and leaves.

After discussing this with various people, including the *Mkuu*, it was conjectured that doubtless the beans had been picked off the bushes by thieves prior to the visit of the *Mchawi*, preparatory to stealing them, but then the *dawa* had been put in place before they had had a chance to take the beans home. The *dawa* now being in place, the thieves had not dared to remove the beans, so had left them severely alone.

CHAPTER XX

Preaching to the Unconverted?

During the course of my safaris throughout the district, I stopped one day at Mikumi on my way through. I stopped by our instructor's house there, Yonah Michael, overlooking the crossroads, to catch up on all the *habari* with him. Now Yonah was a keen Christian, and during the course of our conversation, he suddenly asked me if I would please arrange to be in Mikumi on safari one Sunday, so that I could conduct some sort of service, as the Christians in Mikumi never had any sort of services there, never having seen any missionary for months. I promised Yonah that I would see what I could do and let him know.

There was no rest house in Mikumi, so that if I were to stay there, it would have to be in my tent.

It so happened that a week or two later, I needed to go to the Mikumi area, so let Yonah know that on a certain Sunday, I would be able to organize some sort of service in the village. I took my tent and set it up near the edge of the village, well away from the dust of the busy Morogoro-Iringa road.

On the agreed Sunday, I went to Yonah's house, expecting him to accompany me to an open-air gathering, as I knew there was no sort of mission church in the village. I was astonished, however at what I found later. Yonah led me purposefully through the village to what I was sure would be an open-air gathering, but not so!

Yonah suddenly stopped and pointed to a brand new mud and wattle building about the size of an average African dwelling house, built in a similar manner. All sorts of pretty, fresh wild flowers had been pushed into the still wet mud of the walls, especially round the doorway. I was completely astounded at the trouble the local Christians had gone to in building this charming little church for just this occasion. Yonah invited me to look inside, and there stood wooden benches for about fifteen people, facing an 'altar' table at one

Peter M Wilson
Bwana Shamba

end. At one end of the roof apex, a neat cross, made up of two
sticks, had been erected.

There were by then only about five minutes to go before the
appointed time for the service, and very quickly the fifteen places
inside were taken. But that was not the end of the arrivals. Thick
and fast, from every direction, inhabitants of Mikumi kept arriving at the church. Since there was no more room for them
inside, they simply squatted down on the dusty ground close to
the entrance to the little church. By the time we were ready to
start the service, I estimated there were close to a hundred men,
women and children sitting in the overflow congregation outside. Yonah bid me enter the little church to start the service.

He introduced me as the 'Bwana Shamba, Mkristo mzuri sana'
I wondered how he felt I was a 'very good Christian', but let it
pass. Having remembered to bring a Swahili prayer book with
me, borrowed from Kilosa church, I started to read from it in
Swahili, following the modified Matins service, and hoping my
Swahili was up to par. At the appropriate moment, I asked Yonah
to read a lesson from the Bible, which he gladly did, using the
Swahili Bible my mother had given me before leaving England.
Then it was time for me to preach the sermon I had prepared
in Swahili. I had some trepidation as to whether or not my
Swahili would be up to coping with a sermon. I was just starting,
when I was interrupted by someone from my indoor congregation, asking if we could please sing a hymn. Since we had neither
hymn books, nor any means to making music, I asked how and
what they wished to sing. Their response immediately brought
about the start of a few people in a sort of impromptu choir
singing 'The Lord's my Shepherd' in Swahili to their rendering
of Crimond. I was astounded. The large congregation outside
quickly followed suit and soon Mikumi was resounding to the
strains of this fine hymn.

The hymn finished (they evidently knew the words off by
heart) it was now my turn. I started the sermon by introducing
my text. I read from my Swahili Bible. I chose as my text a
subject I thought would be close to their hearts, the parable of
the sower. I was extremely nervous as I started preaching in
Swahili, but once I got going, my confidence built up rapidly,
especially when I kept seeing various heads nodding in agreement with what I was saying, as well as receiving encouraging
smiles. I forget for how long I preached, but after I had finished,
the impromptu choir sprang to its feet once more and immedi-

ately burst into another hymn. This time it was 'Now thank we all our God', once more sung with gusto in Swahili to its familiar tune, the outdoor congregation again joining in. I finished the service with a few more prayers, including an impromptu one in Swahili, after which I was delighted to hear Yonah add one of his own too.

I read the Grace out in Swahili from the prayer book, and it was all over. Everybody wanted to shake my hand. Numerous 'Asante sana!' expressions of thanks were given me as my hand was shaken by countless warm grips.

Yonah bid me follow him outside, where another tirade of 'Asante sana' and firm handshakes followed.

It was not until some time later that the realization came to me, that I had actually preached a whole sermon in Swahili. I am not going to claim that it was pure 'Swahili safi', but I felt confident that it had all been acceptable and understood. Then I remembered the passage in the Bible that promises that at appropriate times believers have the gift from the Holy Spirit to speak 'in foreign tongues'. I felt very humbled and privileged to have been blessed by the Holy Spirit in this way on this occasion.

Certainly, I knew that back in those days, my Swahili would not have been up to preaching in that way, without considerable assistance from the Holy Spirit, so I gave thanks to God for his help and have never forgotten the thrill and privilege of leading the inhabitants of Mikumi in Christian worship that very special day.

On my next visit to Mikumi several weeks later, when I called on Yonah, he greeted me with glad news that his wife had just given birth to a son. I felt very privileged and humbled when Yonah went on to tell me that they had decided to name him 'Wirisoni' after me.

Peter M Wilson
Bwana Shamba

CHAPTER XXI

Village Safaris

I now established a routine of visiting as many outlying villages as I could, not necessarily those where cotton was grown. Whenever possible, which was on most occasions, I took Dorothy and the family with me, staying in rest houses.

One of the villages I stayed in fairly often was Kidodi, right down in the south. They had a Roman Catholic mission there with a huge brick-built church which would not have looked out of place in any English town. The village *Mkuu* always wore his colobus monkey ceremonial headdress, whenever he came to greet me at the rest house as soon as I arrived there.

He did, however, have one weakness, charming though he was. He was very keen on his rice *pombe*. I had been warned that if ever I needed to make sensible conversation with him, it was advisable to have it before ten o'clock in the morning while he was still sober.

Unfortunately, his bad example led many of his fellow villagers to follow suit, to the extent that the cotton crop which they had taken the trouble to grow was rarely harvested, since the farmers themselves were generally too intoxicated either to care or be able to harvest it.

It was unfortunate that the rice matured for harvesting before the cotton. Had it been the other way round, it might not have created any problem. Thus one of the tasks I set myself was to try to persuade the *Mkuu* and his people to lay off the rice *pombe* at least until they had harvested their cotton. This was very much easier said than done, and I had to continue to see, with great sadness, many acres of good cotton lint fall to the ground, unharvested and abandoned to total ruin by dirt and insects. I could not even find any *Wakulima stadi* to persuade at least to harvest the cotton they had taken the time and trouble to grow. I am afraid that in this respect I had to write Kidodi off as a dead loss. Our frequent visits to Kidodi had started what became a regular routine. No sooner had we pulled up by the rest house, than a queue would immediately form of people with all manner of minor ailments, cuts, bruises, complaints of a headache etc. etc.

This custom had started when on our first safari, someone had come to ask for some suitable *dawa* for a nasty cut he had on a finger. Dorothy had on that occasion therefore got out our First Aid box and applied some *Germolene* to the cut, then fixed a plaster over it. She had barely finished this task, before then too, a queue had formed of people seeking the same sort of attention from the *Bwana Shamba's memsabu*. We always dealt with the various complaints in the same way, cuts and bruises with *Germolene* with or without a sticking plaster, headaches with aspirin and tummy aches with *Rennies*. If ever anyone turned up with a genuine serious problem, we would always do our best to persuade the patients to '*Nenda hospitali*' (go to the hospital), but from the expressions on their faces, we knew perfectly well that they had no intention of going there, having much preferred the idea of my *memsabu* giving them some *dawa*.

Many other villages we visited adopted the same practice, so that we always made sure we were well stocked up with our *dawas* before setting off. I rarely encountered this experience when alone on safari.

An interesting experience for me at any rate, as a keen railway enthusiast, was visiting the villages along the railway line.

Kidete was a case in point. There was neither station nor rest house at Kidete, so everything I took with me, tent, tent poles, food trunk, etc, etc all had to be loaded loose in the guard's van and carried by porters from the track side where we had alighted to a suitable camp site.

The return journey from Kidete was always an interesting experience. Although it was an official stopping place for passenger trains, it was necessary to hail the driver to stop, much as one does for a bus, by putting the arm out. The problem I experienced was that I really needed to be in several places at once for this exercise. I needed to be at the place where the locomotive generally came to a stand, to hail it to stop, and I also needed to be right at the back part of the train to ensure all my possessions were loaded onto the guard's van. The answer was surely to get the instructor to hail the train for me, but then on one occasion, the train failed to stop for him, so I had

Peter M Wilson
Bwana Shamba

no alternative but to remain at Kidete for another day, repitch my tent and try again the next day.

One of the most amazing safaris I experienced was one I made to Kibedya, a village in the northern part of the district. On that occasion we had Diane with us, still at that time but a few weeks old.

No sooner had the village *Jumbe* seen that I had even thought his village worthy of bringing my young baby to it, he was so moved by what he considered to be the greatest compliment I could have paid him, that he immediately instructed his people to look after us in every detail. The first and most useful act they performed for us, was to go to the considerable trouble of digging a *choo* for us, which involved digging a deep pit, over which they built a mud and wattle hut. This involved a great deal of very hard work by a large proportion of Kibedya. Throughout our stay there, there was a constant stream of people bringing us all manner of *zawadi*. We had eggs, live chickens, maize cobs and even, just before we left, a live goat given to us. I was quite thunderstruck by all this generosity and kindness, especially as when I first arrived in the country, someone had told me that the days when a *Mzungu* visited a village and was showered with *zawadi* were gone. I certainly never found this to be the case, and on the contrary, was always showered with things like eggs, maize cobs, coconuts and live chickens wherever I went.

There was a sort of price to pay for all the generosity in Kibedya. It transpired that nobody in the village had ever seen a white baby before, so that Dorothy had constantly to pick up Diane to show her to the constant stream of admirers who came to see her, some even asking to hold her in their arms. Diane however did not seem to mind at all, and gave one of her heart warming smiles to all and sundry, to everyone's delight.

I did not, however, always take all my family wherever I went in the district. There was one particular place, where I was extremely glad not to have done so, having been warned against it beforehand, and that was to the village of Mauzi, pronounced (Ma-uzi). There was a decent rest house, which was the only point in its favour. The village lay right in the lowlands of the district, and was therefore right in amongst the wetlands where rice was grown in profusion. In Tanganyika, where there is standing water, there are *mbu* – mosquitoes. And, boy, were there ever some mosquitoes in Mauzi!

The walls of the rest house rooms were painted white, yet when I entered, they were black. On closer examination, it was clear that they were black because they were covered in *millions* of mosquitoes, literally. I would never have believed that there could have been so many, had I not seen them myself. I had fortunately brought with me the mosquito net for my folding *Hounsfield* bed, as well as a supply of *dawa ya mbu* (mosquito spray) for my mosquito spray gun.

Before doing anything else, I gave the room a good squirting with *dawa ya mbu*. The resultant noise was deafening, as close a million mosquitoes took to the wing, having been rudely disturbed from their slumber by some evil smelling spray. It took quite a while for the noise to abate, as one by one the survivors settled once more on the walls. Thankfully, I had reduced their numbers somewhat, I estimated there were now only about half a million instead of the previous million. I went off to see to my agricultural business in Mauzi, leaving Frank to makeup my bed and mosquito net and prepare my supper etc.

Upon my return around dusk, I preferred eating my supper outdoors, rather than in the mosquito den. Even outside, much of the local mosquito population through it only fair that as I was having my supper, they should be having theirs, naturally comprising my blood supply.

Figuring that I would be safe from mosquitoes inside my mosquito net, I retired early to bed to read awhile, I gave the room one last squirt of *dawa* before retiring under the net. Once more, I was nearly deafened by the buzz they generated. Inevitably, once I was tucked inside my mosquito net, I found a few wayward specimens who thought they too should have the privilege of being inside a net. I found it impossible to swat them, so in the end gave them a close-up squirt of *dawa*. I found that I had to take care not to let any part of my anatomy rest against the net on the inside, lest swarms of mosquitoes swooped on me, letting their friends know it was feeding time. I therefore had to be sure I was well within the bedclothes, which in a hot, humid environment was not the most pleasant of ordeals.

Eventually, I decided to settle down and try to get some sleep. I put out the light, put my book away and did my best to re-tuck the net in under my bedclothes.

I soon found there was another problem. My hosts soon found that the exterior of my net made a very good roosting site and settled upon it in their droves. The problem that manifested

Peter M Wilson
Bwana Shamba

itself, was that whenever I made the slightest movement in my bed, I was woken wide awake by the noise of the odd thousands of mosquitoes taking off in disturbed flight. Then, of course, there was always the odd pesky *mbu* which found its way inside my net, and insisted on flying with its high-pitched whine right by my ear. I kept trying to swat these brutes every time I felt sure that one was right on my ear, and all I got for my efforts at giving it a good hearty swat with my hand, was sore and singing ear.

I am sure in retrospect that my night at Mauzi must surely rank as the most unpleasant and uncomfortable night I have ever spent anywhere in the world. And I am determined always to avoid any such location again in the future. I quickly finished my visits around Mauzi the next day, and thankfully packed up my belongings and returned home the following day, pleased at last to be able to leave the tiny inhabitants of Mauzi to their own buzzings.

On another occasion on safari down at Mikumi, as I was getting ready for the night in my tent, one evening, Yonah came to tell me that the had heard there was another *Mzungu* on safari in the game reserve just to the east of the village.

I was curious to know who it was, so went in search of him, I entered the game reserve, which I understand is now a National Park. It did not take me long to spot him. He was staying in a tent, and I could see he was tucking into a meal sitting at his folding table in the entrance to his tent.

As I approached he saw and recognized me, and beckoned me to join him. I went across to his camp and took up his invitation to join him for supper. His safari boy brought me a similar meal, that I could see he was enjoying. My host was Bill Rees, a game ranger. I tasted the meat he was eating, and was immediately struck by the very pleasant and tender taste. When I asked what sort of meat it was, he surprised me by telling me it was wildebeest, or gnu, meat. When I enquired how he came by it, as, being a ranger in the game park, I could not exactly see him shooting a wild wildebeest just so that he could eat some for his supper, Bill replied that it was lion-killed meat. He had seen some vultures circling when he arrived, so went to investigate, and found some lionesses tucking into a wildebeest meal. He told me he chased them off (he did not say how), then helped himself to a prime cut. It was certainly one of the best cuts of meat I had ever tasted, and was truly succulent and tender. I kept eating loads of it, accepting extra helping after extra helping as Bill offered them to me. I could easily understand why lions are so partial to wildebeest.

It transpired that Bill was on safari in the area for several days like myself, so before I left, he suggested that I join him in the morning for a swim in the Ruaha river, not that far away. I would never have dared swim in such a river on my own, so as the idea appealed to me, I accepted the invitation and met up with Bill the next morning.

We, of course dispensed with the wearing of any swimming trunks, and swam in our khaki shorts. The river was quite swollen and muddy from recent rains, but it was certainly a very pleasant and refreshing experience to be fully submerged in its murky waters. Then a nasty through struck me, so I asked Bill,

'How can you be certain that there are no crocodiles in this river?'

'Oh', he replied nonchalantly, 'It's really quite simple, if there are any, they generally get hold of you!'

I thanked him for his encouraging words, then realized that even Bill would not be swimming in such a relaxed and nonchalant manner if there were the slightest risk of being attacked by a crocodile, or even a hippopotamus, so I relaxed too and really enjoyed the experience, which I certainly would never have attempted had I been alone, however hot and parched I might have been.

On my way back from this safari, I decided to stop off at Ulaya to see to a minor *shauri* (problem) I had there. The next afternoon, I went out from the rest house to go in search of my friends, and found Ismael Chande, almost certainly my best African friend in the district. We had a long, and as usual humorous chat about many topics, then he suddenly said, in Swahili, 'Bwana, how is it that if ever we see a really beautiful, fat bullock, you tell us it is a European breed. Or if we see a big fat brown hen that lays many large brown eggs, you tell us it is a European hen, or if we see a new breed of goat that gives us a lot of good milk, you tell us that it is a European breed, yet when you see a big fat black fly you tell us immediately that it is an African fly!'

He roared with laughter at the expression on my face.

He was perfectly serious in his question, but I could see from the delightful twinkle in his eyes, that he meant the question as

Peter M Wilson
Bwana Shamba

a good bit of humour. We had a good laugh, and conversation turned to other topics. But it was typical of the wonderful sense of humour this man had.

He then took me to his *shamba* to show me his cotton crop. We stayed there a while to discuss what needed doing there, then he insisted on accompanying me back to the rest house. As we walked along the main road side by side right in the middle of the village, I was astonished and embarrassed suddenly to feel him take hold of my hand, and continue walking along the road holding it.

I felt acutely embarrassed, then I remembered frequently seeing African men friends walking in this way. There was absolutely not the slightest inference of anything untoward about the action. He merely wanted to let everybody know that he and the *Bwana Shamba* were the best of friends. On the contrary, as a Muslim, he would have abhorred anything with homosexual overtones.

Whilst I found it, at the time, acutely embarrassing, in retrospect, I realize that he could not have paid me a greater compliment, and I felt very privileged. All the same I was glad nobody from Kilosa drove past at the time to witness the occasion.

During all my safaris, I had noticed the profusion of beautiful butterflies that fluttered all over the countryside, so I decided I would take up a new safari hobby, and collect butterflies. I called in one day at Ilonga research station to see the entomologist for advice. He was most helpful and encouraging, and immediately set to, to prepare a cyanide killing bottle for me, or rather for my butterflies. He showed me how to pin them out on special trays, then gave me a couple of spare old trays and a cork lined box in which to keep them. I made myself a crude collecting net out of mosquito netting, and thus became a butterfly collector. It took a little practice to learn the best way to wield the butterfly net, but practice soon made perfect, and over my remaining time in Kilosa built up a considerable and wonderful collection of beautiful butterflies, which I still have to this day. It made a fascinating and rewarding safari hobby.

Hitch-Hiking the Trains

There were a large number of *shambas* up the fertile Munisa-gara valley up which the main central railway went. There was a village a few miles up the line from Munisagara where there were several *wakulima stadi* , farming, principally, tobacco, for the local Tanganyikan market. They frequently asked for assistance from me, so I had cause to go there quite often. It was too far from Munisagara to walk to and from it each time, so I was left with two alternatives, as were the villagers from the area. One was to cycle, as most people did, it seemed, along the very edge of the railway track. This meant that in at least one direction, it involved cycling with one's back to oncoming trains, the main line being a single 'reversible' track.

I tried cycling in this manner on one occasion. Although I kept looking behind me for trains. When I did once look round, I was petrified and shocked to see one bearing down on me at great speed, but fifty yards behind me. I had not heard anything of it at all, despite it being a great steam monster, as it was coasting downhill at the time. I was truly frightened by the experience and vowed never to travel that way again.

The alternative way to reach the village I required, was to hitch-hike on the trains. Amazingly this was officially acceptable, though not necessarily in the way I was to adopt. The official way to hitch-hike was to get a ticket in the normal way, and ride in the guard's compartment at the rear of the passenger train, having told him which kilometre peg was required, in my case I think it was kilometre 210 from Dar es Salaam. In order to stop the train, officially, the guard was supposed to hang a red flag out from his window, and hope that the foot plate crew would see it and stop. Unfortunately, I experienced several occasions, when we went many kilometres past my requested stop before the driver spied the flag and stopped. When I complained about this to somebody on the railways, his reply was,

'I did not tell you this, but my advice to you is to ride on the footplate of the engine then you can tell the driver where you wish to alight.' I needed no prompting to put this good advice to the test. The next time I needed to go up the line, therefore, I went up to the engine and requested a footplate ride to reach kilometre 210. Fortunately the crew agreed, so up I enthusiastically climbed aboard. This method worked like a charm, so I repeated it many times. The disadvantage of this safari, was that I could not get any trains to stop for the return journey, so it meant I always had to walk the several miles back to Kilosa, usually along the track.

On one of the last occasions I did this safari, as I climbed aboard the footplate, asking for kilometre 210, the driver said to me,

'Well, you've seen me do this often enough before. *You* drive it and stop where you want!' I needed no second bidding as I sat in his seat, opened the regulator, and away we went. I knew kilometre 210 was right on a sharp curve, so when I spied a sharp curve ahead of us, I applied the brake and we slowed down. As I braked to a complete stop, I realized, too late, that it was not the right curve and that I needed to go on at least another kilometre. So, I had to do a re-start, reopening the regulator handle once more. (It was a genuine mistake I made in stopping too soon, I promise!) Although it was always an enjoyable adventure hitch-hiking the trains up the Munisagara valley, I never went there without good reason, I promise that too!

During my eighteen years in Africa I had many adventures, mostly illicitly, on various steam locomotive footplates, not just in Tanganyika, sometimes driving, sometimes shovelling coal. It was a paradise for such a railway nutter as myself.

Musical Soirée

When at school in England, I had spent a great deal of time and parents' money taking both piano and organ lessons. I dearly loved playing either of these instruments, so when I knew I was coming to Tanganyika, I realized that carting even a piano around Africa with me was not going to be a practical possibility. My brother therefore suggested to me that I buy myself a piano accordion, and teach myself to play.

I took it with me on numerous safaris and had made quite good progress at playing it, even managing to master the buttons on the left-hand side of the bellows.

On what turned out to be my last solo safari to Ulaya, I was sitting on the veranda of the rest house one evening, playing quietly to myself, when after a while, I realized that I was not alone. In the light from the pressure lamp I had on the veranda, I could see numerous pairs of eyes looking at me from the outer darkness beyond the range of the pressure lamp's light.

I therefore put the instrument down, and looked carefully out to see who was there. I nearly died, for sitting in all manner of attitudes all round the front of the rest house was a throng of close to a hundred men, women and children.

When I stopped, the *Jumbe* appeared from nowhere and pleaded with me to continue. I therefore continued with my 'concert' playing all the pieces I had successfully taught myself, such as 'Daisy, Daisy, Give me your answer do' and 'Any umbrellas, any umbrellas to mend today'.

I had to repeat most of the tunes I had already played as I had already exhausted my repertoire, but this did not seem to worry my audience. I played on for several minutes more, then put down my instrument again. The crowd immediately once more pleaded with me to continue. Since all I could do was play the same tunes all over again, I did just that, yet again.

The thought then struck me that maybe I could teach the

Peter M Wilson
Bwana Shamba

people of Ulaya to sing these songs. So that is exactly what I did. We spent the next hour or more learning to sing them, until they were able to give a fair rendering with me accompanying them on the accordion.

These songs now 'learnt', the crowd then wanted to teach me one of *their* songs, so I happened to have some manuscript music paper in my accordion case, and while they sang the tunes to their songs over and over again for me, I endeavoured to write the melodies down. With this, I was later able to make a fairly recognizable rendering of their songs, which they sang with great gusto as I played.

Thus we all whiled away the evening hours, thoroughly enjoying our musical soirée. It was close to midnight before the crowd gradually dispersed and I was left alone once more on my veranda.

That evening remains without doubt one of the happiest, if not *the* happiest of my safari years in Tanganyika.

CHAPTER XXIV

Don't Take it for Granted!

One of the first lessons I learnt in Tanganyika was not to take anything for granted when teaching Africans, such as there is a tendency to do when teaching in England. Africans are no fools by any means, yet it is very easy for us to take it for granted, when dealing with them, that they have the same wide realm of experience that we do. Let me cite several examples.

A good friend and colleague of mine, Roger Morton, who ran a Farmers' Training Centre of the slopes of Kilimanjaro, told me of a classic example of this very matter.

He had, in the classroom with him, a group of coffee growers who were attending a short course on coffee culture. Being coffee growers, they were therefore already thoroughly conversant with coffee bushes.

In the introductory lecture he was delivering, he projected on the screen a colour slide of a close-up of a cluster of coffee berries round every leaf node on the stems, the average berry size being that of a rose hip.

Roger then said something like,

'Well, you all know what these are!'

'No!' they replied, screwing their faces up trying to recognize what they were looking at. Some ventured, 'Coconuts?' Others, 'Pawpaws?'

When Roger corrected them and told them that they were coffee berries, they all collapsed in mirth, saying 'Oh get along with you! Who has ever seen coffee berries that size?'

Because the projector had increased the magnification of the slide across the room, the farmers could not appreciate this fact, and thought the image on the screen was life size. Roger therefore took the projector right up to the screen and focused the image down until it *was* life size. When he then asked them what they now saw, they replied 'Well of course we know! What do you take us for? They are coffee berries! We grow them, don't we?'

Peter M Wilson
Bwana Shamba

So Roger demonstrated that the further back he stood with the projector, the larger the image appeared on the screen. Only then did the penny drop with the coffee growers that the projector had enlarged the image to coconut proportions, when an 'Aha!' ran round the room. In England, of course, most teachers would doubtless assume that everyone would understand the magnification principle involved. Not necessarily so in Africa.

A similar example I heard from an entirely different source, concerned a poster which had been prepared and put up all over the place.

Because of the tremendous force of water that falls as rain in Tanganyika, terrible erosion of soil can result. In an attempt to reduce this erosion, it was always highly recommended that whenever ridges were created in a field such as are generally prepared for crops like potatoes, it is vital to 'tie' these ridges, to prevent the troughs becoming raging torrents in a rain storm, especially if the ridges are on a slope.'Tying' means making a sort of mini dam of earth across the troughs every five or six feet apart. This has the effect of trapping any water present, rather than letting it run away in a torrent, thereby eroding the soil away. It has the added advantage, that it gives the soil a better chance of retaining the moisture instead of losing it as run-off. A poster had therefore been prepared illustrating tied ridges, retaining water by each 'dam', or 'tie'. Since water is notoriously difficult to illustrate in a colour picture, the artist had portrayed the water as being blue.

When an instructor on one occasion was explaining all about the importance of tying ridges to a group of farmers gathered around one such poster, he could tell, from the looks on their faces, the farmers were not 'with him' as he explained in detail the intricacies of tie ridges. Then one of the farmers raised his hand and asked.'I think I can understand what you are saying, but what do you put in the water to make it blue?'

The third example I can cite concerning this problem did not take place in the classroom situation.

Whilst I was at Tengeru in subsequent years, a large cash grant was received from abroad with which to make improvements to the facilities at Tengeru. Most of this cash grant went on building new lecture theatre blocks and a splendid new library. With the remnant of this grant, it was decided to improve the students' toilets, replacing the old 'Asian type', with 'Western type' flush lavatories instead.

Within a few days of the students' return one term, the staff were shocked beyond words whey they saw that most of these brand new flush lavatories had been terribly vandalized. The seats had been broken and the pans were full of numerous large stones. The fact of the matter was, that it was not vandalism at all. It was due solely to the staff having taken it for granted that the students would know how to use a 'Western' type flush toilet.

When in the villages, an African uses a toilet, he has to stand with his legs each side of a hole in the ground, over which he squats. There is, as you can imagine, no toilet roll, nor toilet rollholder in such a *choo*. So instead, Africans traditionally collect a few smooth stones to use instead of paper. Having used the stones in this manner, they are discarded down the hole.

There are, in addition, some modern 'Asian' type flush toilets around here and there, but they are designed to be used just like the bush *choos*, and have foot stands each side of the ceramic flush pan, upon which to stand while squatting.

So what the Tengeru students had done with the brand new 'Western' type *choos*, was simply use them in precisely the manner to which they were accustomed. They stood on the seats each side of the 'hole', thereby smashing the seats. Having used the toilets, they then used stones as they were accustomed, then as quite normal, disposed of them down the 'hole', not having the slightest idea how this 'new contraption' worked.

It had been taken for granted the students would know how to sit on this type of toilet and use the paper provided.

Peter M Wilson
Bwana Shamba

CHAPTER XXV

Cottoning On (Pamba)

With the arrival of Dickie Brown from Mwanza, and our new directive from Morogoro, concerning our new policy in Kilosa district, our method of working took on a dramatic change in 1961.

We were to pick a particularly promising village in a good cotton growing area, where there was a good chance the local farmers would be receptive to new ideas and improved husbandry.

There was no doubt at all in my mind that the chosen village should be Ulaya, where I had encountered nothing but enthusiasm and interest for anything new which was likely to benefit the farmers themselves in the long run.

Now the cotton plant is an annual, whose plant when mature can reach waist height with its woody stems. When growing, however, it is generally knee high at flowering time, when it produces a dozen or more yellow trumpet-shaped flowers on each plant. When fertilized or pollinated, the flowers form green buds. These are called bolls. Initially the bolls are about a quarter of an inch across, but all being well, they grow rapidly until they are the size of a large walnut. As they mature they change from bright green to pale ochre, then brown.

When fully mature, they burst open into four quarters, releasing bright white cotton lint. Inside this lint are buried the seeds, which are black and about one centimetre long. These seeds are eventually combed out of the lint in a ginnery, a sort of mill, specializing in removing these seeds, then baling up the lint for export.

Unfortunately, there can be few field crops in the world which are more susceptible to damage by such a profusion of species and numbers of insect pests than cotton. First of all there are beetles which can eat and devastate the actual flowers. Then there is the wretched boll moth, which lays its eggs on the developing bolls. Upon hatching out, these eggs produce a caterpillar called a boll worm, which immediately burrows into the boll, causing it to drop off if still immature, or if already a maturing boll, ruining the lint inside by rendering it black with its droppings. Any lint which survives this onslaught, once it has been released from the boll, when it opens up at maturity is immediately attacked by a bug called a cotton stainer. These are from the order Heteroptera, and have bright red backs, with black spots on them. They are a sucking insect, and like most sucking insects, regurgitate a certain amount of their saliva to get their sucking action going. It is this regurgitated saliva that causes the yellow staining. Any lint either stained yellow or soiled by boll worms commands rock bottom prices and is therefore totally uneconomic to harvest. Unless these insects are controlled, the lint has very little, if any, value at all.

Because of the profusion of insects which attack cotton, both in species and numbers, a regular weekly treatment with insecticide must be applied either as a spray or dust, if the cotton is to have any chance of producing a worthwhile harvest. As if all these insects were not enough, the younger plants can also be attacked by aphids, which of course weaken the plant. In order to combat these multitudinous insects, the recommendation we put out was to spray the entire crop at weekly intervals for a total of seven weeks, starting as soon as the flower buds appeared.

Alternatively a DDT type dust could be used. One of the entomologists at Ilonga research station, called Swain, designed a cheap but highly effective home-made duster, which we called the Swain duster, after the entomologist's name, made up of two large tins, connected by a piece of car or lorry inner tube, depending on the size of tin, to act as bellows when pumped to and fro. A simple spout soldered onto one of the tins completed the gadget, which worked very effectively indeed.

The cost of the insecticide either in spray or dust form, plus of course the cost of an actual knapsack sprayer, was a very great deterrent to most cotton growers from following this regime. And our foremost task was to demonstrate that unless the cotton crop was treated weekly as recommended, then growing the crop at all was virtually a waste of time, energy and space.

The only possible alternative, and it was explained that this was a very poor option really, in comparison with following the

Peter M Wilson
Bwana Shamba

The Ulaya cotton grower prizewinners with their prizes put up by the Kilosa ginnery. On the extreme right is Shomari Mjomba and to his right is Ismael Chande. Dead centre with fez hat is the Ulaya Mkuu.

spraying programme, was to harvest the cotton very carefully, keeping clean and dirty or stained lint totally separate at harvest by putting them in separate bags one on each shoulder. Otherwise it was necessary to sort through the harvested cotton and separate clean from dirty as soon as possible after harvest. All these routines took a great deal of persuasion and convincing of their importance to cotton growers, especially when financial outlay was involved. The best method to convince growers was to grow demonstration plots, grown by selected farmers themselves, not by an instructor, or even ourselves, otherwise the successful crop grown in the correct manner would be deemed successful only because *we* had grown it. They, the farmers themselves, would never be able to achieve the same results.

It was not always that easy to be able to persuade even the *wakulima stadi* to grow such demonstration plots, even though we tried our best to explain that they themselves would reap the advantages of the good quality cotton they had grown. This was where our friends Ismael Chande and Shomari Njomba came in very useful as they very quickly volunteered to grow demonstration plots for us. Their plots, of course, produced top quality cotton which went a long way in persuading others to follow suit.

Peter M Wilson
'Mr Agriculture'

CHAPTER XXVI

Filmrover

Despite concentrating so much of our time on Ulaya village, we still of course, had to continue with our normal duties throughout the rest of the district. And since the whole district was a cotton producing one, we were able to capitalize on our successes in Ulaya to encourage other areas to follow suit.

To help us achieve this, we were issued with a Filmrover. This expensive, thoroughly versatile vehicle was fitted with a 240-volt generator under the front passenger seat, directly driven from the engine. It was fitted with facilities to erect a cinema screen on its roof, loudspeakers, and other film-showing facilities, and also came equipped with a 16mm film projector, and a studio-type reel-to-reel tape recorder.

We made very good use of all this equipment, and in particular the tape recorder, by establishing inter-village rivalry by sending messages to and from their respective *Wakulima stadi*, and also on occasions, recording full scale village *ngoma*, native dances. These were all played at the other villages we visited, who immediately countered like for like. Both Ismael and Shomari were leading lights at Ulaya in this respect, and proved invaluable to the exercise.

The main use we put the Filmrovers to, however, was for their prime purpose, showing 16mm films outdoors. Having learnt the lesson of never taking anything for granted, the first step to take before getting down to showing the cotton growing films we were planning, was to get the villagers used to the principle of seeing films out of doors.

To this end the British Council sent us a selection of travel films, etc, just anything for us to project to get people used to seeing films. Most of the ones we received were prepared by the COI in Britain.

I remember nearly falling off my stool when looking at the first film we put on, which suddenly showed a full-face close-up of Stanley Clark, the farmer in Buckinghamshire for whom I had been farm manager before coming to Africa. He had been picked out in the crowd at the Banbury agricultural show, as a typical English farmer.

We did also manage to get hold of two locally made feature films, *Chalo amerudi* (Chalo has returned) and another *whodunit* – *Muhogo mchungu* – type film in which the new vice-president starred, Rashidi Kawawa, thereby giving the film a flavour of Ronald Reagan.

For our first filmshow night, we obtained the use of the school football field in Ulaya and set up the Filmrover between the goal posts at one end, erected the screen and loudspeakers and with the tape recorder played the recording of one of the *ngomas* we had recorded. We hoped that this would attract people from far and wide, but to our surprise, it did nothing of the sort. The only people on the field by the time we were ready to start were the few who had come initially out of curiosity to see what we were up to while we were setting up the Filmrover.

No sooner did we start playing the music, however, than even these people disappeared.

I wondered if perhaps the volume was too high for the music, which had been set very high indeed. After turning the volume down a little, a few people did drift in from all directions.

When at last we had an audience of sorts, we decided to put on the first film, a black and white travel film about England. To our utter astonishment, almost everybody stood up and ran off in blind panic, never having seen the like of this sort of magic before.

We did not shut off the projector, but just let it run on to see what happened. Bit by bit, people then started to drift back and settle down on the grass. We put on several films including *Chalo amerudi*. By the time we had finished showing films for about an hour and a half, we decided to call it a day, so we put the lights on. We were pleasantly surprised to see the entire field covered with squatting villagers, with hardy a blade of grass visible. Now, the boot was on the other foot, and some of them pleaded with us to show some more films when they saw us packing up. So we told them to come again the next evening. In fact we put shows on every evening for over a week just to ensure they were thoroughly used to seeing films. The two feature films were by far the most popular, and they were requested every evening, the one starring Rashidi Kawawa being especially popular and creating hoots of laughter when he was to be seen running about on screen.

At the end of this period, we were confident that the people of Ulaya were now quite used to seeing films, and were therefore ready to see the cotton growing films we had planned all this groundwork for in the first place.

Peter M Wilson
Bwana Shamba

CHAPTER XXVII

Film Making

Having satisfied ourselves that the people of Ulaya were quite used to the concept of film shows, we were ready to start making the actual cotton growing films for which all this preparation work had been done.

We intended to make seven films in all, the seven steps in successful cotton growing. These were cultivation, sowing the seeds, thinning and weeding, the seven-week spraying programme, harvesting, and grading and selling. To help us shoot these films in 16mm we obtained the services of a film man, Mr Swann.

We had had expert assistance in planning these films, and so we started to recruit potential stars. Fortunately, we were not hampered by annoying things such as Equity cards when it came to choosing our actors and actresses. By this time there was no shortage of volunteers to star in our films. These included Ismael and Shomari naturally.

The first film was shot successfully and sent off for processing and editing as necessary.

Then it was time to start shooting the second one dealing with sowing the seeds. Our actor on this occasion happened not to be a cotton grower. This of course made no difference as far as making the film was concerned, but it just meant that perhaps he needed a little more direction than an experience grower might have needed.

Both Mr Swann and Dickie Brown were on the roof of the Filmrover for the filming session, the latter armed with a battery powered megaphone with which to direct the actor. As usual there were crowds of onlookers standing on the fringes of the field, so Dickie used his megaphone repeatedly to ask them to keep back out of film sight. In this particular sequence the actor was to enter the field, check the pegs marking the proposed cotton rows, walk up the field a little way, drop his bag of seed down, then get ready to start sowing.

The shooting started and Mr Swann bent over his camera to start shooting the film. Dickie stood next to him shouting the directions to the actor on his loud megaphone in Swahili.

'Enter the field!' 'Walk to the middle!' 'Look up the field!' 'Check the pegs!' and so on, the actor responding very favourably and competently.

Then, when the actor got to the middle of the field where he was supposed to toss down his bag of seed, Dickie blazed out the instruction,

'*Shusha mbegu!*'

At this point, everybody in the field, the actor included, literally fell about with laughter. Dickie wondered whatever had caused all this mirth. What had he said to double everybody up? There was absolutely nothing wrong whatever with the Swahili Dickie had used which meant 'Drop the seed!' The trouble was, Dickie did not realize that that very phrase in Swahili also means, 'Ejaculate!'

It was quite some time before order was restored and filming could continue, but later in the evening, many of the farmers pulled Dickie's leg unmercifully about the brick he had dropped unintentionally. It was a long time before Dickie was allowed to forget his *gaffe*.

A week or two later we had completed all seven films.

For the last film on selling cotton, we had had a very large traditional mud and wattle building put up as the set for the cotton co-operative. At that time, the country's president, Mwalimu Julius Nyerere, was pushing for *Ujamaa* (family to-getherness) which was another way of expressing co-operatives. By having this building erected, we killed two birds with one stone, by creating a set for our film, and also by supplying Ulaya with a cotton co-operative building, which stayed in perpetuity after the filming.

Our seven films completed, we were able to show them at the appropriate times the following cotton growing season, and they worked extremely well.

There was at first, naturally, much mirth and bantering when Abdallah, Ismael or Ahmed appeared on the screen, but once they got used to seeing their friends on film, they settled down and took to heart the very messages we aimed to convey.

CHAPTER XXVIII

Ox Ploughing

We had great success amongst the Ulaya cotton growers in getting them to improve their husbandry techniques with the crop, so Dickie decided it would be a good idea to call in all the field instructors and have them in for a conference. This would not only allow us to bring them all up to date with what we had been doing in Ulaya and elsewhere, but would also allow them to bring to our attention all the problems and difficulties they were experiencing in the field throughout the district. Thus we found ourselves besieged by over fifty instructors from all over the district. As luck would have it, the majority seemed to have friends they knew in Kilosa, so we had no problems whatever in arranging accommodation for them for the con-

The sum total of Kilosa's agriculture department staff gathered together for the conference, squatting front row left to right: the author; Dickie Brown; Carmichael Mpupua.

ference. The district commissioner kindly made a large room available for us for the occasion too, in the *boma*.

Dickie addressed the gathering entirely in Swahili, being totally fluent in the language. I learnt a great deal from listening to him on this occasion, and it helped a lot to know what he was actually talking about in Swahili.

In due course the floor was opened to the instructors for them to recount *their* problems and/or progress. The main problem that appeared as a result of this useful session, was that many of them had questions asked as to the possibility of their being able to prepare greater acreage for cotton production.

Most farmers were very limited as to what acreage they could prepare, since every acre had to be cultivated by hand, using their traditional *jembe*, a heavy duty drag hoe. The principal question every farmer wanted to know, was if there was any possibility of a tractor being made available to them for ploughing etc, through, maybe, some sort of co-operative.

This was of course out of the question, the cost being prohibitive, not only in acquiring the tractor in the first place, but in the costs of running it. So that idea was shot down in flames right from the start. Dickie did, however promise to look into the problem and see if we could come up with any sort of solution. Other relatively minor problems then came to light, one being the prohibitive cost to cotton growers of the insecticides and sprayers needed for the seven week spraying treatment programme. We promised to try and find a practical solution by organizing some sort of loan or hire purchase arrangement for them. Thus each suggestion or minor problem that came up was dealt with by some means or another. The conference duly ended, and was pronounced highly productive and useful. Without a doubt the main problem that had come to light was that of being able to put greater acreage under the plough. Dickie and I discussed the matter at length, and we finally came up with the idea of using and training oxen for the job.

Oxen were successfully used elsewhere in the country for ploughing, so why not in Kilosa?

The idea developed in our minds until at last we decided to give it a go. Dickie organized the arrival of a trained ox-trainer to come to Kilosa to help us get the idea off the ground. We designated two instructors to be trained by him in ox training, obtained a few suitable oxen, and away we went the scheme.

After a few weeks, we had several well trained ox teams of

Peter M Wilson
Bwana Shamba

The ox ploughing demonstration at Gairo.

two beasts, as well as a couple of competent instructors trained in the art of training oxen.

We therefore arranged a giant field demonstration up in Gairo in the north of the district, an area well suited to cattle and where such a demonstration day would be eminently practical. We organized a fleet of GT lorries to ferry interested farmers up to Gairo for the occasion, and organized a massive field day. Several hundred farmers from all over the district duly turned up, and the working pairs of oxen were yoked up in readiness to start ploughing.

No sooner was the first furrow cut in the unploughed land, that several hundred jaws gaped wide open in astonishment at the sight they saw. Never before had anyone seen a *ng'ombe* (ox) pulling a plough. (Nor had they ever imagined such a thing was even possible.)

There was great excitement and celebration when the farmers immediately envisaged the almost boundless possibilities that appeared with these trained oxen, and the day ended with practically everybody wanting to get hold of a pair of them …

The actual day ended with a true African-style celebration in the form of an impromptu *ngoma* starting up, Dickie and I being the guests of honour, the dances being largely offered to us.

Peter M Wilson
'Mr Agriculture'

The celebrations lasted well into dusk, and as darkness

descended the GT lorries took everybody home, happy and highly optimistic about what the future might bring for them. Dickie and I declared the day highly successful and profitable.

The local tribesmen at Gairo preparing for their dance in our honour.

After that, requests for help in training oxen arrived in our office from just about every cotton producing village in the district, and more besides.

With such a wide interest in the development of ox training, we had to ensure we had not bitten off more than we could chew. Since we only had two trained instructors in ox training, our first priority was to train up some more ox trainers.

There was another problem we had to face too. Cattle, unfortunately, are susceptible to all sorts of nasty creepy crawlies and *wadudu* (pests) capable of infecting them with a wide range of cattle diseases, many of which are fatal to cattle. The two worst *wadudu* are ticks and the infamous tsetse fly.

To help us take measures to combat this threat, we called in the assistance of the veterinary department. If we wanted our cattle to have the slightest chance of surviving these diseases, especially the common tick-borne diseases, it was vital, as with cotton, that they be regularly treated with insecticides. The most effective way to do this was by dipping the cattle at frequent and regular intervals. If no dipping troughs were available, then it was necessary to spray the cattle, giving them a good

Peter M Wilson
Bwana Shamba

drenching with insecticide to kill off all the wretched ticks and other parasites.

The tsetse fly was a different problem, and much more difficult to prevent. Ideally, the best measure to prevent decimation by the lethal fly, is to destroy the fly's environment, the bush, which therefore requires all bush and scrub over a wide area being totally annihilated. But this was virtually impossible to achieve in a district like Kilosa. We asked the veterinary department to stand by with courses of injections for the cattle, either to protect or cure the potentially fatal tsetse-borne disease *trypanosomiasis* or *tryps* for short.

Initially, we decided to concentrate on establishing at least one ox team in Ulaya, where there was the greatest response and interest. Both Ismael and Shomari, as expected, bought a pair of oxen, so we sent our ox training instructors to Ulaya to train them there. We also arranged a loan for these two men to purchase an ox plough apiece. The population of Ulaya could not believe their eyes when they saw the newly trained oxen there ploughing Ismael's *shamba* with effortless ease. After that everybody wanted a team of oxen, but that included also, alas, the tsetse flies in the area. It was sickening to see these beautiful trained oxen upon which so much care, time, money and attention had been lavished, succumbing to the wretched tsetse fly.

We urgently called in the veterinary department to come to the rescue, but alas, it was all to no avail. The vets did what they could, but though they did doubtless prolong the lives of the affected oxen, they were by no means optimistic. In due course all our hopes and aspirations died along with the oxen.

At about this time, we heard a politician make a somewhat apt statement. He said, 'There is a mistaken belief in Tanzania, that President Mwalimu Nyerere rules this country. This is untrue. Tsetse flies largely rule Tanzania!'

Sad, but true.

Maybe there was something to be said for tractors after all?

CHAPTER XXIX

Half an Onion

On a narrow terrace below my house in Kilosa, there was a short drive leading to a carport. This comprised six wooden upright pillars supporting a corrugated iron roof. Beneath, there was an inspection pit covered with planks.

One afternoon, I decided to clean out this pit, to discourage snakes and other nasties from lurking in there. As I threw the planks to one side to open up the pit, I unfortunately threw one of them against one of the uprights. This resulted in a loud *boom* as the vibration spread to the corrugated iron. Up on the underside of this roof, a number of hornets had built their nests. Their habit was always to hang upside down on their nest, in appearance a pale sort of small honeycomb about the size of a half golfball hanging by a short length of fibre.

One of these hornets took exception to being so rudely woken up by the loud *boom* and vibration to the roof, so that without a moment's hesitation, it swooped down and stung me right on the end of my nose.

The African hornet is very odd compared to its European cousin. Its body and abdomen are only slightly larger than that of its cousin, but there the similarity ends. Connecting the thorax to the abdomen is a long elongated segment, similar in diameter to a pin. Their wings are also somewhat longer. I have no doubt also that their sting is rather more *kali*, fierce.

After I had been stung, I felt distinctly 'woozy' and my eyes started watering profusely. I decided it would be wise to go up to the house to get over this setback. When Dorothy heard what had happened, she went immediately to fetch a small first aid book I had been given by Crown Agents, whose green cover had been treated, a small notice warned us, with poisonous insecticide. The first aid advocated in this booklet for hornet stings, was to rub the affected area with half an onion.

I went to lie down on my bed to get over my wooziness.

Peter M Wilson
Bwana Shamba

Page: 145

Dorothy soon appeared triumphantly bearing half an onion which she gave to me to rub on my nose. The relief was instantaneous! I could not believe that onion juice could have such an immediate effect. In retrospect, I realize that I must have looked a proper Charlie, as I lay back on my bed, rubbing half an onion on the tip of my nose, a look of sheer ecstasy and delight on my face as I did so.

Having rubbed the half onion on my nose for several minutes and got the relief I needed, I carefully placed the half onion on my bedside table and dozed off to sleep. That evening, having totally recovered from my stung nose, we decided to go to see a film in the cinema in Kilosa.

When we came out, I was surprised to see an old school friend and his wife plus a friend of theirs waiting for us as we emerged from the cinema. They were on their way back south to Mbeya having successfully climbed Kilimanjaro, and were scrounging a bed or two for the night. Having heard we were in Kilosa, they had gone to the gymkhana club to look for us and then been told we were at the cinema. We immediately agreed to put them up for the night, and went up the hill to our house.

We very gallantly relinquished our bed for their use that night, and I joined the menfolk in the lounge, sleeping, like them, in my sleeping bag on the floor. Dorothy slept in the children's room.

It was not until long after our visitors had gone next morning that Dorothy discovered the half onion still on my bedside table. We had a good laugh about it, wondering what our guests had thought about our half onion and why we kept it by our bed, wondering if perhaps they thought we had stumbled across a new type of aphrodisiac.

We disposed of the offending half onion, and as we remembered the episode in getting ready for bed, had another good laugh about it. I don't know whether or not an onion is any sort of aphrodisiac, but I do know it is highly effective in relieving the pain from a hornet sting!

CHAPTER XXX

Spots Before the Eyes

In my opinion, unquestionably the most beautiful of wild animals found in Tanzania is the leopard. It is a magnificent and majestic beast with the most exquisite fur imaginable. I have to add, though, that there is no doubt that a leopard skin coat looks a million times better on a leopard than on any Hollywood actress.

While I was stationed in Kilosa, I was on my way back to Ulaya from Juani one night in the dark, driving my GT. My headlights dipped downwards as I cleared the brow of a small hill, and there, caught in the glare of my headlights, I saw a beautiful full-grown leopard just starting to cross the road.

As soon as he saw my headlights, he just sat down right in the middle of the road staring into them. He sat there a full ten minutes, before slinking off into the shadows at the side of the road. I could have stayed there all night admiring him, he was so beautiful.

Talking about Juani brings me to the next encounter about which I heard involving a leopard. Bjorn Graae told me that one night he and Daphne heard a commotion in their chicken run. Bjorn picked up his rifle and went off to investigate. It was not until he was actually in the chicken run, that he found there was a fully grown leopard in there with him.

He was too close to use the gun on him, and in any case his first instinct was to spare its life. The leopard, however, did not seem to appreciate Bjorn's consideration, for it suddenly leapt for him, placing one of its paws right on top of his head. Having extended its claws, it completely scalped Bjorn's head, then ran off. When Daphne came down later to see what was happening, she was shocked to find Bjorn with his scalp hanging down in front of his face.

Daphne calmly flipped the scalp back over the top of Bjorn's head again and led him up to their car. She then drove him the ten miles or so to Kilosa hospital. There the surgeon managed to suture the scalp back into place and also to close up a couple of deep scratches on his forehead.

Bjorn had had a very lucky and narrow escape from his close encounter of the leopard kind. All he had to show for his experience were a couple of deep scars on his forehead.

Another amazing story I heard whilst in Kilosa, involved a couple who were sitting in their lounge one hot and balmy evening. Because it was so hot, they had opened wide their French windows giving out onto the veranda. They had a dog which was fast asleep on the mat right in this doorway.

The couple were sitting in easy chairs one each side of this open door. All of a sudden, the dog woke up with a start and gave a deep growl whilst sitting up looking intently at something outside. Then as cool as a cucumber a full-grown leopard came in through the open door and helped himself to their dog, running off with it. The couple never again saw either the dog, nor the leopard.

This story confirms the fact that one of the leopard's favourite delicacies is dog. On that occasion, the leopard never even gave the couple, sitting only inches away, a second glance.

Snakes Alive!

Despite my dread of snakes when I first came to East Africa, I soon learnt never to give them a thought as I busied myself walking around *shambas*, nor indeed in the *bundu*. In actual fact I feared and dreaded *upupu* far more than any snake.

The most frightening experience I had with a snake was in my own garden in Kilosa. On that particular evening, I realized I had left my best torch in my car parked at the far end of the drive terrace outside my house. All I had with me in the house was my second best torch, whose batteries in any case were just about dead.

I thought it better to have the security of my best torch in the house overnight in case of emergencies, so, taking my dim torch with me, I went out into the pitch darkness to collect my best one. I was about three quarters of the way to my car, when I heard a hiss. I froze, not daring to put down my left foot which at that moment was fortuitously poised in the air.

With the aid of my dim torch, I looked down by my feet. To my utter horror, I saw that my right foot was about two inches from the tail of a fully grown puff adder.

Had I stepped with my left foot at that moment instead of my right, I would certainly have trodden fairly and squarely on the brute, and might indeed not be alive to tell you this tale now.

The puff adder is a deadly snake provided it can get a good bite in its victim. Had I trodden on it, wearing only flip-flop shoes and no socks, it would certainly have managed that on me all right. It is what is known as a back-fanger, which means that its poison fangs are situated right at the back of its mouth. This means that to inject its venom in a large dose, it has to open its mouth wide in order to get its back fangs to bite the victim. Again, had I trodden on it, it would easily have managed that.

The puff adder is the most likely snake in East Africa that anyone might stand on. Most snakes are far more frightened of humans than humans are of them, and whenever possible, a snake will flee for its life on the approach of a person or animal. But because of its obese size, the puff adder is generally unable to move away to safety fast enough, therefore it is the most likely of all snakes to be trodden upon. When fully grown, as this one was, it can measure up to four and a half feet long. But where it differs from most other snakes, is in its girth. Most snakes have a circular body cross-section, whereas the puff adder had a compressed oval body cross-section, up to four or five inches or so wide and one and a half inches deep, hence its inability to escape quickly. It does have, however, one of the fastest strikes of any snake, particularly if trodden upon.

With my weak torch, I quickly looked around to ensure there was no other snake around, then went quickly to retrieve my best torch. Now armed with my best one, I had a good look at the puff adder, then picked up a large boulder and with it dispatched the snake to oblivion, thanking God for having spared my life on this occasion.

Behind the servant's quarters at my house on Tengeru, there was a redundant *choo*. It had an outside door and made a very useful and practical wood shed. One day I went there to fetch some logs for the fire and opened the door. The logs had been neatly stacked up to just over waist high. As I was about to reach forward to pick up some logs, I was horrified to see not one, but two hooded snakes rear up to threaten me. I hastily closed the door and thanked God for sparing me yet again. The snakes, which had clearly been copulating in there, were spitting cobras, nasty pieces of work who, as the name suggests, spit venom into the eyes of their victims prior to striking them. These vile creatures can spit their venom with amazing accuracy, over quite some distance, even being able to reach a man's eyes from ground level.

Many a person has had their eyes spared from its venom, because they happened to be wearing a wrist watch. Many are the tales of spitting cobras aiming for a wrist watch as they have spat their venom, believe it to be an eye. I was wearing no watch that day, but mercifully God restrained these snakes from spitting at me. Had they done so, I would undoubtedly have received a double dose from those two.

The recommended first aid for venom in the eyes is to wash them thoroughly with milk, Mercifully I had no need to pursue this first aid.

Not liking the idea of spitting cobras lurking around my house and garden, I wondered how to be able to dispose of both of them. Then I remembered that one of my neighbours had a 12-bore shotgun. I therefore went straight round to his house and explained the situation. He immediately agreed to come with his gun. We went to the woodshed and while he prepared himself with his loaded gun at the ready, I gently opened up the woodshed door. No sooner had I done this than, as before, two evil looking hooded heads reared upwards. There was then a deafening BANG! As my friend let fire with both barrels. Suddenly there were just two stumps sticking upwards when they then flopped sideways, mercifully dispatched to oblivion. The remains of their still writhing bodies were removed and safely disposed of.

My third experience with a snake was extraordinary and occurred in the Ulaya rest house.

Dickie Brown and I made frequent joint safaris to Ulaya and in doing so we always used to stay at the rest house, staking our claim to one of its rooms each. It turned out that we both were keen chess players, and consequently, we spent many evenings locked in fierce chess battles. We used to play on the fixed table I had put in my room and upon which we also used to have most of our meals. One evening, Dickie's safari boy/cook, Kiberenge, arrived with our supper just as we had finished a game. So we hastily piled all the chessmen into their box. But because Kiberenge was waiting to put our meals in front of us, instead of sliding the lid onto the box, I just left it balanced loose on top. We then had our suppers and afterwards retired for the night to our respective rooms.

The next evening, after we had been back at the rest house for an hour or two Dickie challenged me to another chess game, so he came and sat at the table in my room. I soon came to join him, sitting in the chair opposite. He had already opened out the chess board, so I casually took the loose lid off the box of chessmen and was about to put my hand in to retrieve a handful when I recoiled in shock. Right there, curled up and virtually knotted up in amongst the chessmen was small light brown snake, almost perfectly camouflaged in amongst the untidy chessmen as it was. I did not care what type it was. As far as I

Peter M Wilson
Bwana Shamba

was concerned it was a snake, and I'm afraid my attitude is that the only safe snake is a dead snake.

I know many people abhor those like myself who kill a snake *then* look to see what kind it is. I am afraid that my strict policy was always kill first *then* see what kind it was. I adopted this tactic on this occasion, tipping it out onto the floor then stamping on its head as it tried to wriggle away. I never did find out what kind it was. As far as I was concerned it was now a harmless snake because it was dead, and that was all that mattered. How it had managed to climb up a bare table leg and get up onto the top of the table, then knot itself up like that in my chess box, I shall never know.

Oddly enough, the last time my family had an encounter with a snake was right here in England. We were all on a camping holiday in Cornwall in the extreme south west of the country. One day, we were walking along the beautiful cliff path for which the county is famous. The path follows the edge of the cliffs and, for much of the way, passes through fairly dense patches of gorse bushes.

Yvonne, who happened to be leading us along the narrow path, suddenly stopped and stooped to pick something up.

'Look, Daddy!' she said triumphantly, holding aloft a wriggling beast by its tail, 'I've found a slow worm!'

With horror I instantly recognized the markings on its head.

'Put it down!' I yelled urgently, 'That's an adder!'

Yvonne screamed and tossed it hastily away, mercifully unharmed. It would have been ironical, to say the least, had she escaped all those years in Africa untouched by a snake, only to have experienced her first venomous snake bite in England.

As a safety measure, whilst living in Africa, I banned all forms of plastic snakes in our house, because I was afraid that the children would get so used to seeing plastic ones and picking them up that one day they might pick up a *real* snake assuming it be only a plastic one.

CHAPTER XXXII

Kwa Heri Ulaya! Jambo Ulaya!

The end of my first three-year contract approached with surprising rapidity. The first sign of its approach was heralded by a letter I received from Dar es Salaam. It informed me that if I intended to renew my contract for a further tour, my future posting was to be Mafia island, of all places. For a start, this posting would have been almost unprecedented, as I, a mere Field Officer, to have been given a district to take in charge. This was normally strictly the job of an Agriculture Officer (normally a graduate), and one grade above mine. In addition, this posting would have been foremostly one concerned with commercial fishing. I would have been responsible for the actual island of Mafia in the Indian ocean some miles south of Zanzibar, and also the Rufiji delta directly opposite Mafia to the west, and all the fishing involved in those waters. My experiences of fishing were strictly limited to trying to catch fish with a worm on a bent pin in the rivers around Sedbergh when I was a boy. True, there would have been some agriculture on the island itself to see to, but fishing would have been the first and main priority.

However, my posting to Mafia island, which I am sure would have been a very pleasant one, was not to be. At about that time, a head office circular came round, asking for volunteers to go in for teaching agricultural subjects in one or other of the training institutes either at Tengeru or Ukiriguru, near Mwanza. Successful applicants, the circular went on to say, would be given the necessary training.

Much as I adored all the safaris I undertook in Kilosa, they did mean that I was away from home practically all week, every week, except week-ends, which, for a family man such as myself, was not a good thing. Believing that in a teaching post, I would be more likely to be at home every night, I applied.

Peter M Wilson
Bwana Shamba

To my delight, I was accepted. I knew that nevertheless I would in many ways desperately miss my safaris, especially those to Ulaya where I had made so many very good friends amongst the Africans. But strictly speaking, I knew I should put family first, so I did.

The 'necessary training' turned out to be attendance at a 'crash' course at Moray House College of Education in Edinburgh. The fees were to be paid by the Tanganyika government. The course, however, was to take place during my next home leave, the leave to be lost being added to the actual time spent in the UK, so that I would not lose out by it. Our home leaves worked out at just over 3 days per month served, at the end of each 3-year contract.

Before going on home leave, I decided to 'have a go' at the higher standard government Swahili exam, having set my sights on the promised bonus if I passed it. It was not actually required of me in accordance with General Orders. A long time previously, I had taken, and sailed through, the lower standard exam, and had therefore lost no salary increments. I knew that as far as the higher standard exam was concerned, it was now or never, if I was going to try and pass it at all. I therefore applied, sat the exam, faced the oral interview panel, and mercifully passed it, thereby receiving my promised bonus.

The time to say farewell to Ulaya village and its inhabitants came all too quickly. It seemed the people of Ulaya were as sorry to be losing me as I was them. They arranged a special day to bid me and Dorothy a fond farewell.

Dorothy and I duly turned up on the chosen day. The *Mkuu* had arranged a special lunch in the *baraza* building on specially laid out tables for the occasion. Dorothy and I were sat at the top table, next to the *Mkuu*. We were served with a traditional African meal with all the trimmings.

There was first and foremost, obviously, a huge dish of the traditional *ugali*, their staple maize meal 'stodge'. This was rendered more palatable by the presence of a large dish of boiled chicken, served in abundant gravy.

The meal started and everybody tucked in. The first thing Dorothy and I noticed was the total absence of cutlery, even to serve out the *ugali* and chicken. We therefore observed how our hosts dealt with the meal before us.

First, a small handful of *ugali* was taken with the right hand. This was kneaded into a small sausage shaped mouthful, which was then dipped into the chicken gruel, trying to take a piece of chicken meat in the process; this was then popped into the mouth.

Watching this procedure, I was reminded that there is a special verb in Swahili for 'to wash face and hands' implying 'before eating'. The verb is *ku-nawa*. I had observed that for many Africans *ku-nawa* before eating meant they would only really wash their right hand, virtually ignoring the left one.

It was clear to see why, in watching my friends eating this meal. Only the right hand was being used, and therefore, it would have been 'pointless' to wash the left one, as not required for eating. Furthermore, the Swahili for the right hand, or indeed the right as opposed to the left is, *mkono wa kulia* – the 'hand for eating', or the 'eating hand'. Dorothy and I tucked into the meal, eating in like manner. We were pleasantly surprised how tasty the meal was and we thoroughly enjoyed it.

Then the *Mkuu* noticed we had nothing to drink, so he dispatched somebody to go and fetch us a Coke and a Fanta orange drink at the Ulaya shop.

The meal finished and we well replenished, we all moved over to the large new mud and wattle building we had built for the filming of a grand *'baraza'* meeting. The place was filled to capacity so that it was almost bursting at the seams. It was standing room only inside.

Dorothy and I were asked to stand on a sort of podium along with the *Jumbe* and the *Mkuu*. Then started a whole series of long speeches in Swahili, started by both the *Mkuu* and the *Jumbe*, then the meeting opened up as a sort of free-for-all during which many of the *wakulima stadi* with whom I had had dealings came forward to make another length speech.

The content of most of the speeches was repetitious, everyone saying virtually the same thing in slightly different ways, some more verbose than others. Expressions of regret for our leaving were mostly said, along with profuse thanks for everything I had done to help the Ulaya farmers grow better and more crops, thereby helping them to earn more money. We were wished long life, happiness and good health etc. etc. etc. It was all highly complimentary and I felt quite moved by it all, even wiping away the odd tear.

Then it was my turn. So I thanked them for their constant kindness and generosity throughout my many safaris to Ulaya along with the numerous generous *zawadis* I had always been given. I also expressed deep regret at having to say farewell to

Peter M Wilson
Bwana Shamba

the good people of Ulaya, promising that I would pay them a visit if ever I returned to Kilosa for any reason.

The speeches finished, the *Mkuu* wanted us to shake everybody's hand before we left. So queues were formed outside for everybody to shake Dorothy's hand and mine. The handshakes were the traditional 'three-fold' handshake, in which initially a conventional grip is made, then one which grips the wrist, then thirdly, another conventional grip. This obviously takes three times longer to carry out than one normal handshake, and with close to a thousand hands to shake each, this operation was clearly going to take hours.

Then we came up with a solution to hasten the operation. It was agreed that all the women present would form a queue to shake Dorothy's hand, and similarly all the men would queue up to shake my hand. So this was quickly organized by the *Mkuu*, and thus we completed the ritual in only a fraction of the time.

It was a memorable and moving day for everybody, and I had many tears in my eyes as I made the final *Kwa heris*, especially to Ismael and Shomari who had been such good friends to me, and also to Seif Rukemo, the faithful Ulaya agriculture instructor.

With heavy hearts, we shook the *Mkuu's* and *Jumbe's* hands, climbed abroad my Landrover and off we went, saying *kwa heri* (Good-bye) to Ulaya village possibly for the last time ever.

Back in Kilosa, we had set about packing up each and every one of our possessions in wooden crates, ready for shipment to wherever we would be posted on return from UK leave, as we would doubtless not be returning to live in Kilosa.

We went around to many of our friends' and colleagues' homes for a farewell evening meal, during our last week or so in Kilosa. I was fortunately able to pass Bigears on to our friend, Marcel Contoret, who already had a pet monkey, and was pleased to acquire another. Then it was time to leave Kilosa for good. It was with mixed feelings that we made a last tour of our house and garden with its exquisite view.

Then came the time to say '*Kwa heri!*' followed by more three-fold handshakes to Frank, Juma and Maria, our *yaya* or children's nurse.

We had berths booked on the 1 a. m. mail train to Dar es Salaam to catch our flight to the other *Ulaya*, (Europe) and the UK. We sold our old car, then we were ready to leave Kilosa for ever.

As evening approached, we packed our cases into my faithful GT. I drove down to the *boma* for the last time, transferred our cases to Dickie's Holden car, officially handed in my beloved GT, then Dickie kindly took us up to his house till it was time to catch our train.

At the appointed time, he ran us down to catch the train to Dar. I had booked a double cabin, that is to say two ordinary cabins, each with a two-tier bunk bed. The two cabins were connected by a communicating door. This arrangement allowed us to put our excited children to bed as well as ourselves.

The final *kwa heris* followed to Dickie and his wife Joyce, and we were on our way. We spent one night in Dar in the New Africa hotel. The following day, one of the head office drivers drove us to the airport in a GT, we boarded the East African Airways Comet jet airliner, and we were on our way back to *Ulaya* – Europe.

My mother met us at what is now Heathrow Airport, being delighted to see us and her grandchildren, including of course, Diane, whom she had never yet met.

We went down to Crystal Palace in south east London, to stay with her for our leave. I only had a couple of weeks or so before I was due to start my course at Moray House. I had managed to get 'digs' in Musselborough for the first term up there, as I intended initially to leave Dorothy with the girls at Crystal Palace for the first term.

My digs in Musselborough were first rate, and were within walking distance from Moray House, which was an advantage. My landlady always fed me with enormous, nourishing meals, so that I often found myself in difficulties managing to eat them all up. At Moray House our course assembled, and I was pleased to find that a friend and colleague from Dar es Salaam, David Brewin, was also participating. The actual course rejoiced in the name of Chapter VI (agriculture) and if successfully completed would qualify us to teach as qualified teachers anywhere in the world, except, curiously enough, in Scotland, where we would only be classed as 'probationary teachers'.

The course we attended had only about six of us on it, and we all enjoyed it very much, though I admit that, after a period of some five or six years since I had last had to swot up for exams, I did find it very hard going having to concentrate on working for them.

Once our written exams were completed satisfactorily, we had

Peter M Wilson
Bwana Shamba

to go to do our practical experience. We were all posted away to various 'recognized schools' for our teaching practice. I was posted to the Technical College in Cupar in Fife, with 'digs' arranged in the village of Ceres about five or six miles away from Cupar. By this time it was winter, and a hard one at that. During my first 'observed' lesson, a chemistry one, a raging snow storm was visible outside. I remember the tutor who observed my lesson wrote in his comments about my effort,

'He coped well with the distraction of a snow storm outside'.

Next morning, however, there was snow several feet thick, plus many deep snow drifts, so that I had to walk into Cupar over the top of all this snow.

For my second term at Moray House the family joined me, and we decided not to live in Edinburgh, so I set about finding suitable accommodation.

I eventually found a suitable furnished flat, not in Edinburgh, but in North Berwick a few miles to the east.

By that time I had taken delivery of my brand new car, courtesy, at last, of a good loan from the Tanganyika government. It was a Morris Oxford Traveller of the latest model. It was a lovely car, easily able to accommodate us all. With this car, I was therefore able to commute daily to and from Moray House, together with, as it happened, Vanessa and Yvonne.

We had fortunately been able to get them both accepted into the Moray House demonstration primary school, which was extremely handy, allowing the three of us to go together to Moray House in the Royal Mile in Edinburgh daily.

Then one evening, poor Diane started screaming at bedtime, uncontrollably. It was clear that she was in considerable pain, but we were at a loss to see why or where. We called the doctor in post haste, and he immediately diagnosed a hernia in her abdomen. He summoned an ambulance and poor Diane was carted off to a children's hospital in Edinburgh. Fortunately we were able to go with her, following the ambulance in our car. Diane was immediately admitted, so with aching hearts we left her in the good care of the nice ward sister.

She was successfully operated upon next day and thankfully, has never again had the slightest bother with her former hernia since.

A few days later she was allowed home, so thankfully we were able to resume our new routine in North Berwick. My dreaded swotting continued as the final exams drew near. I had managed to get my dissertation out of the way, written around a book entitled *The Uses of Literacy*, which actually I found very interesting and absorbing. Our graduation day finally came, for which we had to appear in mortarboard and gown, followed by the inevitable photograph clutching the rolled-up certificate on parchment, and we were then officially postgraduates with Certificate in Education.

One most interesting digression occurred during that second term, and that was Tanganyika's Independence on the 9 December 1961.

As it turned out, I feel sure we were able to celebrate this occasion better than I would have done, had I actually been in Tanganyika at the time. Edinburgh University arranged a vast dinner for the occasion, curiously enough actually organized by a few Nigerians in the university. It was well attended by anyone having anything at all to do with Tanganyika Territory as it was then called. Incidentally, it did not change its name to Tanzania at independence. That came several years later when it merged with Zanzibar after the latter's abortive 'coup'.

At the end of the dinner we were each presented with a very nice commemorative medallion featuring a bust of Julius Nyerere on one side, and the new coat of arms on the reverse. Its short ribbon was in the colours of the new national flag. A black stripe bordered with thin gold lines, flanked by green stripes of the same width as the black. If my memory serves me right, the black represents the black population, the green the agricultural wealth of the country and the gold lines, actually a very pale yellow on the true flag, the European population which contributed so much to the country's independence.

While all this was going on in Edinburgh, far away in Tanganyika, the new national flag was being hoisted precisely at midnight, on a special new flagpole on the very summit of Kilimanjaro. The person given this honour was none other than my old friend from my Swahili course days at Tengeru, now Brigadier Sam Magai Sarakikya. A special new postage stamp was issued, featuring Sam hoisting this flag at the summit, renamed Uhuru peak ('Independence peak'), from its former German name, Kaiser Wilhelm Spitz.

At last our Moray House course was over, and we returned to my mother's flat at Crystal Palace in London.

After a lengthy period back in Europe, and having used up

Peter M Wilson
Bwana Shamba

our extended leave in Ulaya – Europe, by touring Switzerland in our new car, it was time to return to Tanganyika, now, of course independent.

Because we had our new car to take back with us, we opted to return by sea, rather than fly. We booked passages in an Italian vessel of Lloyd Triestino lines, a very smart, modern air-conditioned ship the *m. v. Africa.*

Fortunately we had been tipped off that if we asked to board her at Trieste, her home port and starting point, we would be able to use the ship as our hotel when she called in at Venice for three days to pick up cargo. Had we boarded in Venice we would only have been allowed to do so an hour or two before sailing time. So we of course booked to board at Trieste, after which we spent three wonderful days visiting Venice, where we found the temperatures just like those of Dar es Salaam, hot and very humid. On our way south via the Suez Canal, we called at Brindisi, Port Said, Suez, Mogadisciu, then Mombasa where we got off together with the car to drive to Tengeru, of all places, my new posting. It was a wonderful trip and very relaxing, on board the *m. v. Africa,* the children making maximum use of the swimming pool on deck. We made the trip back to and from the UK for leaves several times subsequently by Lloyd Triestino ships, which included the *m. v. Europa.* These trips always included a stop at Aden, then a 'free' port, which meant we could buy all manner of electrical goods etc at only a fraction of 'normal' prices.

A fancy dress competition was held on board on the trip, and it so happened that I won it. I had managed to borrow a girl's black one-piece bathing suit and had miraculously managed to squeeze myself into it. I borrowed some goggles from one of the engineers, pinned a notice on my back that said,

'It's quicker by Lloyd Triestino!'

It being my first time to 'Cross the Line' at sea, I volunteered to get 'the treatment' as we crossed the equator southbound. This meant allowing myself to be arrested by King Neptune's soldiers, who then forced me to eat salty spaghetti. Ugh!, then have some more rubbed into my hair, then be thrown into the pool to wash it all off. Foolish, but fun nevertheless. Dorothy dressed up as a Lloyd Triestino sailor in a borrowed outfit.

Dorothy and the girls 'chickened out' of this 'baptism' by King Neptune, on this occasion.

CHAPTER XXXIII

Swahili Tutoring

We were delighted with our new life at Tengeru. Only some seven miles down a good tarmac road in Arusha, was a first class primary day school, Arusha school. We were able to send both Vanessa and Yvonne there, and later Diane too. They all loved it, making numerous friends there. They were also very proud of their first school uniform, bottle green dresses and a grey felt hat.

To get all the Tengeru children to and from the school every day, we had organized a very efficient school run rota in which all the Tengeru parents participated. This, too, was a wonderful way for all the Tengeru children to get to know each other, and for us to know them as well.

One morning, however, I experienced a great adventure on my school run to Arusha. It was the morning after the abortive *coup* in Dar es Salaam, when the army had revolted. Apparently a few wayward soldiers had escaped from the army barracks just north of the capital. As they fled, their vehicle had run low on petrol, and they had allegedly murdered a garage attendant in order to steal petrol.

As I cleared the last brow on the tarmac road just before Arusha, I was horrified to find myself staring down the muzzles several rifles pointing directly at me as I sped down the hill towards the road block ahead of me. I managed to stop alright, but it was, nevertheless, an anxious moment. As soon as I had stopped the armed police ordered me to open my window which of course I did without a moment's hesitation. One of the policemen immediately poked his doubtless loaded rifle straight in my window while he scrutinized the occupants of my car. Having satisfied himself that I only carried children, he withdrew his rifle and bade me continue on my way. It was sometime after that my heartbeat returned to normal. Amazingly, the children seemed not in the least perturbed by the incident.

Shopping on Arusha
market.

The social life at Tengeru was very varied. Bryan Down, the then Institute's principal, and his opposite number in the Research Station opposite, the late Brad Houston, had managed to get official permission to use one of the empty staff houses in Tengeru to use a social clubhouse. We called it the Tengeru Club. It was a huge success, and through its many activities, which included regular dances, open club nights and parties of one sort or another, plus its well stocked bar, it enabled all us staff really to get to know one another, as well as having a thoroughly good time in doing so.

Additionally, both Dorothy and I also joined as active and acting members the very lively Arusha Little Theatre club, which put on regular plays in a beautifully converted large service garage, making a sizeable, well equipped theatre.

Our social life was by no means limited to Tengeru's boundaries, and we often found ourselves socializing in Arusha, Moshi or even further.

Whenever there was a full moon, Dorothy and I packed our bags and set course in our car for the coast at Mombasa, only

Peter M Wilson
'Mr Agriculture'

some two hours' drive away. Once at the coast, we either stayed in a tent, or in one of the many comfortable hotels right on the coast. We often used to go on these trips with our good Canadian friends and neighbours, Wally and Chris Redekop.

Lecturing to agriculture students in the new large lecture theatre at Tengeru.

Tengeru was also very conveniently sited for quick and easy access to most of the well known game parks, as well as Nairobi too, all of which we frequently visited, all being a couple of easy hours' drive away.

The immense pleasure of living at Tengeru at that time was nothing, however, to what it was about to become for me at that period.

When I first arrived at Tengeru from the UK, having completed my PGCE, at Moray House College of Education in Edinburgh, I was taken on the staff of the Agriculture Institute. I taught crop husbandry and other agriculture related sciences to the African students, most of whom were destined to become agriculture instructors out in the field. There were also many veterinary students at the Institute, but I had little or no involvement with them.

Peter M Wilson
Bwana Shamba

I very much enjoyed teaching and found it very rewarding work. During the course of my teaching duties at Tengeru, I noticed that scattered about all over the place, in hidden cupboards, in old store rooms, etc, were numerous visual aids of one sort or another. It was clear that nobody knew anything about all these useful teaching aids. So I took it upon myself to collect them all up, catalogue them, and develop proper library storage for them all. In connection with this too, I rescued the 'forgotten' Institute museum, and tidied it all up, establishing some new exhibits for it too. In connection with this I also established a living crop museum of small plots each growing a different crop found in the country. I later increased it to include different grasses too. It was all very rewarding and challenging. As a direct consequence of all this involvement with visual aids one of the Institute's vets, Bryan Down (destined to succeed Tony Markham, who was at that time the Institute's principal), and I were sent to attend a visual aids course at the Overseas Visual Aids Centre at Tavistock Square, in London during our next home leave.

I had been teaching at Tengeru for about two years, when the post of Swahili tutor fell vacant. Because I already had passed the higher standard government Swahili examination, and had taught one or two short evening class courses, I was asked if I was interested in taking over the Swahili tutorage. It seemed like a good idea at the time, so in a rash moment I said I would.

Teaching agriculture students on my museum plots.

Peter M Wilson
'Mr Agriculture'

As it turned out, it was undoubtedly one of the best decisions I ever made in my work, for it led to many years of a blissfully happy career, though initially, I certainly got many *'colli-wobbles'* before I actually started teaching it.

One of the first considerations I had to think about, was what textbook to use. There just was none generally available that was suitable. True, there was Ashton's Swahili Grammar, but that was far too advanced for beginners. After much deliberation, I realized there was only one way open to me, and that was to write my own.

I was already quite a proficient 'two-finger' typist, so before long, my little Tengeru office was resounding to the tap, tap, tap of typewriter keys as I hammered out my own Swahili notes.

By the time the first intake was due to arrive for my first Swahili course, I had only completed less than half of the notes I would require to take me through a complete course. I was really beginning to get a large collection of Lepidoptera specimens in my stomach by this time as the first course loomed ever nearer. Besides actual Swahili tutorage, my responsibilities were also to look after all the administration for the Swahili courses coming to Tengeru, which included accommodation, catering, visits, visiting speakers, etc, etc.

Fortunately there was an excellent rest house on the Tengeru estate comprising a dozen or so individual rooms, which were invaluable in accommodating the core of most of my Swahili courses to follow. Catering was largely solved by coming to some contractual agreement with one of the nearby hotels. Unfortunately the Lake Duluti Tearooms, where my 1958 course had eaten, was by then defunct.

As luck would have it, the very first course I was to teach at Tengeru comprised only about a dozen expatriates from as many different countries, which helped considerably reduce the butterfly collection in my stomach. Armed with only the first few chapters of my notes, I launched into my maiden Swahili course. In order to keep at least one step ahead with my notes, in between classes I had to work furiously on my typewriter composing subsequent chapters.

Fortunately, it being such a small course, there was a very relaxed atmosphere in the classroom which worked marvellously for building up my confidence. The courses were to be of seven-week duration, during which time students were to be given a full background on the grammar of the language, plus learn a little elementary conversational Swahili too.

It was very satisfying to be responsible for helping these dozen or so *Wazungu*, who knew not a word of Swahili when they came, to get a practical hold on the language and eventually be able to hold simple conversations with them. I soon found myself loving the challenge and interest of the job.

My first course ended, and this gave me the opportunity to work more on my notes, adding to them and perhaps more importantly, improving them, where I had encountered snags or difficulties in the classroom.

My second course loomed on the horizon. It was to be a huge course of over fifty students. They were all to be British volunteers from the excellent VSO organisation (Voluntary Service Overseas). Most were graduates, though later VSO changed its policy and in due course *all had* to be graduates.

Had this course happened to be my first ever, I am sure I would have died a thousand deaths. All being brand new graduates, the ink barely dry on their degree documents, they were very astute and quick to winkle out any errors or discrepancies I might make, but the atmosphere in the room was most relaxing and encouraging. In due time I was to teach such a class almost

One of my smallest VSO Swahili classes at Tengeru, with a few extras including a few Japanese volunteers. (The three people in the inset were VSO latecomers to the course.)

every year, and always found myself looking forward to it immensely.

During all these courses, I established two new traditions. The first was to invite all participants to my house for open house musical soirées almost every week. For these evenings, anybody could come to our house from the course primarily to listen to classical music, as I had quite a vast collection of classical records plus a good quality radiogram upon which to play them. I made two principal rules up for those present: no smoking, and no noise or talking.

Thus once a week during courses, our lounge was filled with prostrate figures in all the seats and all over the carpeted floor, lost in the music. Many of them were to be seen swotting up on their Swahili vocabulary lists at the same time. Towards the end of each evening Dorothy and I would serve tea or coffee to all.

The other tradition I started on all courses was a mammoth end-of-course party, sometimes held in our house, or sometimes in one of the nearby hotels, depending on the size of the course. I could at this point, perhaps appropriately add a third 'tradition' for each course, because for most courses from that second one

My home at Tengeru, near Arusha.

onwards, I took all interested students up Mount Meru, myself acting as guide.

Of the end-of-course parties, the most memorable (just) was undoubtedly that at the end of the Russian course. I had been asked to teach eight Russian veterinary surgeons, together with each of their interpreters. For the party, the Russians had organized for us all liberal supply of the genuine, real McCoy Russian vodka, *Stolichnaya*. They would have none of that Smirnoff rubbish, as they considered it. The party was held in the local hotel where they had fed during the course. Dorothy and I duly turned up, a 'polite' half hour late.

What we did not know, nor could we even suspect, was that it is the established Russian tradition, that if the guest of honour arrives late for a party, then every round of drinks he/she has missed by being late is put aside for him/her to drink upon arrival.

Furthermore, no one else is allowed any further drinks after his/her arrival until he/she has 'caught up' by drinking the put-aside drinks.

When Dorothy and I therefore arrived, we were each presented with a tumbler full to the brim of neat, pure *Stolichnaya*. Furthermore, as we were given it, we were *told* to drink it up as quickly as possible, as nobody else could have further drinks until we had caught up. The prospect of having to drink all that neat vodka was a daunting one, but after a few small sips, we found our sips getting larger and larger as we grew accustomed to the taste and by the time we got half way down the tumbler, it tasted just a little stronger than water.

No sooner had we disposed of the tumbler-full than it was replaced by a genuine vodka glass, which was kept perpetually charged up with vodka as we drank it.

How I managed to drive home the half mile down the Tengeru drive after that party, I shall never know, but I did. The most amazing and wonderful thing about that party, was that despite having put away considerable quantities of vodka that night, neither of us had even the slightest whisper of a 'hangover' next morning.

It was just as well, because we had drunk a considerably greater quantity of vodka than we might perhaps have wished, but one just doesn't argue with a Russian who offers you a drink of real *Stolichnaya*. And how many Russians have ever been known to turn down a genuine vodka?

It is almost impossible to single out any one of my numerous students over the next few years that I taught the language, but there is one who does stand out in my memory as undoubtedly unique. She was VSO girl, and I am still amazed at her achievements. Her name was Jenny McHarg, a graduate of, I think, history. Nothing very remarkable about that, I hear you say, except that Jenny was totally blind and had been so since birth. I have never met anyone, either fully sighted or not, who had the 'guts' that Jenny did. All the while I was lecturing in the classroom, I could hear a constant clicking sound, like someone knitting loudly, as Jenny took everything I said down in Braille notes with a little gadget she had.

To assist her in learning vocabulary, I used to read out vocabulary lists onto cassette tapes for her. One evening, I called in at the rest house to deliver one such tape. I knocked on the door of the room she shared with another girl. Upon being bidden to enter, I did. Poor Jenny, in bidding me enter, did not know that her room mate was in a state of undress, so that I got an unexpected view of female anatomy as I entered. This latter girl later told me that frequently when she woke up in the night and put her light on, she would find Jenny sitting up in bed studying her Braille Swahili notes in the pitch darkness.

Amazingly, when it came to the trip up Meru, Jenny was one of the first to express interest in climbing the mountain. She was one of the few on that course to make it the very summit, and that despite not having the reward of the spectacular sunrise on reaching the summit.

Many of the African students at the institute could not or would not believe Jenny was blind, such was the confidence with which she used to find her way around the compound to and from the lecture room and staff room for coffee breaks and so on. Such was Jenny's popularity that it was interesting to notice the young men on her course 'queuing up' to go out with her. In fact, she eventually married someone from her Swahili course, Mike Revel, and they now have a family of their own.

It was mostly due to remembering Jenny McHarg, that when I ran the London Marathon in later years, I collected sponsorship for the Guide Dogs for the Blind Association, raising £2,300 for it.

Another VSO student who stands out in my memory, was a charming young man called Richard Bamford. He used to spend a great deal of his spare time at our house enjoying playing with

Peter M Wilson
Bwana Shamba

and spoiling our three daughters. He was from a close family himself, and thus loved spending time with mine.

After his course ended, he and a few others from the same course went to the coast at Mombasa to do some 'snorkelling' and just enjoy a happy, relaxing seaside holiday. We were totally devastated, however, when a few days later, we received the tragic news that this charming young man had drowned whilst snorkelling. It appeared that he had drowned in a clear shallow pool only knee deep. Several people, when they discovered him, spent a long time trying to revive him by various means of resuscitation, but, alas, to no avail. Everybody was totally shattered at this news, not least my three daughters who had grown dearly to love him after all the attention he had lavished upon them.

There is another VSO student who stands out in my memory, though for an entirely different reason; he was a young man who went AWOL within two days of arrival. He just disappeared on the third morning of the course and nobody had a clue where he might be. I had no alternative but to advise the British Council about this, since they had overall responsibility for VSO affairs. It eventually turned out that this young man had 'done a runner' to South Africa. It transpired that he had allegedly left a young lady in Britain 'in the family way' and was running away from his responsibilities. For myself, it was at least a relief to know he was not running away from me.

Then there was another VSO girl who spent the night on Meru sharing her sleeping bag with one of the Egyptians on the same course. I also remember a German girl of slightly overweight appearance, clapping her hands in glee when, on studying the course time-table, she saw that every afternoon was designated for 'Exercises', imagining that this might help her possibly lose a few pounds.

The atmosphere on all the VSO courses, as I have said, was always wonderful and full of humour. I well remember a nurse called Bridget Connery, on one such course. In order to help me retain names, a definite weakness of mine, I always asked my students to complete a prominent name card to place before them where they sat. For some reason I could never fathom, I could never get the unfamiliar name of Connery fixed in my mind and over the course of several days started to call her Miss Cummins. I knew, at least, that her name began with a C. One day, I spotted her ever so surreptitiously replacing her name card upon which she had inscribed the name Cummins. This action was enough to jolt my memory as I knew there was no Cummins on the course, so that at last the penny dropped regarding the *gaffe* I had made, but at least it taught me the lesson, and from then on she was always Miss Connery. That little bit of mischief, however, typifies the wonderful humour and atmosphere on those courses.

I have one other lasting memory connected with VSO.

One day, Tengeru was honoured to welcome the Hon. Barbara Castle, MP, when she was minister for Overseas Development in the British government.

Bryan had organized a staff sundowner party to welcome her to Tengeru. During this party, she 'button-holed' me for a long chat as she wanted to know, for some reason, my opinions about the VSO volunteers. During the course of our conversation, she asked me how I set about teaching Swahili.

At that very period, it just so happened that I was about half way through the course for Russian vets, so without particularly thinking about its implications, I invited her to come in and sit in my class the next day for a few moments. Next day, she duly turned up and sat at the back of my class for ten to fifteen minutes, then left.

It was not until some years later that a friend of mine in the British High Commission, whom I had also taught Swahili, as it happened, told me that on arrival back in the UK parliament Barbara Castle had asked a question 'in the house' about me. 'What was a British OSAS officer' (that was I) 'doing in Tanzania teaching Russians?'

My friend told me that she was quickly reassured that there was nothing 'subversive' about my actions.

I once added up all the different nationalities I had taught Swahili to over the years and was astonished that the total came to some twenty or so!. This total included Russians, Japanese, Czechoslovakians, Germans, Scandinavians and also Africans from Nigeria. It almost came to the point where the list of countries *not* represented was shorter.

My students, of course, took their notes away with them, and from then on, I started receiving a deluge of letters from hundreds of people 'who had seen so-and-so's Swahili notes, and could they please buy a copy for themselves.'

Such was the deluge that I spent almost all my spare time in the duplicating room, churning out hundreds of copies of my 'book' until, one day Bryan (who was by then the Principal) suggested to me, that since it was proving so popular I should try and get it published. It was certainly an appealing idea to get revenue from the book after all the time and effort I had put into it. We were only selling the duplicated copies for cost price of the paper plus a bit extra for my time in printing it out. I therefore went through the book modifying it here and there, adding further notes where I had found my students experiencing difficulties, then added a liberal quantity of exercises for each chapter. Then I approached various publishers, including Longmans, but got nothing but refusals from them all, 'because they did not wish to compete with *Teach Yourself Swahili*.' As far as I was concerned, of course, it was no competition.

After weeks of searching for a friendly publisher, at last the East African Literature Bureau in Nairobi agreed to publish it under the title *Simplified Swahili*. It was soon declared a best seller by them. A few years later, unfortunately, the East African Literature Bureau folded up along with the East African Community, of which it was part, so that I had to find another publisher. This second time around, Longmans seized it at once, it by then having a proven 'track record' and it has flourished ever since. A year or two later I translated it into French, under the title '*Le Swahili Simplifié*'.

If reading this chapter gives you the urge to rush out and buy a copy of *Simplified Swahili*, please feel free to do so, by all means. But please rush out and buy a Longmans (now Addison Wesley Longman) copy (ISBN 0–582–62358–8).

CHAPTER XXXIV

Singing for Joy

After we had been settled in Tengeru for a couple of years or so, the local representative of the Dar es Salaam university extra-mural department, David Edgington, took it upon himself to create a choir. Since the choir comprised largely of people from both Arusha and Moshi, it was logical to call it the Arusha-Moshi choir. It proved to be not only great fun, but most popular as well, not only with us, its singing members, but with our public.

The very first work we sang as founder members of this choir was the beautiful and moving Requiem by Gabriel Fauré. I opted to sing bass in this choir and so generally found myself seated next to my friend and colleague Bill Andrews. Our first class piano accompanist was Diana Down, Bryan's wife, who also played some exquisite solos during the interludes.

Diana had obtained her LRAM at the age of 16. She had then studied at the Royal Academy for a further four years. She was thus well able to support the choir with her expertise on the piano.

I had been selected to sing the bass solos in the Requiem, so Diana very kindly coached and rehearsed me for these.

When we were ready, we performed this work both in Arusha and Moshi.

The choir grew from strength to strength and we undertook a variety of works including Hiawatha and, what was perhaps our greatest achievement, Handel's Messiah. In the latter I was again asked to sing the bass solos for which, once more, Diana kindly coached me.

We were fortunate to have some excellent soloists for Messiah, not the least of which was Charlotte Hartwig, an American housewife, who had the most exquisite contralto voice I had ever heard, either before, or indeed since. Even now, whenever I hear Messiah being performed, I still 'hear' her beautiful voice singing those magnificent solos in this fine work.

Peter M Wilson
Bwana Shamba

We once had the privilege of singing Messiah in Nairobi cathedral.

One venue of note in which we sang was in Moshi itself. When our planned venue fell through at the last minute, the only place David was able to secure was the Hindu Mandel, so that on that occasion we sang Handel in the Mandel.

After each concert, we generally celebrated our success with a small party during which we presented our conductor, David, with a small token present of thanks and appreciation. I well remember, fortunately during a rehearsal, we came across a word ending in -st. David quite rightly made much of good diction in our singing (an important facet sadly neglected by many a choir.) Wishing to stress our enunciation of the − -st at the end of the word, David mouthed an exaggerated −st at us in his conducting, and in so doing spat out his false teeth. It so happened that he was standing on a table at the time, so that his teeth proceeded to bounce off the table as well, for good effect.

It therefore logically followed that at the party following that particular concert, David's present was a tube of denture cement.

The Arushi-Moshi choir was not our only source of making music. A friend and colleague on the Institute staff, David Gooday, also formed a singing group in Tengeru in which we sang madrigals and folk songs and the like. We never did perform in public, but just sang for our own enjoyment. The only exception to this was one Christmas time when we several times put on a concert of exotic carols and Christmas music. It was all great fun, and we were most grateful to both Davids for giving up so much of their leisure time to encourage us to sing, which gave us so much great joy.

Dolly

No account of my years in Tanganyika would be complete without mention of my faithful Alsatian (German Shepherd) bitch, Dolly.

I had been at Tengeru about a year, when out of the blue, someone asked me if I would like to have an Alsatian puppy. I immediately assented as I have always loved dogs as pets even though I had never before had an Alsatian. The bitch puppy was about eighteen months old when I received her and was already named Dolly. I saw no reason to change her name, so she kept that name for the rest of her life.

From the very first day, she was a perfect pet and never gave us any problems whatsoever. From her first day she showed a great love for ball games and chased her tennis ball with boundless energy every time I threw it across our one-acre garden for her.

She very rapidly became very attached to me, an attachment which became, in time, a complete devotion, never wanting to leave me out of her sight. By the time she grew up, she followed me everywhere, even to my office, and often, even into the classroom, where should sit quietly for hours, her head resting upon her front paws, without stirring one inch, just so long as I was there.

The Africans tended to fear her as they often fear any dog, but especially a larger *kali* (fierce) dog like an Alsatian.

Under normal circumstances Dolly never bothered about anybody within 'our' territory. But she was an excellent guard dog and always barked loudly if ever anybody black, or white, ever came into our garden.

The only time she ever bit anybody, was when she was nursing her litter of three puppies on our back veranda. At that time a neighbour's three-year-old son took it upon himself to go and look at the puppies, despite having been severely warned by his parents not to go anywhere near them.

Dolly awaiting her
next game of 'squash'.

He was barely twenty yards from the veranda when Dolly, without warning, suddenly leapt up and gave chase, the poor terrified boy screaming as he took flight. Dolly then gave him a sharp nip on his posterior, which naturally produced screams and voluminous tears from the three-year-old. It was not a proper bite, but merely a warning nip from Dolly that her pups were 'off limits' to anyone.

The only person she allowed near her pups at that time was myself. She really seemed to delight in my going to admire her puppies, and used to wag her tail at me enthusiastically if ever I congratulated her on her fine family as I stroked one of them. In due course, I was able to find good homes for all her pups, including one to our neighbours at that time, Wally and Chris Redekop.

Thus, being next door neighbours, Dolly was able to see one of her puppies whenever she wanted. In fact I often used to see them romping and chasing each other round and round the garden, having a whale of a time together.

The front veranda of my house was about twenty feet long and seven feet wide. Its ends were a part of the house walls, and its garden side was made up of a low wall, full of rockery plants.

The place where the house wall joined the concrete floor of the veranda was curved into a concave to facilitate sweeping it out, without awkward angles. Dolly and I regarded this veranda as our 'squash court', as I called it. The object of our game was, that I 'served' the tennis ball by throwing it hard at the concave curve at the base of the end wall. If my shot was accurate, the ball bounded back on a reciprocal trajectory straight back at me. If the ball was too high or too low, it bounced against both walls and floor then flew back in my general direction. Whichever way the ball bounced, the object of the game was to see who caught it first, Dolly or me.

Dolly used to make the most extraordinary and spectacular jumps in her endeavour to catch the ball, which was surprising considering the slippery floor from which to take off. Occasionally, as she leapt, she would slip as she did so, resulting in her sometimes falling quite heavily on her side. But she never seemed to care, and was as keen as ever to leap high again for the next ball.

Our scores were remarkably well matched.

Very often, no sooner had I set foot in our garden on my way back from work, than Dolly would come charging up to me, her ball in her mouth. I could almost hear her urging me to hurry, saying

'Come on! Hurry up! Let's have another game of squash, right now!'

As soon as I took the ball from her mouth, her tail would almost wag itself off, then she would give an excited bark as if to say,

'Well, I'm ready! Get on with it!'

Then we would start to play our game, often for at least half an hour, myself tiring before Dolly did.

It was definitely a case of a mutual admiration society between Dolly and me, and we both knew how much we loved each other. Most of our friends loved her too, and whenever we went away on home leave or went away and had to leave her with someone else, she would quickly settle down and feel totally at home, knowing that because her new temporary master or mistress was my friend, he/she was therefore a friend of hers too.

One particular friend who often looked after Dolly during our home leaves, especially after we moved down to Dar es Salaam, was Bridget Connery. She too greatly loved dear Dolly, and Dolly and she hit it off superbly from the word go, to the extent that I think Bridget was often sorry to see us return from leave.

On one occasion a few weeks before I was due to go on home leave from Tengeru, Dolly came on 'heat' but, alas, her bleeding went on for weeks and weeks, and showed no signs of abating. In the end, we had to leave for England and leave her to her devices. On that occasion, we left her with Wally and Chris who had very kindly agreed to look after her.

Apparently, we heard later, once we came back from leave, the bleeding continued on and on, if anything getting worse. So, Wally, realizing that something was clearly amiss, mentioned this to Bryan, himself a qualified veterinary surgeon.

There was, at that time, another vet. on the station, Stuart Watson. So with these two vets in attendance, Dolly was operated on for something like three hours, because it transpired that poor Dolly had a terrible cancer of the womb. Bryan did tell me later that they seriously considered the possibility that they would have to put her down, but, remembering how dearly I loved her, they decided to see if they could save her by cutting away the cancer, which, thankfully, they succeeded in doing, but not until they had cut away an enormous amount of her reproductive organs, plus several large tumours. Fortunately, and this is all credit to both Bryan and Stuart, Dolly made a full recovery, and by the time we returned from that leave, she was able to greet me with all her usual excitement and warmth.

The only difference I noticed in her after that operation, was that, when getting up from lying down, she visibly winced as she struggled up. It also seriously curtailed her ability to leap for the ball during our games of squash, but this in no way diminished her keenness to play.

When in due course I was transferred to Dar es Salaam, she of course came with us, and took the change in her environment without 'batting an eyelid'. Dolly loved Dar, doubtless because I was also there. She loved to go into the sea for a swim.

After about three years in Dar it was time for me to go on leave again, possibly even terminal leave. I arranged for her to stay with our old Kilosa friends, Marcel and Theresa Contoret, who lived right on the coast just north of the city. They also agreed to look after my faithful old Ford Corsair car, and to give it the occasional run.

We returned to England, and I felt a real wrench at having had to leave my beloved Dolly.

As things turned out, I did not return to Tanganyika to work, but managed to find myself a new agriculture civil service job in Botswana.

I therefore booked a sea passage from Dar es Salaam to Durban, so that I could take both Dolly and the Corsair with me, and drive up to Botswana with my Corsair. I had business to see to in Nairobi, so I flew to Dar, stopping off in Nairobi for a night on the way.

When I reached Nairobi, I phoned up the Contorets, to let them know I was in Nairobi and hoped to reach Dar the next day to collect the car and Dolly.

Therese interrupted me with,

'I'm ever so sorry to have to tell you, Peter, but Dolly died yesterday.'

I felt as if I had been pole-axed. I was absolutely shattered. I heard later, that whenever Dolly heard my car, she used to get all excited, but when she realized it was 'only' Marcel driving it, she used to flop down again all dejected.

It seems that the 'official' reason for her death was heart worm infestation, but also, because she was pining for me so much as well, this doubtless weakened her will to live. I therefore had to catch my ship to Durban without my beloved Dolly.

She was buried near the soft white sandy beach where she had so loved to romp and play.

I still miss her terribly to this day.

CHAPTER XXXVI

Scouting for Boys

One day as I was walking back home from my office at Tengeru, I was surprised to see a scout camp in full swing in the dell next to the Tengeru chapel.

Subsequent enquiries revealed that the local scout commissioner, Tom Lane, QC, from Arusha, had requested permission from Bryan Down to use the handy site for a scouting PTC or Provisional Training Course, this being the preliminary training course for scoutmasters, before they could go on to get their Woodbadge course. This course, therefore, was a *must* for all potential scoutmasters.

Later on I wandered back up to the scout camp out of curiosity. There I met Tom Lane, a charming gentleman and mad keen on scouting. He wasted no time in doing his utmost to pass on his enthusiasm for the movement and when I told him that at preparatory school, I had been very active in the Cubs, he changed his strategy to doing his utmost to persuade me not only to take up scouting, but to go several steps further and take over from him as Regional Scout Commissioner when he left the country in a few weeks time. Such was his enthusiasm that I soon found myself truly wishing to get involved. What with one thing and another, Tom organized another PTC course within the next few weeks, largely so that at least I could get that part 'under my belt'.

I have to admit that I found it great fun getting personally involved in boy scout activities, such as camp cooking, tying knots and all manner of typical scouting activities, including the camping itself.

I now had attended a PTC, so was qualified to go to the next step, the Woodbadge course itself. This had to be held in one of the main training camps in one of the respective countries. In my case it was to be Rowallan camp near Nairobi. The world camp for this type of activity is Gilwell Park on the edge of London.

Peter M Wilson
Bwana Shamba

Tom therefore arranged for me to attend a Woodbadge course at Rowallan. It was a large course, involving about forty other potential scouters. Once more we all camped in tents for the duration of the course which covered every type of scouting activity concerning boy scouts. It was quite strict and tough, ensuring we attained certain strict standards. On one of the days during the course, we were privileged to have a visit by Lady Olive Baden-Powell, the widow of the late Lord Baden-Powell of Gilwell, the founder of the Scout Movement.

This grand old lady went round greeting everybody on the course. When it was my turn to shake her hand, without thinking, I proffered my right hand. As soon as I saw her proffer her left one, I quickly substituted my hands and just got my left hand out in time to shake hers. I was terribly embarrassed and had totally forgotten that boy scouts shake hands with the left hand.

At the end of the course, I was given my Woodbadge certificate, then offered the Woodbadge beads themselves, a couple of small wooden elongated beads mounted on a leather thong to be worn round the neck, together with the special Gilwell scarf and woggle.

I returned to Arusha with the good news for Tom that I was now the proud owner of a Woodbadge. This had been an essential prerequisite qualification before I could be nominated as Regional Scout Commissioner.

I was astonished when, about ten days later, I received a smart green warrant card appointing me as Regional Scout Commissioner, Northern Region. The warrant was signed by Leader Stirling, Tanganyika's Chief Scout. Tom had wasted no time in getting this organized as his departure date was approaching fast.

After that he spent almost all his spare moments telling me all about what was going on regarding scouting activities in 'my' region. After Tom left, (I was very sorry to have seen him go, as together with Dorothy and his wife Mary and our respective children, we had spent many happy afternoons socializing together on picnics and so forth.) We had become very good friends. So there I was, still feeling like a total novice, responsible for all scouting activities in northern Tanganyika.

I later also recruited Dorothy's assistance as she took over the role as Akela leader (Cub scout leader) for a small pack of Cubs which was in the process of getting going as an active pack on Tengeru.

With the Lane family
by one of the
Momella lakes.

Some weeks later, by which time I had settled into my new responsibilities, I organized and started up a Rover Scout group for several of the students from the Tengeru Institute who had expressed an interest in getting involved, for which I had the great and welcome assistance of at least two of the VSO volunteers, who had been posted to the staff on Tengeru, in the running of it. I was particularly pleased that I was able to put the name forward for one of these African Rover Scouts to attend a Rover moot in Sweden. He duly attended and later related many accounts of his wonderful experiences as he obviously had had a wonderful and memorable time out there.

After only two months after I had expressed an interest in getting involved in scouting, I received a message that I was to make myself ready to receive and entertain the World Chief Scout, Sir Charles McLean. I was asked to meet his private aircraft at Arusha airport and entertain him for a period of up to two days.

I quickly therefore organized a scout camp on Tengeru, so that he could get a taste of scouting in the area. On the appointed day, I duly turned up at Arusha airport to await his arrival. I went there in my new Morris Oxford Traveller. Right on time

Peter M Wilson
Bwana Shamba

Sir Charles arrived, complete with kilt and sporran. He also carried a long sort of crook.

He was a thoroughly pleasant gentleman, ultra polite and considerate. I had decided that in order to show him a little of northern Tanganyika, I would take him up to Ngurdoto crater, which by then was a properly organized National Park with decent roads, fit for cars, such as mine.

I took him first to my house for a wash and brush up. I introduced him to Dorothy and our daughters, including poor

Sir Charles Maclean talking with local scouts.

Peter M Wilson
'Mr Agriculture'

Diane who was quite ill at that time and in bed recovering from a nasty bout of acute nephritis, having had sojourns in hospitals both in Arusha and Dar es Salaam as a result of this frightening illness.

Sir Charles stood in the doorway of her room, and greeted her warmly from where he stood, in case of spread of infection either way

I took Sir Charles and Dorothy up to the rim of Ngurdoto crater and fortunately plenty of big game was in evidence and clearly visible, as was Kilimanjaro's exquisite ice cap, positively sparkling in the brilliant sunlight. Sir Charles was delighted with the tour and showered us with thanks. I then took him round the scout camp I had organized on Tengeru, and he took a keen interest in everything and everybody there. He spent quite a long time chatting to both African and Asian scouts who were present.

I then took him back to the airport, and he was gone. I had been greatly impressed by his charming manner and genuine interest in everything and everybody he met.

I was even more astounded when I visited the Scout shop in Buckingham Palace Road in London a few years later, on my next home leave. Almost as soon as I entered the shop, I bumped into him. Without hesitation he greeted me by name then asked,

'Oh, by the way, how is Diane?'

I was totally astonished that he should have remembered not only my name, but that of my Diane and that she had been very ill in the few seconds that he had met her all that time before, in spite of the hundreds of other people he must have met officially in the intervening period.

He then very kindly invited me to join him for lunch.

A few weeks after Sir Charles' visit to Tengeru, I received another message to be ready to welcome and entertain the commonwealth Scout secretary, Mr Cook.

I therefore quickly organized another scout camp on Tengeru to coincide with his visit.

I had then, for that visit, some forty-eight scouts from all over the region, camping on Tengeru in eight different tents. I had even arranged for a proper flagpole to be erected to site, so that we could have the proper flag-breaking ceremonies on the camp site each morning.

I duly met Mr Cook and took him to his hotel in Arusha.

It just so happened that very Friday evening after I had

Peter M Wilson
Bwana Shamba

attended to the evening routine at the camp site, Dorothy and I had been invited to a friend's wine and cheese party in Arusha. I was determined that I would only take a moderate quantity of wine at that party, and all through the evening kept on turning down offers of more wine. I was determined to 'Be Prepared' for my next day's duties.

Next morning, however, when the alarm went off, to my horror and dread I found that I had the mother and father of all headaches. I had the most appalling hangover despite my attempts to prevent one the previous evening. There was no way I would be capable of entertaining a VIP with a head like that, let alone conduct the morning camp procedures. I therefore sent a message down to the scout camp that I was indisposed and regrettably would be unable to be present at the site.

After a couple of hours, or so, as I lay on my bed, I heard the commotion of somebody arriving at our house. I heard Dorothy's voice welcoming our visitor, I knew not whom at that moment. A little while later, there was a knock on my door, and horror of horrors, there stood Dorothy and Mr Cook. He had come up to my house to express his condolences at my 'illness' and wish me a speedy recovery. I did not know where to look, my head still being unmercifully hammered from within by those nasty little gremlins.

My VIP chatted with me for a few minutes from the doorway, then bidding me all the best, he departed whence he had come. A moment later Dorothy re-appeared to tell me he had gone. She also told me that my room positively reeked of stale alcohol. I was truly ashamed, the more so because I had miserably failed to 'Be Prepared' despite my earlier attempts to be so.

During my subsequent responsibilities as commissioner, I became aware of a particular weakness in my experience, and that was in things pertaining to Cub scouts. I therefore determined I would put this right by attending, if possible, a Cub Woodbadge course. First of all, of course, I had to attend a relevant PTC course. As luck would have it, there was one at a convenient time at Rowallan camp in Nairobi, to which I presented myself. I was now qualified to attend the Cub Woodbadge course itself. I applied to Gilwell Park in England for a place on such a course and was lucky enough to be offered a place on one during my next leave, which I duly attended.

I was delighted with it, and it was all great fun to be back to 'little boy' activities such as I had been much involved with when I was at preparatory school. I made many new friends on that course, including Helen Reeves, a very keen Akela leader from Macclesfield, in Cheshire, amongst others.

Upon my return from that leave, I soon received another warrant, again signed by Leader Stirling, appointing me to the country's official scout training team, to which Roger Moisey, an amazingly energetic and keen scouter had recommended me. This qualified me to wear four Woodbadge beads around my neck. As it happens, I was never called upon to serve on the training team after that, but I still proudly possess my four Woodbadge beads.

Peter M Wilson
Bwana Shamba

CHAPTER XXXVII

On Top of Africa

Within the first year of my stay at Tengeru, it was decided that the Institute would organize an expedition up Mount Kilimanjaro.

This was to be for the benefit of both staff and students alike.

I immediately applied to be included on the expedition, as did my friends and colleagues, Bill Andrews and Hussein Mongi, a Tanzanian Agriculture Officer, a Makerere graduate. Bryan Down also put his own name down. In due course ten of the institute's students also put their names forward. We all trained like mad for the five-day trip, three for the way up and two for the descent. Early on the appointed morning for our departure, we all piled into the Institute's GT green Commer minibus and away we went with all our climbing gear and sleeping bags.

We were to tackle the mountain by following the usual 'tourist' route up the eastern foot, starting at Marangu. On the way, we stopped at the Marangu hotel to collect our guide and assistant guide, two charming Wachagga tribesmen, the tribe living on the mountain's lower slopes. We had decided to dispense with porters, preferring to carry our own modest loads, packed in small rucksacks.

The minibus was able to take us about three quarters of the way up a good, initially tarmac road, which changed to murram half way up to the forest reserve boundary. We were delighted to be able to ride that far up, since the road becomes very steep. This therefore saved us an hour or two of stiff climbing.

When it was clearly time to get out, we all wearily alighted, the knowledge of a long, tiring climb ahead of us. No sooner had we started to walk and the minibus disappeared, than we saw an astonishing sight. It was an African lad, skimming down the road on a home-made wooden bicycle.

Fortunately he stopped, by dragging his bare feet along the road, which allowed us to admire his contraption. Everything

Peter M Wilson
'Mr Agriculture'

Page: 188

was made of wood, including the wheels. These were not exactly a geometrist's idea of a perfect circle, but as the young lad had ably demonstrated, they were nevertheless capable of a fair turn of speed. It had no means of propulsion, clearly depending solely on gravity for forward movement. It also had no brakes in evidence, hence, the use of scraping bare feet to slow down and stop. It was a real work of art and we all admired it immensely, never having seen the like of it before. Once we had finished admiring it, the lad remounted and disappeared at alarming speed on it down the steep hill.

We continued on our climb, each of us carrying a small rucksack on our backs. These contained spare clothing, a water bottle, a limited amount of food, and our very light-weight sleeping bags. The road continued its relentless course uphill zig-zagging to and fro. Some of us took a short cut path that struck a straight line uphill between each zig and each zag in the road. After about half an hour's climb, we espied our first objective, Bismark hut. It was a long low bungalow type structure mounted on a thick concrete foundation plinth, and was roofed with corrugated iron.

Because we had ridden in style in the minibus much of the way up from Marangu, there was no need for us to spend a night in this hut. Climbers who walk all the way up from Marangu, on the other hand, are well advised to sleep there for their first night on the climb.

We sat down on the edge of the large concrete veranda and had a drink. We were already at approximately 9,000 ft, so that we already felt somewhat breathless from the altitude.

We admired the vast view ahead and way below us, looking south-eastwards. Most of the extensive plain below was covered in a vast blanket of cotton wool clouds. Away to the south we could just see a long mountain range which demarcated the Lessogonoi plateau and the Masai Steppe beyond.

Much of the road we had followed up from Marangu had been flanked on both sides by thick banana plantations, in amongst which we frequently saw large circular houses built entirely of banana leaves, the traditional house of the local Wachagga tribe. As we left Bismark, we approached a forest of giant heather trees. Most of these were draped with lichen which hung down like so many giant cobwebs. There was a narrow footpath which led us up through this forest, but it was very tiring work, as we had constantly to stride over protruding tree roots and boulders.

Peter M Wilson
Bwana Shamba

Bryan Down, Tengeru's Principal, left, entertaining the Tanzanian President, Mwalimu Julius K. Nyerere, right, on his official visit to Tengeru in the mid 1960s.

On each side of this path grew an abundance of wild flowers such as I had seen nowhere else in the country, wild gladioli being prevalent, along with busy-lizzies galore.

After about half an hour's stiff climb we suddenly emerged from this forest, to find ourselves, at just under 10,000 ft. on the edge of a vast plateau. Directly above us, towered Mawenzi's jagged peak, which, from where we stood, did not look anything like its 17,000 ft. altitude. It had a light fall of snow on its summit. Over to our left, therefore westwards, we could see our beautiful ultimate objective, with its exquisite flat-topped peak, glistening as its white cap caught the morning rays of the sun.

We continued on our way along a fairly easy narrow footpath that found its meandering way through the rough scrub, comprising dwarf heather and numerous varieties of brown dried grasses. The climbing was far easier now as the path was, in fact, almost level across the first part of this plateau.

About half an hour later, we saw our next objective, Peter's hut, built entirely of corrugated iron. This too shone brightly in the morning sun. Our path steepened very slightly as we approached this hut. It followed in and out along the contours as we crossed several small streams.

Peter M Wilson
'Mr Agriculture'

Along this section we passed several small groups of climbers on their descent, their porters carrying enormous headloads wrapped in giant sheets, with apparent ease. As we plodded slowly up the path to conserve our energy for the real climbing later, we noticed our two guides also carried their small loads on their heads rather than in a rucksack as we did.

Another three-quarters of an hour later saw us arriving at Peter's hut. Inside we found permanent two-tier bunk beds, liberally covered in dried scrub from the area around us.

We staked our claims for our respective beds, then congregated outside to partake of more food and water. Round the back of the hut was a corrugated iron shed containing a *choo* which we all made use of. Far below us to the south we could see the level steppe, by now almost devoid of cloud. We were now easily capable of seeing the town of Moshi immediately below us, shimmering in the haze. We were now close to 12,000 ft. and already were able to feel the slight effects of altitude, though of course, we had worse to come.

We therefore turned in to rest for the night quite early on, long before daylight even threatened to leave us. We gladly slipped into our sleeping bags and tried to make ourselves comfortable on the wooden bunks, trying to position the dried heather scrub into its most comfortable position.

A few of us, myself included, carved our initials in the wooden sides of the bunk beds, adding ours to the already numerous initials carefully carved over, doubtless, many years, by numerous climbers eager to leave their mark on Kilimanjaro.

As we settled down to elusive sleep, we could hear the constant wind whistling its way round the hut, seeking out every slightest crack and gap in the hut walls. It was already decidedly cold at this altitude and we were glad of our snug sleeping bags. I am confident in saying that I don't believe any of us had a good night's sleep that night, but we did nevertheless have a good rest. The bright morning sun, however, lured us out of our sleeping bags and into the glorious morning sunshine, which after the relative gloom inside the hut, had us all squinting our eyes, despite wearing sunglasses or goggles.

The persistent icy wind still blew up the slope at us.

The steppe below us had again become covered in cloud. Despite the beautiful spectacle to our south, we found it very difficult not to keep our eyes to the west, where the Kibo peak,

Peter M Wilson
Bwana Shamba

our ultimate destination, beckoned to us to hurry and rejoin it. It looked absolutely gorgeous, illuminated as it was by the morning sunlight. Its flat snow-covered peak sloped gently to the left from our viewpoint.

After breakfast outside in the sunlight, we loaded up our small rucksacks and resumed the climb, which still followed a narrow smooth footpath. Scattered all around us grew numerous really weird plants, which looked like some sort of giant prehistoric cacti. These were, we found out later, giant groundsel.

The path was by now considerably steeper than we had encountered the previous day since leaving the heather forest. We were now on the south western foot of the Mawenzi peak, and a large and impressive rock outcrop stood on our left as we plodded up the slope. After about a quarter of an hour, we passed a small dribble of clear water tumbling down the rocky slope. Someone had prepared a large crude notice and fixed it nearby. It read 'LAST WATER'!

We therefore thought it wise to replenish our water bottles. This gave us an excuse for a brief rest, after which we carried on, deliberately plodding very slowly, as we had been warned of the essential need to conserve energy for the final assault on Kibo. Half an hour later, we found ourselves on the very edge of the vast saddle which separates the peaks of Kibo and Mawenzi.

It is almost level across its length but with a very slight concave depression in the centre. From north to south it curves down the slopes in a convex shape. It is a barren desert of grey volcanic ash, totally devoid of any vegetation at all. Stones and boulders are scattered untidily all over it, with an occasional small rock outcrop, otherwise it is totally smooth. We could see our footpath making its way across to our next objective, Kibo hut, another corrugated iron building away over on the western end of the saddle, right at the foot of the Kibo peak.

With no protection whatever from Mawenzi by now, we were totally exposed to a strong icy wind which whistled past us mercilessly. It was bitterly cold, as we rummaged in our rucksacks to search for and don any spare clothing we could find, our anoraks being unable to prevent the wind from finding its way to our shivering bodies. The saddle is some five or six miles in length and on average about a mile wide.

Just as we were about to move off, our guide summoned us to follow him as he walked purposefully over to our left away from the path. He stopped after about a hundred yards and triumphantly pointed to the ground were he stood.

We followed him over and were totally astonished to see spread on the ground, perfectly preserved, as we were already above the perma-frost line, the corpse of a horse. Our guide explained that it had had to be put down, as it had finally succumbed to the cold and altitude. It was one of several horses which had been used to carry up the equipment needed to be used on Kibo's summit in 1961 to celebrate Tanganyika's independence, when its new flag was hoisted on the special flagpole taken up there for the event, to enable ~~Sam Sarakikya~~ *{Alexander Nyirenda}* to hoist the flag precisely at midnight that night. It could be said, therefore, that this poor horse died for the country's independence. We stood around gazing at this poor creature's frozen corpse for a while then decided it would doubtless be warmer to walk. We continued our our way, picking up the meandering smooth footpath across the saddle. The icy remorseless wind blew at us across the exposed saddle till we felt totally frozen.

Even though it was virtually level walking, we nevertheless walked ultra slowly to conserve energy for the next day's assault on Kibo. It therefore took us a long time to reach the diminutive Kibo hut, which, like Peter's hut, contained two-tier bunk beds covered in dried scrub. Opposite the hut, a few yards away, was a small corrugated iron-covered *choo*, upon which someone had inscribed 'This is the highest and coldest *choo* in Africa!'

I can assure you that this was no exaggeration as at this spot, despite being tucked right up by the base of the steep scree leading up to Kibo, the icy wind whistled and blew with great intensity freezing us all through. I was frozen through to the bone in no time.

There was certainly no lingering with the daily newspaper in that *choo*!

There was also no lingering outside to admire the view of Mawenzi's massive jagged bulk towering over the eastern end of the saddle. From Tengeru this peak looks small and insignificant. There was nothing small nor insignificant about it from where we now stood.

Unlike the Kibo peak we were due to climb next day, which really just requires energy and stamina to climb, not requiring any mountaineering skills whatsoever, the Mawenzi peak, however is quite another story. It is composed of very crumbly and jagged rock for most of the way from the saddle. In this case

Peter M Wilson
Bwana Shamba

climbers need to be very experienced in climbing hazardous rock such as this, if they are to stand the slightest chance at all of reaching its jagged peak.

Somewhere on its north-eastern shoulder, there is doubtless still the twisted wreckage of an East African airways Dakota which crashed there in the 1960s with no survivors.

We all hastily entered Kibo hut to stake our claims for a bed, preferring to eat inside, rather than outside in the bitter wind. There being nothing to keep us up for, we soon wriggled into our sleeping bags, looking in vain for sleep.

The intense cold, plus the incessant wind whistling round the hut with an eerie moan, on top of the anticipation of the struggle that lay before us the next day, meant that we all found sleep totally elusive. Bryan kindly issued us all with sleeping pills, but since these had little or no effect, poor Bryan was kept awake most of the night issuing us each with additional pills to try and coax some sleep to come our way. Our worst enemy that night was the bitter, bitter cold that froze us right through.

The guides slept in a separate triangular roofed shed a few yards away, and at the appropriate time came to arouse us ready for the final assault. We needed no awakening through, as despite all Bryan's pills, I don't think any of us slept for more than one hour in total that night, if that. As for the rest of us, we drank a little water and ate a little of our food, then set off to take up our battle with the scree.

The assault on the scree was a thousand per cent easier than Meru's scree for the very good reason that there was a firm well-trodden zig-zag path up it, so that there was positively none of Meru's two steps up and one down business.

Nevertheless, due to the starting effects of altitude we were all constantly fighting for breath and had to take frequent pauses to regain it. One good point about our assault on the steep scree, it did at least at last warm us up.

By and by, the sky lightened as the sun's effect gradually made its presence felt. The view was awe-inspiring as we looked down across the vast expanse of the saddle to Mawenzi's enormous, jagged bulk, even now towering higher than where we stood. To each side of the saddle, the lower slopes and the plains beneath were blanketed in thick cloud. About three quarters of the way up this scree, we came to a large cave. Its interior was blissfully devoid of the icy wind that outside still fought to freeze us solid. Its floor was liberally covered with fine volcanic ash.

We paused in there to drink some of our water. Personally, I found that thirst was a constant consideration, whereas hunger never made its presence felt at all on the climb.

As we lay prostrate on the cave floor, the assistant guide told us that this was the point of no return. Anybody who did not feel they could go on to the summit, was advised to go back down the mountain here, accompanied by the assistant guide, the main reason for having brought him with us.

A few of the students decided to call it a day and turned back at this point, leaving us to carry on up the steep scree.

Just before we reached the first summit, called Gilman's point, as on Meru, we found ourselves on solid rock over which we had to scramble from one level to the next. At last, totally exhausted and breathless, we arrived at Gilman's point, a small mini-peak, right on the south, south east edge of the vast crater rim.

As on Meru, there was an aluminium box on the top, placed there by the Sierra club, containing a book for us to sign. Most of us delayed this honour until we had admired and/or photographed the unbelievable panorama about us.

Immediately to the south east of us stood a glacier of mammoth proportions. The sheer wall of ice facing us towered twenty or more feet vertically upwards along the whole of its length, as it lay diagonally down the south eastern slope from the crater rim. Directly opposite us on the north eastern corner, stood a most spectacular glacier, laid out in giant steps of different levels. This glacier is often referred to as the wedding cake. To the west of us, was the vast actual volcanic crater, with its wide flat cone directly in its centre. I estimated the crater to be between one and two miles in diameter. Here and there within this vast crater stood what looked like icebergs, which was all that was left of previous glaciers.

Having signed the book we held a 'council of war' to decide who, if anybody, wanted to continue on to Africa's highest peak, then called Kaiser Wilhelm Spitz, now called Uhuru peak (Independence peak) at 19,341 feet above sea level and some two miles further round the southern crater rim.

We finally decided that only Bill Andrews and myself felt inclined to make the final assault, accompanied by the guide who was still with us.

Bill and I therefore followed the guide, who led us a few feet down towards the crater's interior, leaving Gilman's point in a

Peter M Wilson
Bwana Shamba

spiral anti-clockwise descent. After a few feet, we came to an horrendous obstacle. It comprised giant ice spikes which were too weak to hold our weight. This meant that we had very tiringly to make giant strides over these eighteen inch to two foot cones, which at close to 18,000 ft is not exactly an easy obstacle course to undertake.

We had about a hundred yards of this exhausting obstacle until at last we had reached the far side, totally exhausted and breathless. Our guide then led us up a fairly steep grade back up on top of the crater rim. Once we were up on the rim, it was a thankfully almost level walk along the slowly curving crater rim to Kaiser Wilhelm Spitz, where had been erected a crude cairn of large stones.

Oddly enough, even though we were effectively right on the very roof of the African continent, there was hardly a breath of wind high up on that exposed crater rim. We followed the reasonably easy walking and level rim for the couple of miles or so to the summit, with its inevitable Sierra club aluminium box and book. The actual summit was far from spectacular, being little more, apart from its cairn, than a minute plateau barely higher than the surrounding crater rim. But it *was* the very highest point of the vast African continent, and here Bill and I found ourselves totally devoid of energy. We both lay down in order to summon the energy with which to sign the book.

As for myself, I wondered whatever I was doing up in this seemingly Godforsaken spot, and all I wanted to do was to get back down the mountain.

Altitude sickness affects different people in a variety of different ways, and the guides have been trained to be on the alert for very odd behaviour on the summit. Some climbers have even made a move to step off the crater rim and jump into the crater, a fall of several hundred feet. I did take a few photographs and some cine film, but I have no recollection whatever of doing so, and in fact I was pleasantly surprised when I eventually got my slides back, to see what a good selection I had miraculously taken. One photo I did take was of Mount Meru, fifty miles away to the east. It looked just like a tiny insignificant triangular shadow, somewhat different to the obverse, of Kilimanjaro seen from Meru's peak.

Having taken all the photographs I wanted, all I wanted to do was to get down, down, down. I therefore left Bill and the guide to their rest on the top, and proceeded with all haste to return towards Gilman's. I had gone no more than a hundred yards when I collapsed or fell, I know not which, then promptly vomited. Having done this I fell fast asleep where I lay.

The guide, still looking after Bill, left him and hastily came to wake me up, as it is dangerous when not acclimatized to it to sleep at that altitude, lest one forgets to breathe.

Having woken me up and stood me on my feet again, the guide then noticed that Bill had also fallen asleep. He therefore left me and hastened back to see to Bill. This then set the pattern for our poor guide until we safely reached Kibo hut once more. Both Bill and I alternately fell fast asleep, causing the unfortunate guide to have to shuttle back and forth between us to wake us up and set us back on our feet each time. Eventually our faithful and devoted guide saw us both safely back to Gilman's point, where we found our friends waiting for us in the morning sunlight, the sun being well up above Mawenzi's peak by then.

It was now time to descend the scree. This time we missed Meru's soft and cushioned scree, as we could not by any means take the same 'seven league strides' and leaps down the steep scree slope as I had done on Meru.

Kibo's scree was littered by numerous sharp boulders and rocks instead. We had no alternative but to follow the zig-zag path downwards, up which we had climbed. For our poor guide, it was still the same routine, with both Bill and I alternately falling fast asleep, possibly caused at last by Bryan's pills? At any rate we were in due course all safely back at Kibo hut, into which we staggered and fell on our bunks, this time falling fast asleep before even spreading ourselves out on them. It was, of course still bitterly cold there as before, but we were so shattered and exhausted we were almost past caring about that small detail.

We slept for well over half an hour, when our guide aroused us and told us we had to be continuing down the slope as we still had to get back down to Peter's hut before nightfall.

Crossing the almost level saddle after Kibo's scree was blissful to say the least. We no longer needed to walk ultra carefully to conserve energy as we had on the way up, so that we could now walk as fast as we felt we had energy reserves to use. It therefore only took us a fraction of the time to reach Mawenzi's foot before turning right to follow the path back to Peter's hut.

We all paused again by the water spring for a long drink of refreshingly cool water, and again replenished our water bottles.

Peter M Wilson
Bwana Shamba

Then at last we were back at Peter's hut, and again flopped, exhausted, onto our bunks. On this occasion, however, we did not have it all to ourselves, but found it already occupied by a small ascending party. There were fortunately plenty of bunks for each of us, so that it was no hardship.

As on the way up, we breakfasted next morning out in the sunshine, admiring, for the last close-up time, Kibo's beautiful snow capped peak, feeling very pleased with ourselves at the realization that we had 'been up there'.

After a really good night's sleep we felt totally invigorated, so that we were able thoroughly to enjoy the descent from then on.

When we got back down to the giant heather forest, we lingered frequently as we picked many of the abundant wild flowers until our shirt pockets were bulging with vast bunches of them. We still had to stride cautiously over the endless exposed tree roots and boulders, which we did find tiring, but nothing compared to what we had already experienced higher up.

At last we were back at Bismark hut, where our guide who had hurried on ahead through the heather forest, came back and presented each of us with the traditional crown of woven ever-lasting flowers. These were ceremoniously deposited on our heads, either directly, or first having been woven round our caps or hats, as was Bill's. I understand that nowadays, this crowning ceremony has been discontinued in order to preserve the ever-lasting flowers growing in that vicinity.

Then it was the long trek back down to the Marangu hotel where our minibus awaited us. The trek back down the actual road seemed endless and was a huge anti-climax after what we had seen and achieved beforehand. By the time that at last we reached the Marangu hotel we were tired and weary, immensely relieved finally to be back 'in civilization'. We each of us sported a five-day growth of beard and moustaches. The minibus finally drove us back to Tengeru, jubilant and triumphant. Tired but contentedly so. Proud to have stood 'on top of Africa'.

CHAPTER XXXVIII

Lock, Stock and Kitchen Sink

1967 was a year of change. The Arusha Declaration had taken place, and we all wondered what was coming next,

The local *hazina* had asked Bryan for an up-to-date list of all the residents at Tengeru, house by house. This we knew, or thought we knew at the time, was in connection with a suggestion that we should all have to pay the new local taxes. Bryan therefore, as requested, sent a full list of all Tengeru's houses, advising them who was in which house. The list went something like this:-

House No. 1 Mr & Mrs B. C. Down
House No. 2 vacant
House No. 3 vacant
House No. 4 Mr & Mrs Joe Bloggs
House No. 5 Rest House
House No. 6 Mr Joe Soap
House No. 7 vacant
House No. 8 Mr & Mrs P. M. Wilson

... etc, etc, etc. A few days later back came a batch of tax demands for Mr & Mrs B. C. Down, Mr vacant, Mr Rest House, Mr Joe Bloggs etc.

After this we did have to pay our local taxes.

Although we suspected we were living on borrowed time as it were, and that changes were inevitable, we were totally unprepared for the next big change when we first learnt about it.

Bryan had called an urgent extraordinary staff meeting. We all gathered in the staff room, a little apprehensive as to what Bryan might have to tell us. We were all utterly shocked and speechless by his announcement that fateful day.

Tengeru was to close. Lock, stock and barrel, and even certain fixtures such as kitchen sinks had to go. *Everything* had to be

Peter M Wilson
Bwana Shamba

packed up in wooden packing crates, ready for transport to somewhere else in the country, as yet, he knew not for certain where. It just did not seem possible. Everything we had all worked so hard and dedicatedly for, to build up the Training Institute to a good, well-run institute, especially poor Bryan doubtless felt the most sick of all of us.

All the brand new buildings, the new lecture theatres, the new library, the new kitchens and students' facilities, the new veterinary laboratories and surgery rooms were all to be wiped off the map at the stroke of a pen. It seemed criminal to us, and still does, and a complete and utter waste of time, money, investment and everybody's dedicated and ethusiastic efforts over the last decade or so. And for what? As yet we did not know, but it had better be a good reason!

Then later came the other bombshell when we learned the reason that Tengeru had to be dismantled. It has been decreed that the headquarters of the new East African Community should be in Arusha, where the new purpose built Regional *boma* office block had already been closed down for take-over by the EAC which was to be the best thing created since sliced bread. The politicians decided that because more staff houses were needed for the EAC staff working in Arusha, the Tengeru staff houses should be vacated and made available.

Was this the good reason to close down a good, efficient, training institution and wipe it off the map? We didn't think so. I still don't. Especially so, with the benefit of hindsight. As it turned out, the EAC was a five-day wonder, or rather maybe a five-year wonder or thereabouts. It certainly didn't last that much longer.

Tengeru is now a ghost station. Termite mounds now dominate the modern new kitchens, dormitories and indeed much of the Institute compound. Most of the beautiful houses that were our homes are now derelict and abandoned. Naturally we knew nothing of all this at the time we were instructed to pack everything up.

The first job was to go into Arusha with the Institute's GT lorries and collect as many empty wooden crates as we could beg, borrow or 'steal' from businesses in town, for us to crate up our beloved institute. We had to start this mammoth task as soon as possible, if not sooner.

As for the staff, we duly received our transfer notices a week or two later. We were being scattered to the four winds. Even more extraordinary, was that Dorothy, being listed as the principal's secretary, found that she was to be transferred to Dar es Salaam, and I was to go to Ukiriguru near Mwanza! A phone call to head office soon put that one right, however. Phew!

Later it transpired that I was, after all, to be transferred to Dar es Salaam to work in Pamba House, the ministry's new head office in the heart of the city. I was to be assigned to the training department as an administrator.

But I am a trained teacher!

Trained as such at considerable expense by the Tanganyika government!

So?!

Then the painful business started of packing absolutely everything we could lay our hands on. Many of the fixtures had to be dismantled before we could pack them up, blackboards and the like taken down, laboratory sinks de-plumbed etc. etc. etc. None of us had ever had to undertake anything quite so painful in our lives before. We were dismantling everything we had worked so hard to build up to something we could take a pride in.

Morale as you can imagine had never been as low as that ever before. But ours was not to reason why, etc. etc., but even that didn't help us much. Poor Bryan must have felt the most demoralised of any of us. In fact, not surprisingly he fell quite ill before we had even all yet departed, so that as it turned out, I was asked to return to Tengeru, having settled into Dar es Salaam, to help him see to his own packing and transfer. I wasn't altogether surprised.

Not surprisingly, nobody's heart was in this mammoth packing job. Poor Chris Redekop had worked so hard and so devotedly to build up the new Tengeru library, so that it had become the envy of many of the country's training establishments and all who saw it. Chris had meticulously classified and sorted all the books subject by subject. She now had the job of dismantling it all and dividing the books to be sent to different addresses. Since she had no way of knowing what to send to where, she had no alternative than to mix them all up in a giant heap in the library, then divide them by 'pot luck' into separate crates as she picked them back up at random from the jumbled pile. Enough to break anybody's heart.

At last, the last of the crates was packed and its lid nailed down ... Then we had to sort out what had to go where. Some

Peter M Wilson
Bwana Shamba

had to go to Ukiriguru, the sister institute near Mwanza, and some to Morogoro, not necessarily to the newly established agriculture university faculty there, but towards the creation of a new agriculture training institute there. No comment.

Then it was our turn, the staff. We had to pack and crate up all our own personal belongings, so as to leave the houses totally empty.

Whilst all this tragedy was taking place, it is very sad to relate that another painful tragedy was also unfolding at that very time, as if we didn't have enough sadness to contend with at that terrible time. It came to our ears that poor Mike Owen, who had been on 'my' Swahili course back in 1958, and who had been posted to the Tengeru research station and was therefore still at Tengeru, had contracted leukaemia and was therefore gravely ill at his home with this terrible and often fatal condition. Mercifully, our 'powers that be' allowed him and his poor wife to remain in their home at Tengeru indefinitely and did not insist on them vacating their home immediately, as even the Tengeru research station had to undergo a similar dismantling exercise. It is very sad to relate that within a week or two of Tengeru Training Institute's demise, poor Mike succumbed to his illness and died. It was a sad and terrible shock to everyone, especially as Mike had been so truly likeable and was everybody's friend. It was, of course, even worse for his poor wife who had to bear her painful bereavement on top of having to move out of Tengeru.

My own belongings packed and sent to Dar, we all piled into my car, including Dolly and our beautiful Persian/Siamese cats, and drove down to Dar es Salaam. There, I was allocated a brand new ground floor flat, in the Sea View area, close to Selander bridge which basically divides the business end of the city from the residential end. As the name suggests it was close to the Indian ocean, about five hundred yards, in fact, so that we could even hear the sea and also benefit from its refreshing breezes through the louvre windows. Having settled in there, I then had to return to Tengeru to help poor Bryan. On this occasion I opted to fly up. Interestingly, as the Dakota aircraft approached Arusha, it flew right over Tengeru, giving me a wonderful aerial view, which I photographed.

It was sad and strange to be back at Tengeru's ghost, yet not be living there. It was certainly a wrench to see our old, now deserted, house.

It took me about a week or ten days to see to Bryan's packing, who by then knew he was posted to Morogoro to take over the new institute being created there instead of Tengeru …

I then had to fly back to Dar.

I caught the 'Milk Round' flight as the local East African Airways flight was affectionately known which called, from Nairobi, at Arusha, Moshi, Mombasa, and Zanzibar, then Dar es Salaam. This flight was generally made with one of their fleet's Dakota (DC3) aircraft. A good old faithful steed.

Unfortunately, as we approached Mombasa, there was much violent turbulence causing me for the first and only time in my life to be violently air sick on the final approach. Now Mombasa is situated on an island, having a sea inlet right round it. The airport at Mombasa starts right on the end of this inlet, and due to all this adverse wind and turbulence, no doubt, there was almost certainly an adverse eddy of wind caused by the cliff just before the runway started.

There must have been a sudden break in the wind just as we cleared this cliff, for no sooner had we passed over the beginning of the runway, than the Dakota lurched and landed heavily on its starboard side. This caused us to veer off suddenly to the left at 45 degrees to the runway. Before we had even turned back onto the runway, I was most impressed to see that the crash tenders were already racing alongside us and escorted us back to the terminal apron.

As usual, I got off as at all transit stops to stretch my legs. I nearly always met people I knew by doing so. This certainly made me feel 'I belonged' in Tanzania. Once in the terminal, I worried about that bad landing. I had visions of the undercarriage either not retracting properly next time, or worse, folding, then being unable to open up for the next landing, after its exceptionally hard landing. I looked at the flight departure board, and had just noticed there was a Comet flight due to Dar early in the afternoon. I had just decided that I would abort this Dakota flight and wait for the Comet flight, when they announced over the public address system that passengers on my flight should proceed to the aircraft and collect their hand baggage as this flight was now cancelled.

As I climbed the steps into the aircraft, I said to the steward in true RAF parlance,

'What's the matter, have you bent it?'

To my surprise he answered 'Yes!'

Peter M Wilson
Bwana Shamba

'What have you bent?'

'The propellers!' I looked at the starboard propeller, and was aghast to see that each of its blades had been bent back through 90 degrees!

We had actually hit the ground with that propeller as we landed. We must have been very close to doing a forward somersault. A truly lucky escape! Praise the Lord! We were subsequently all transferred to the wonderful Comet flight which barely took ten minutes to Dar, cutting out Zanzibar however. The Comet was sheer luxury after the old Dakota.

CHAPTER XXXIX

Dar es Salaam and Home

The name Dar es Salaam means, as I have said, Haven of Peace, which as soon as one sees it, strikes one how appropriate the name is for the country's capital. The harbour and waterfront must surely rank as one of the beautiful, if not *the* most beautiful in the world.

This is more than can be said for its climate.

As soon as one emerges from the cosy atmosphere inside an airliner on arrival at Dar, one is struck by the unpleasant hot, and very humid atmosphere of the place. Although the average temperature in the city rarely exceeds the 80s F, the humidity is a different matter. This remains almost constantly throughout the year in the upper 90s per cent.

Such a climate takes a long time to get used to. It means that just about every day, all day long, one is literally dripping with perspiration, so that one can even feel it constantly running in rivulets down the back.

Many of the city's public buildings are thankfully air conditioned, and this included Pamba House. As for my flat, I was fortunately able fairly soon to buy a second-hand air conditioner which I wasted no time in getting installed in our bedroom. If one can at least get a good, cool and humidity-free night's sleep, it helps to cope with the heat the humidity during the daytime. Even though this machine made a loud whirring noise all might, it was well worth it to get a comfortable night's sleep.

Whilst in Dar, I again joined as an active member of the Dar es Salaam theatre group which boasted a large purpose-built theatre. As a member, undoubtedly my personal highlight was performing the lead part as Emile de Becque in South Pacific. Although Dorothy and I were active members of the Dar dramatic society, we also frequented many of the activities in the Dar es Salaam gymkhana club.

On one occasion there, the tennis courts there were graced

My complete family just before we left Dar. Left to right: Myself, Dorothy, Vanessa, Yvonne and Diane holding Toffee, her Persian/Siamese cat.

by the presence of world tennis aces, Arthur Ashe and Stan Smith, who played a few demonstration singles matches followed by a game of doubles with our club's top players. Through this club, we met most of our best friends in Dar, in particular 'Satch' Brandon Menzies Sacher who was a harbour pilot. He along with his charming wife, Alison, soon became our best friends in Dar along with Tim and Trilly Keating.

We also made much good use of the wonderful beaches of the Dar es Salaam coast, although most of the time we spent on the beautiful pure white soft sands was at weekends. It was sheer delight to be able to wade straight into the lovely warm sea, without so much as the slightest flinch because of unpleasant sea temperatures. The children just loved it, and just about every weekend, we all practically lived in the Indian Ocean.

I well remember, and so, no doubt does poor Yvonne, one afternoon in the sea. Yvonne used to love, like her sisters, diving into the sea from off my shoulders, and on one such occasion, she surfaced a few yards away screaming blue murder. It just so happened that she had surfaced right under a Portuguese Man 'o' War jelly fish, so that its tentacles were dangling all over her poor face. These tentacles being poisonous had caused her face to become covered in nasty red weals, looking just as if she had been lashed repeatedly across her face. It was a long time before the pain from these stings abated, and in the end we were able to soothe the stings a little with *Nivea* or some suchlike cream Dorothy happened to have in her handbag. Even this episode did not deter any of us from frequenting the sea whenever we could. In fact I remember one particular Christmas day, when we spent practically the whole day up to our necks in the Indian Ocean.

At low tides, when part of the coral reef was almost fully exposed, we used to go out looking for shells, of which there was an abundant supply of beautiful and varied specimens. Whenever we walked out in the coral shallows however, we always made sure we all wore plimsolls, which I had fitted with tin innersoles, to protect our feet from the deadly barbs of stone fish which are so well camouflaged as to be invisible. If alarmed the stone fish is able to erect its poisonous dorsal barb which is easily able to penetrate the sole of a tennis shoe. We never, to our knowledge, ever trod on one, but if we did, the tin innersole certainly did the trick. But we did collect a beautiful array of shells of many different species.

Peter M Wilson
Bwana Shamba

Back on the beach, the perfect white sand was ideal for shaping into works of art. Our favourite was when I used to carve our quarterscale, or thereabouts, Landrover, which was immediately dubbed a Sandrover. I used to make it facing the sea, so that the children could sit in it and 'drive' it into the rising tide.

Our old Kilosa friends Marcel and Therese Contoret had their home just north of the city, and we often used to go out there to spend time with them, and even stay a weekend or so in their guest house next door occasionally. When we visited the beaches to the south of the city, which entailed crossing the harbour inlet by ferry, we generally used to come back home with a bucket full of fresh prawns.

While we relaxed on the beach, a constant stream of hawkers, usually children, used to come and offer us buckets full of shrimps. The more we refused to show an interest, the faster the price tumbled. If we kept up the refusals until we were ready to leave, more often than not, the price dropped to fifty cents for a full bucket. At this point we usually bought. They were certainly beautiful prawns, as were the lobsters we often bought too, or rather they were crayfish, which are just the same, but minus any claws.

As a diversion from sea swimming, for much of our time in Dar, as Dorothy worked in the brand new vast Kilimanjaro Hotel in Dar es Salaam, which had an Olympic sized swimming pool at its rear, our children spent afternoon after afternoon swimming and diving in this open-air pool while Dorothy and I were at work.

My new job in the capital, in Pamba House, the Ministry of Agriculture's new modern head office, which took the place of the old thatched compound I had first visited, was to assist in general administration in the training office. I had as my assistant a young VSO graduate, a most pleasant, shy man called Ray Purcell.

At any one time, the ministry had up to one thousand students studying either abroad or within the country. Our job was to keep full records of all these students for quick reference if ever information was required about any of them for any reason. I introduced the useful Kalamazoo system and designed a special form for it upon which we could store all the information we were ever likely to need regarding any particular student. It also involved keeping an up-to-date statistics board on the office wall. I won't say it was the most exciting job I have ever had, but it had its rewards. I still ran the occasional Swahili course when the need arose, of which at least two were exclusively for Japanese volunteers. By a strong coincidence, the very last Swahili course I conducted in Tanzania was at Ilonga, just outside Kilosa, of all places.

Though these last few courses were very pleasant, they never caught the atmosphere of those held at Tengeru.

During one of the end-of-course parties at our flat, when it was fully of Japanese, we were treated to a demonstration of Karate, which was certainly something different from the norm. Due to the extreme kindness of these friendly people, I acquired a well equipped Pentax camera set with all sorts of accessories and interchangeable lenses etc, which I still have and use.

After about six months in Dar, I had cause to go to Morogoro for a day. Whilst I was there, I had lunch at the hotel in the town. What I did not know at the time, was that there had been some sort of typhoid epidemic in Morogoro recently.

A week or two later, I began to feel really ill in my office in Pamba House. I tried to stick it out, but felt worse and worse as the morning wore on. I knew I had a fever, so in the end, I decided I had better go home and lie down. I was just able to drive myself home, switched on the air conditioner and put myself to bed.

I lay there for several hours dozing some of the time, yet feeling thoroughly miserable. After a while I thought I had better present myself to a doctor. So I got back into my car and drove myself to the Ocean Road hospital, only about half a mile along the sea front road. At this time, of course, Dorothy was away at her secretarial job at the hotel.

I was looked at by a very efficient Goan lady doctor who took a blood sample and put me straight on to the antibiotic Chloramphenicol, as she suspected straight away that I had typhoid. When the blood test rest came back, it was confirmed that I had indeed got typhoid. I was ordered to stay in my bed and not get up. It was at this time that our air conditioner really came into its own, for without it, what with my temperature and the high humidity as well, it would have been unbearable having to remain in bed in those circumstances without it.

It was fortunate that before coming abroad, I had had an anti-typhoid injection. Though these injections were always very unpleasant and made the upper arm most tender and painful afterwards, it had been well worthwhile, for, even though I had

Peter M Wilson
Bwana Shamba

never had the necessary booster injection, the injection I *had* been given nevertheless kept my typhoid in check, so that it never developed into the often fatal third phase. I well remember while in bed at that time hearing live on my radio that memorable occasion when Neil Armstrong spoke those memorable words from the moon, 'One small step for man, but a giant leap for mankind'.

After several weeks on my antibiotic, my Goan lady doctor was very worried and perplexed that, though the antibiotic had certainly checked my temperature, in as much that it did not go on rising, it never brought it down completely, which in theory it should have done by now. She therefore decided to do some tests on my batch of antibiotic.

The result of that test confirmed that it was a faulty batch and had been, incidentally, manufactured in the USSR.

My doctor immediately ordered a fresh consignment from the UK and as soon as she received this, passed it on to me to take instead of the previous batch. It worked like a charm, and in no time, my temperature dropped right down to normal and stayed there.

I felt very much better for this, but after so long in bed with a high fever, I felt terribly weak, so that I could hardly even stand up. I certainly felt very much better than I had for a very long time. Unfortunately, either my typhoid or the antibiotics had left me with a very painful and unpleasant recurrent cystitis.

Having managed to stay out of hospital with my typhoid, it was this cystitis which finally got me into hospital and I was admitted to the enormous Muhimbili hospital in Dar, where as it happened, my former VSO Swahili student Miss Connery, alias Miss Cummins worked. It was very nice of her to visit me in my ward there occasionally. Despite feeling very sorry for myself when I was there, I was well looked after in that hospital even though they did not manage to fix my cystitis. I could well have done, though, without being woken up in the middle of the night on two different occasions by an African nurse, once to ask if I would like a laxative, the other to ask if I wanted a sleeping pill ...

The cystitis continued month after month without showing any improvement despite having been put on umpteen different antibiotics to try and nail it. If anything it got worse and caused me a great deal of pain and discomfort.

I was still having problems with it when I went home on my

next home leave. I went into the hospital in Hastings, to have a cystoscopy. In the end, my cystitis was finally cleared up with the antibiotic Penbritin and I have mercifully never ever had any reoccurrence since then.

I was still terribly weak, though, so when I returned to Dar for my next tour, I decided to take up squash rackets to try and rebuild my strength. I played on the good gymkhana club courts, mostly with a very energetic Welshman of senior years to myself, called 'Taffy', Doug Delahay.

He, like myself, was a virtual beginner at the game, but we played so often and so hard that we both 'grew up' together in the game, and improved by leaps and bounds as a result.

Doug and his wife Kathy, and Dorothy, became very good friends all that tour, until Kathy and 'Taff' left on terminal leave.

My squash had improved so much that before the end of that tour, I was elected squash captain for the club. We played squash matches against any other club we could find, which were not many. In actual fact, the club we ended up playing most against was the army, or the TPDF, the Tanganyika Peoples' Defence Force, whose barracks were just to the north of Dar es Salaam. We had some very good matches against them, both at home and away at their barracks. Their squash captain was, by extra-ordinary coincidence, none other than my old friend, now General, Sam Magai Sarakikya.

I remember once when we had gone to their barracks for an away match, we found their squash court had had its floor polished so efficiently that we just could not stand up on it. Our match had therefore to be postponed as a result. An orderly had been asked to clean out the court in readiness for our match, and not knowing any different had polished it until it looked like a mirror. It was certainly clean.

I had, on my gymkhana club team, an elderly gentleman who had a permanently bent knee. He was undoubtedly our best player despite his knee. He used to stay put virtually on the T, from where he would reach out to left or right as necessary, and deliver a drop shot here or a drop shot there with pinpoint accuracy. These lethal shots would be intermixed with a hard drive into either of the back corners. If ever he could not reach a ball from the central T, then he would just leave that one and accept the lost point. But he almost always won his games.

I remember one particular match when we played the TPDF at home, I teamed him up against one of their sergeant majors, a short, squat young man, bristling with energy and fitness. I could see as they went out on court, that this sergeant major was most offended to be matched against this 'decrepit' old man. The match started, and as usual, before long, our 'old' man had his opponent running all over the court until the latter was just about on his knees with exhaustion.

As expected, our 'old' man won his game against the sergeant major with ease. After the match, I had difficulty in preventing myself laughing as I watched this sergeant major, all the time he was towelling himself down, he kept looking at the 'decrepit' old man from the corner of his eye, and I could almost hear him thinking, 'How on earth was I beaten by *that* old man?'

It was about this period in Dar that my responsibilities in the head office were changed. My new job was to become the editor of the ministry's Swahili newspaper *Ukulima wa Kisasa* (Modern Farming). The paper appeared monthly, and was packed with reports and advice on better farming methods, keeping up with the latest government decrees pertaining to farming.

It was a most interesting and challenging job for which I was ably assisted by a first class African staff. Our editorial office was out of Pamba House, well out towards the suburbs. One day, I was approached by a charming young African who was seeking a job. He was from Zaire, formerly Belgian Congo, a graduate from Ohio university in the USA where he had an American fiancée.

We hit it off together from the very first moment, doubtless helped by the fact that we were both fluent in all three of our common languages, English, French and Swahili. He turned out to be very useful in our office, and we quickly became very good friends. His name was Denis Saxo-Songolo.

As it happened, I had just about completed the project of translating my *Simplified Swahili* book into French, so I mentioned this to Denis, who immediately helped me adapt my French translation to suit the language changes and variations as used in central Africa, that is Ruanda, Burundi, eastern Zaire, and the very southern part of Uganda. The book was published in this format under the title of Le Swahili Simplifié, by the East African Literature Bureau, the book appearing in print literally hours before the EALB became defunct with the collapse of the EAC.

Very much influenced by the British radio farming programme serial, the Archers, I introduced into my Swahili newspaper a serial story, entitled *Adamu Yakobo*, which featured a *Mkulima stadi* (go-ahead farmer) called *Adamu Yakobo* and another farmer who never did anything right, nor even followed government advice etc. He was called *Sijala Maskini* (I have not yet eaten, broke).

The Adamu Yakobo did not mean anything in Swahili, but it was carefully chosen, however, so that it suggested neither his religion, nor tribe. I contributed to the story every month, including as much humour as I could into the story, and it proved very popular within the readership. I certainly enjoyed writing it.

One day, in my capacity as editor of a newspaper, I received an invitation to morning coffee with the president, Mwalimu Julius Nyerere, at State House. I naturally went, and felt very privileged. It was a most enlightening experience as well as most enjoyable.

After I had been editor for about eighteen months, out of the blue I received an urgent request from Pamba House, asking if I could do anything urgently about the ministry's permanent exhibition stand at the Sabasaba permanent show ground on the edge of the city.

I knew nothing of this, so decided to go and look at it. Sabasaba, incidentally, means Sevenseven in Swahili and stands for the 7 July, which is TANU Day, TANU being the ruling political party of the day, the Tanganyika African Nationalist Union.

I found my way to the Sabasaba ground and located the ministry's stand. I couldn't believe my eyes. It was hardly a 'stand' at all, it was really more of a 'collapse' than a 'stand'. In fact it was a miracle that it could stand at all. It was a miserable, decrepit rusty corrugated iron shack which literally fell to pieces the first time I touched it. It was hardly surprising the ministry wanted me to do something about it. The first requirements was obviously to find some money, lots of it. So I went to Pamba House to see what was available for this project.

The simple answer was that there was not actually a brass cent readily available for the project, as nothing had ever been requested, nor of course allocated for it. No such 'vote' existed for it.

Since clearly there was an urgency about replacing the monstrosity on the showground, I resolved to find any spare cash

Peter M Wilson
Bwana Shamba

there might be in a redundant 'vote'. I went to see the ministry accountant, and between us we found a nice fat sum in an old forgotten 'vote' which had been earmarked for a long abandoned project. I asked if I could have it, and the accountant told me to put in a request in writing, listing the good reasons why I should be allowed to have it. I duly did as suggested, and in the meantime 'designed' a rough sketch of what I envisaged the ministry's permanent stand should look like.

In due time I received a point blank refusal to my request. I was very disappointed as I was looking forward to spending this vast sum.

When I returned to the accountant, he was surprised that I expected approval. He told me that such requests always start with a refusal, but that if I repeated my request with additional good reasons why it should be granted, then I would almost certainly get approval the second time.

I did as suggested, and sure enough, back came my approval. There was only one proviso, however, and that was that I should spend the money quickly otherwise I might lose it altogether. This suited me, as 7 July was not that many weeks ahead, and I was determined to complete what I had in mind in time for the next Sabasaba Day. Armed with my provisional sketch, I went to see the chief architect's department and put forward my proposals. As luck would have it, I was shown to a most friendly and co-operative architect, who had nothing much on at that time. Without much ado, he immediately got down to drawing up professional working drawings for the type of building I had suggested.

I then went to Piddlydee (PWD or Public Works Department) which does most government building projects. I begged them to take on my project as soon as I could let them have the working drawings which were promised 'soon'.

The engineer promised to do what he could. I collected a couple of 'spare' bods from my office, two young Africans, who at that particular moment had nothing pressing to see to, and we went off to the Sabasaba ground. First of all, I wanted to get rid of the monstrosity. It literally fell to pieces the moment I tried to dismantle the first corrugated iron sheet. The whole contraption fell in an untidy heap. So we spent the rest of the day dismantling the individual sheets. I wanted to keep these and possibly use them to erect into temporary pens for livestock judging competitions if I could get them organized in time.

I realized that an electricity pole stood right in the way of the building I proposed to have built. Clearly, unless the pole were removed, I would have to have a major change made to the planned building.

Back in my office I wrote to TANESCO, the local electricity supply company, imploring the urgent removal of pole No. xxx and why. Back came the answer that it was a vital pole and much too important to be removed etc. etc. etc. This was a major set back, so I went to the ground to have another look to see if I could get round the problem.

The more I looked at it, the more I realized just how vital it was to get rid of it. Just then, I noticed a man working a JCB tractor digging out some foundation a little distance away. I therefore went across to him and asked him if by any chance he could 'accidentally' reverse hard into pole xxx. He said he couldn't or wouldn't do it, but after a bank note or two had exchanged hands, he changed his tune and said he would see what could be done.

I returned to the site about ten days later, and found that somebody had carelessly reversed with a heavy vehicle right into the offending pole, with the result that it was now leaning at a very dangerous angle and all sort of cables were hanging from it looking very dangerous indeed. I thought I had better report the potential danger of pole xxx at once to the local electricity company.

When I returned to the site about a fortnight later, I was relieved to see that the electricity company had been, and totally removed the offending pole, along with all the hanging cables.

Having had the excellent working plans delivered by the architect the previous day, I was now in a position to start forthwith. I went straight round to the PWD office armed with my precious working plans. I asked if they could get started with building with all possible speed, firstly to complete the project in time for me to fill the building with exhibits for the next Sabasaba show and also because unless I spent my funds quickly, I might lose them altogether. They got the point and got started with astonishing speed.

The building was largely built of reinforced concrete as well as having internal walls of concrete blocks. The next time I went there a day or two later, I could not believe how much had already been done. The foundations were all dug, and the shuttering for the first walls was already in place. At this rate it would be well ready in time for Sabasaba.

Peter M Wilson
Bwana Shamba

The completed permanent ministry exhibition hall on the Sabasaba ground, Dar es Salaam.

The main building was to have two storeys, one at ground level. In the latter I had planned to have two substantial cages incorporated, capable of holding wildlife such as rhino, buffalo, or even a lion if need be, because at that time, our ministry was also responsible for wildlife, so it would be appropriate to have wildlife on display. I had a great deal to do to plan and organize the many exhibits for the Sabasaba show, so wasted no time in rounding them all up. Our ministry was also responsible at that time for forestry and it just so happened that the forestry department of our ministry had designed and perfected a wonderful new timber prefabricated house. Upon research, I found that fortuitously it would just fit on the ground floor of my building, so I decided to make that the main exhibit on the lower floor. I decided I would furnish it completely as an occupied house, filling it with all manner of objects such as one would find in any house, and label them according to the ministry's products they came from, for example cotton sheets on the bed (cotton), cigarettes (tobacco), various containers in the kitchen of rice, maize meal and potatoes, etc, shoes (leather from cattle),

Peter M Wilson
'Mr Agriculture'

sisal mats, and leopard skin on the wall (game department) and so on. I had great fun planning it all out and had much good and competent assistance from Denis and others from the *Ukulima* office. I had already had words with the wildlife people who promised to supply 'suitable animals' for the cages. They certainly came up trumps, for the day before the show was due to open they brought in a lioness and a rhino. Once the show opened, there was no doubt that these two exhibits were the stars of the whole show, and we had constant hoards of eager Africans, in particular, queuing to see these well known animals they had never had chance to see before at such close quarters. Unfortunately, having deliberately left wide spaced bars so as not to impede vision more than necessary, the poor creatures were being constantly bombarded by all manner of projectiles and were also being prodded with sticks, etc. I had hastily to post a couple of game scouts on duty to prevent this. I also satisfactorily had managed to fill the main building with all manner of relevant exhibits concerned with our ministry. On a plinth outside to one side of the building, I was able to get hold of the latest type of fishing boat being recommended by our fishing department. There was one disappointment I did have for this show. There was a very poor response to the entries for livestock judging. I had suitable rosettes made to award to the winners, but due to lack of support, we just did not have sufficient entries to make the idea viable. Instead, I approached a couple of local equestrian clubs, and asked them to organize some horse jumping etc within the main grass arena, which they did, very ably.

Everybody agreed the ministry's contribution to the show had made it a resounding success. Towards the close of the last day, we were privileged to have the visit of Mr Derek Bryceson, a former director of our ministry and now Minister of Agriculture. He was destined to be the last European minister in the new independent government. As soon as he saw me, he came over to shake my hand and congratulate me. Praise indeed!

He toured the show building with interest. It was all very satisfying that it had such a resounding success. I had certainly thoroughly enjoyed the challenge of the project and it was all very rewarding.

Not many weeks after that, it was time to make preparations to leave the country, possibly even for good, as my contract had almost expired. There had been so many repatriations lately, which had meant that the medical staff had been seriously depleted, and with a young family, I thought it a valid point that we needed good medical facilities if we were going to stay on. The ministry did offer me a further contract, but I thought I owed it to my family to turn it down, so I did, much as I loved the life in Tanzania. As the end of my contract approached I made the arrangements for my last passage home.

We had never yet taken the opportunity to see the Victoria Falls, so decided that we had better do it on this trip home, lest we never again had the opportunity. In the end, we organized a fantastic route home embracing many of our friends. We flew out to Lusaka in Zambia, then on to Livingstone where we stayed in the new *Musi-oa-tunya* Hotel (the local name for the Victoria Falls, meaning 'the smoke that thunders').

We spent several days visiting the falls from both the Zambian side and later the Rhodesian (now Zimbabwe) side. The falls were everything we had thought they would be and more besides. It was an unforgettable sight.

To get from Zambia to Rhodesia, which at the period had declared unilateral independence under Smith's regime, we had to walk across the famous Victoria Falls bridge, built by Cecil Rhodes to carry both a road and the railway that he hoped would in time be the Cape to Cairo railway he had dreamt about building but never did. We stayed in an hotel on the Rhodesian side for a couple of nights, then flew to Swaziland via Johannesburg, to see and stay with our friend and Tengeru colleague, David Gooday, who had settled in Swaziland with his own farm there.

After a memorable and interesting stay with David, our old Kilosa friends, Bjorn and Daphne Graae from Juani coffee estate, who were by then settled in South Africa near Pietermaritzburg, offered to come and fetch us by car and bring us back to their place by way of a tour through Zululand. It was an unforgettable journey and wonderful to see the Graaes again after a long absence. We stayed with them in their home near Pietermaritzburg for two weeks during which time Bjorn showed us his new invention, a new type of bicycle pump which needed no flexible connection between tyre and pump, instead using a specially designed grommet. He had already gone into production himself, but for some political reasons, the South African government would not let him market them in South Africa. It was a great disappointment to him, especially as he had loads of the appropriate piping to build the pump. Not to be defeated, he turned to manufacturing a whole range of really attractive candleholders using up the pipe stock he already had for the pumps.

During our stay there, they very kindly took us for a trip through the beautiful Drakensburg mountains on the Lesotho border (formerly Basutoland).

We had booked a trip on another Lloyd Triestino ship, the *m. v. Europa* from Cape Town back home, so to get there, we had booked a trip by South African Railways bus down the 'Garden Route' to Cape Town, a three day trip. This followed the coast all the way from Durban to Cape Town, and in doing this most enjoyable trip it was easy to see why it was called the garden route, it was all so spectacular and beautiful. When we got to Cape Town we found we had a spare day before we were due to sail, so we took another SAR bus tour, this time a day trip to the nearby Cape of Good Hope, not, as commonly considered, Africa's southernmost point. We duly caught our ship home and had another wonderfully relaxing trip. The memory of seeing Table Mountain receding across Table Bay as one leaves dear Africa is a sight one never forgets.

Having found our way to Paris to visit an aunt there on our way home we completed this memorable trip home from Africa by catching the famous night ferry to London, now sadly retired into history.

Peter M Wilson
Bwana Shamba

For Afters

Upon my return to Britain in 1975, we still had our three daughters in boarding school at Wadhurst college in Sussex, so it was imperative to secure a good job to be able to keep them on at their school for continuity's sake.

I looked for another similar post to that I had filled in Tanzania, and after a time I was shortlisted for a similar job in Fiji. But I believe the job was shelved and nobody was ever appointed.

Eventually, however, I did manage to secure an agricultural job in Botswana (formerly Bechuanaland), sandwiched between South Africa and what was then called Rhodesia (now Zimbabwe). The post was that of head of the crop husbandry section of the Botswana Agriculture College, near the capital, Gaborone.

So as to be able to take both my car and my beloved Dolly to Botswana, I booked a sea passage from Dar es Salaam to Durban, flying to Dar, then later driving up to Gaborone from Durban.

However, as already explained, I had to leave Dar es Salaam without Dolly. I did, however, drive up to Gaborone across northern Natal and the Transvaal, and on arrival at the agriculture college, was astonished to see that my appointment at the college was to take over from a former Swahili pupil of mine from Tengeru days, Cyril Eyre. My new posting station, 'Content', as it was called, resembled Tengeru inasmuch as it contained not only an agricultural training establishment, but also an agricultural research station. Upon this research station I had another surprise to find a former colleague from Tanzania and Tengeru, a friend of mine working there, Stuart Irving.

Within a couple of weeks of arrival, I learnt that the brand new Mercedes 220 saloon car I had ordered direct from Germany had arrived in Cape Town. I therefore went down there on a direct train from Gabrone to collect it and drove it back home across the Great Karroo desert.

Once I got into the crop husbandry routine, I discovered all over the college, not visual aids as at Tengeru, but books. I therefore undertook to collect all these up, Dewey classify them and form a proper library. This was considerably boosted later when the college received a large cash grant with which to buy new books, and to build a new purpose-built library.

The house I was allocated was, like at Tengeru, a bungalow. It had almost an acre of garden, so I eventually built in it a murram tennis court and a large, deep, kidney shaped swimming pool. Since my house was the closest one to the college, my daily commuting comprised a walk all of about one hundred and fifty yards between house and office. Life in Botswana was never quite like I had found it in Tanzania, doubtless because of my total inability to speak Setswana, the local language. I did make a half-hearted attempt to learn it but got no further than a few of the greetings.

I therefore only completed just one three-year contract and found I was only just in time to book a passage home from Cape Town on the penultimate Union Castle sailing to the UK. I quickly booked a first class passage, which was my government entitlement, on the massive *Pendennis Castle*, a beautiful liner, and thoroughly enjoyed the relaxation and luxury of that memorable trip home aboard her. My marriage, by then, had sadly gone wrong, so that Dorothy and I returned to Britain by different routes and at different times.

The sea trip was certainly a memorable and fitting departure from Africa, sailing out of Table Bay, seeing spectacular Table Mountain fading away and over the horizon. I did bring home my still pretty new Mercedes car, which cost me only £80 because I was on the ship with it.

Back in Britain, I started looking for a job, and for starters, joined Banstead post office as a temporary Christmas rush postman, being put in charge of a 'walk', for which I had to do all my own sorting and two daily deliveries. Like all good postmen, I even got bitten on one occasion by a dog. After the Christmas rush was over, as they were short of postmen at Banstead, they did offer me the job permanently, but I had already decided I wanted to apply for a job as a London bus driver I had seen advertised.

As a boy, I had always been keenly interested in all things London Transport, so it was with great pleasure that I was accepted for training as a double-decker bus driver once I had

Peter M Wilson
Bwana Shamba

passed the preliminary and necessary 'cab test'. This comprised nothing more than ensuring I could fix my six feet two inch frame into the small bus driver's cab without fouling the steering wheel with my knees.

My driving instructor turned out to be David Weston who, like myself, was an ardent railway enthusiast. We eventually became very close friends, and later, the two of us, and our respective wives (Dorothy and I by then being together again) went for several joint holidays. David later went on to become the mayor of the Royal Borough of Kingston-upon-Thames.

I thoroughly enjoyed the experience of driving an RT type double decker bus all over London, and sometimes even beyond it, in learning how to drive it. Midway through the training, it was necessary to learn skid control on the world famous Chiswick skid pan, now alas, retired into oblivion. First we were made to experience a totally uncontrolled 360 degree skid at 30 miles per hour, after which we had to control such a skid and pull up in a marked rectangle on the tarmac.

After about ten weeks of driver tuition, it was time for the crucial driving test, carried out by a Ministry of Transport examiner. Mercifully I passed, then went to collect my coveted PSV badge, no. N106216, which in those days we had by law to display on our person at all times we were driving a bus.

I was allocated to Sutton garage, and so Dorothy and I bought ourselves a nice house in Carshalton, within walking distance from my bus garage. After an initial period of driving on any or all the routes covered by Sutton garage, I was allotted permanently to route 93, a pleasant route running from north Cheam, via Morden, Wimbledon Common and Putney High Street to Putney Bridge station. Having been allotted a permanent route, I was also allotted a permanent 'mate', my conductor, Arthur Banks. We got on well together, working well as a team and managing well to keep to our timetable.

Much as I loved the driving, I thought I should go in for an administrative job, so after applying for promotion, I ended up driving a desk in London Transport's head office at 55 Broadway, over the top of St. James Park underground station, near Victoria. My first administrative post was in the sports office under the charge of Phil Howard. I was basically responsible for keeping an administrative 'eye' on the numerous LT sports grounds and other LT social club sites scattered all over London. As luck would have it at that time, London Transport met biennially with their Paris counterparts, the RATP, for a sporting weekend, alternately in London and Paris. I had the privilege therefore to be involved in these activities as interpreter between French and English, and so found myself thoroughly enjoying weekends in Paris, travelling by air, at London Transport's expense.

Despite enjoying my new job, the promotional prospects were virtually nil in that office, so, in an attempt to seek better prospects, after two or three years in that office, I moved sideways into the publicity department, being put in charge of the incredible London Transport photographic archives. These contained tens of thousands of old photographs dating right back to the days of horsebuses, horse trams and even steam hauled underground trains.

When I went for an interview for this post, as I walked into the interview room, the chairman of the interview panel, Richard Fagg, greeted me with the words, 'When I read your c. v. I feel that life has passed me by!'

After some six months in this post, I offered to take many of the official photographs myself, if they bought me a proper camera for the job. Hitherto, all photographs had been taken, at great expense, by professional photographers. Thus London Transport bought me a Hasselblad camera to use with interchangeable lenses (considered by many to be the Rolls Royce of all cameras and lenses).

Thus I became London Transport's 'official' photographer, thoroughly enjoying myself being paid to pursue two of my favourite hobbies, photography and transport. I was even given an official permit to ride in the cab of underground trains!

Some of my assignments were quite exciting to say the least. Of these, decidedly the most hair-raising were the monthly 'progress' photographs I had to take of two major construction sites, a huge garage complex in Uxbridge and a large new office block near Earls Court. In order to take these photographs, it was necessary to climb 120 rungs vertically up a working tower crane on each site. Quite apart from other hazards, it was quite an exhausting ordeal to climb 120 rungs straight up, especially when carrying my camera equipment as well. The worst part was getting off, and even more so, getting back *on* the ladder at the very top, where there were no proper handholds, having to grab any convenient spar. All this time, the whole structure shook and trembled, as it continued its normal working.

However, I am still alive to tell the tale, so all was well!

One of the more interesting jobs I was given to do was to photograph every job undertaken on the underground railway system that could only be carried out at night once the trains had stopped running.

On one occasion, I found myself locked in at Oxford Circus station, so had to walk up the Victoria Line tube tunnel (by which time of course the current had been switched off) to Kings Cross station which is always kept open for staff.

On another occasion, Sir Peter Masefield, the chairman, insisted that I myself, as 'official' photographer, should photograph the LT board, a job always previously carried out by an outside professional photographer.

To begin with we just did not have the necessary equipment for such a job, and even if we had, I certainly had not a clue how to set it all up, let alone operate it. With only some four hours leeway, I therefore went quickly to hire all the necessary equipment, then made a frantic phonecall to a professional photographer friend of mine, Rob Brimson, to ask if he would kindly give me a crash course in setting up and using all this equipment. Mercifully he agreed, so I duly turned up with all the gear and he showed me the ropes.

Then came the appointed time to take the photographs. With a fair degree of trepidation, I took the lift to the 'holy of holies' seventh floor at head office and entered the board room with many butterflies in attendance in my tummy. Then, horror of horrors, the complete board was already assembled, all there seated and waiting at the vast polished table!

I therefore had to set up all my flash umbrellas and other equipment under their 'beady eyes' as they watched my every move.

When it was all set up I called out, 'Right, gentlemen, would you please look this way!' and it was FLASH! FLASH! FLASH! The umbrellas mercifully all flashed in unison and thanks entirely to Rob Brimson, my photographs all turned out just fine. No doubt one of them still adorns the boardroom wall.

As official photographer, of course, I was always in at the front row for such auspicious occasions as Her Majesty the Queen opening the new Heathrow Airport station, and Prince Charles opening the Jubilee Line. On that occasion I even rode the 'royal' inaugural train. On another occasion, I had the privilege to photograph the legendary legless pilot Douglas

Bader, when he came to launch a new book to help disabled people in travelling about London.

I was still hankering for further promotion, however, so was casting my net wide to seek it. I eventually found it as deputy 'Tours and Charter Manager' in the office responsible for all tourist services, including the world famous 'Round London Sightseeing Tour', by London bus. It was an enjoyable and challenging post which gave me the grade of Executive Assistant. After about a year or so, the then manageress, Maureen Gaythwaite, decided to quit her job and LT and set up her own similar business. I immediately applied for her post and consequently gained a promotion to manager, a post which held the grade of Senior Executive Assistant. I thoroughly enjoyed the challenge of this rewarding and interesting post, until the time came that London Transport was caught up in the general transport 'shake-up' which was all the rage throughout the country at that period. It was at this stage of my life, in 1983, that I successfully ran the London marathon. I managed it in 3 hours and 57 minutes and collected £2,300 towards the Guide Dogs for the Blind Association, prompted by the thought of Jenny McHarg, the blind VSO girl. As part of my marathon training, I used to run home to Carshalton twice a week, a distance, roughly, of some twenty miles.

All managers having been encouraged to seek further professional qualifications by one of our directors, I undertook the Institute of Transport *viva voce* examinations, which I managed to pass, thereby being accepted as a professional member of the institute to get my MCIT qualification. The reward I received from London Transport for this initiative, was to be offered 'voluntary retirement'. I told my boss flatly that I did not yet wish to retire. So, my responsibilities having already been redistributed to such an extent that I no longer had a job to do, I was told to stay at home *on full pay* 'until they found me a job'. I immediately asked for that instruction in writing, so ended up for just over nine months on full pay (which at SEA level was no pittance) doing precisely nothing except getting bored, until, fearful an excuse might be found not to compensate me, I eventually said 'Alright, give me my compensation, and I'll go!'

I therefore received a useful lump sum compensation, plus a good pension, my last promotion having considerably boosted my pension status.

Peter M Wilson
Bwana Shamba

So I was back to seeking a job. Initially I found one with the excellent government MSC (Manpower Services Commission) scheme of that era. I was given the management post in charge of a project called the Merton Horticulture Project based in Wimbledon. At least this was a step slightly nearer my proper career. The job entailed clearing up and redesigning gardens for handicapped people to enable them to tend them from their wheelchairs. The project also trained its out-of-work members in such skills as brick laying, paving slab laying, etc. It was a good scheme, and did a useful job in the Merton community.

But the government, in its wisdom, disbanded the MSC so once more I found myself looking for a job. As I still had my PSV driving licence, and had so enjoyed bus driving, I decided to go in for coach driving, working initially part time for Epsom Coaches, then for Edward Thomas coaches of Ewell.

My marriage by then having finally and regrettably broken up, I moved to Horley, my present home, and switched to driving for Crawley Luxury Coaches, later deciding to do so full-time. This had the advantage that I was allocated my 'own' coach, a lovely 'executive' Van Hool 53 seater with B10M Volvo engine, or *lump* as it is known in the trade. It was equipped with a toilet, coffee machine, television and video player. It also had a first class stereo system allowing me to play much fine classical music with no shortage of decibels, especially when I had an empty coach. So I felt totally at home in this home from home vehicle, and just loved every minute I drove it all over Britain, as well as in northern Europe. On one pleasant occasion, I had to drive a load of boys from my old school at Sedbergh, back there from Gatwick airport on their return from a skiing trip abroad.

I would doubtless still be driving my 'motor' even now, had I not been struck down by a massive stroke in June 1994 which paralysed my left side and brought about my swift and permanent retirement. Now I am branded a disabled pensioner. Nevertheless, God had blessed me remarkably since my stroke, and I have experienced some wonderful miracles of healing. I have found it very hard to accept that never again will I need to do a paid job for my living.

I have therefore turned to writing to occupy my time. I continue to live on my own, alas now unable to play the piano, nor indeed make the fine-detailed models of trains and buses which I used to enjoy before my retirement. I have also now taken up water colour painting as a hobby through the excellent encouragement of *Conquest Art*, an art society set up specifically to encourage the handicapped in this rewarding hobby.

My three lovely daughters, now all married, have given me seven delightful grandchildren between them, all of whom I manage to see quite regularly, and what with being wonderfully looked after both by my 'fianceé', Beryl, who lives less than a mile away, as well as the Lord Jesus Christ, who lives within my heart, what more could I want?

Peter M Wilson
Bwana Shamba

Glossary of Swahili Words Used Within the Text

Amerudi	he/she has returned
asante sana	thank you very (much)
bado	not yet
bado kidogo	not quite yet
baraza	a meeting or meeting house (generally the Mkuu's court)
bin	son of
boma	a fort, government office block (many of which were sited in old forts)
bundu	not actually a Swahili word. Meaning 'the bush', scrubland etc
bunduki	rifle, gun
Bwana	Mister, Mr (used much as Monsieur in French)
Bwana Shamba	Mr 'Field' ie Mr Agriculture
choo (pronounced 'cho')	toilet, latrine
dawa	medicine, chemical, etc
debe	a 4-gallon capacity tin can, very commonly used in Tanzania
dudu	insect, pest, creepy crawly (strictly speaking should be *mdudu* in singular)
habari	news, chit-chat
hazina	local authority native administration
hema	a tent
heri	good fortune, happiness, blessing
hodari	able, efficient
hospitali	hospital, clinic
huyu	this person
huzuni	sorrow, calamity

jambo!	hello! (traditional Swahili greeting, *hamjambo* – if greeting several at once)
jembe	a heavy duty drag hoe, the African farmer's principal tool for cultivation
jumbe	village headman
kabisa	extremely
kali	fierce, strict
kanga	a guinea fowl; a loose printed colourful cotton cloth, worn mostly by women
kanzu	a white full-length robe often worn by Moslems
karai	a shallow heavy duty wok-like container generally carried on the head
karibu	near
karibu!	Come in!
kiberenge	a small diesel locomotive such as are commonly used on light portable sisal estate railways
kidogo	a little (adverb)
kidole	finger, toe
kikapu	basket
kilimo	agriculture
kipulefti	a traffic roundabout
kisasa	modern, 'now-ness'
kuku	a chicken, hen
kulia	right (side) lit. for eating
kunawa	to wash hands and face (before eating)
kunywa	to drink
kwa	for
kwa heri	good-bye
machozi	tears
maskini	poor, destitute, broke
mbegu	seeds
mbu	mosquito
mbuga	black cotton soil, which becomes treacherous when wet
mbuyu	baobab tree *adansonia digitata*
mchawi	a witchdoctor
mchungu	bitter
mdewa	tribal chief
memsabu	madame, mistress of the household
mkoche	hyphaene or dwarf palm, *hyphaene coriacea*

mkono	hand, arm
mkono wa kulia	right hand, or eating hand
mkono wa kushoto	left hand
Mkristo	a Christian
mkulima	a farmer, cultivator
mkulima stadi	a go-ahead farmer
mkuu	a deputy tribal chief, 'important person'
moja	one
moja kwa moja	straight on
mtoto	child
muhogo	cassava
mwegea	'sausage' tree – *kingelea pinnata*
mzungu	a European, white person
mzuri	good (person)
nenda	go!
ngoma	tribal dance, drum
ng'ombe	cow, ox, cattle
ng'ombe maksai	ox, oxen (castrated)
nyama	meat
nyoka	snake
nzuri	good
pamba	cotton
panga	a machete
pombe	locally brewed beer, generally from any of the cereals
saba	seven
sabasaba	7 July, TANU Day
safari	a journey
safi	clean, pure
sana	very
shamba	field, estate
Bwana Shamba	Mr Field in the sense of Mr Agriculture
shauri	problem, business matter
shoka	axe
shusha!	drop! release!
sijala	I have not yet eaten
stadi	progressive, go-ahead
sufuria	saucepan, often devoid of handles
taa	lamp
tazama!	look!
tia	put!, place!

ugali	stodgy dough made from maize grain – the staple diet of many Tanzanians
uhuru	freedom, independence
ujamaa	family 'one-ness', co-operation
ukulima	cultivation, agriculture
Ulaya	Europe (there is also a village of that name in Tanzania)
upupu	buffalo bean, cow itch, mucuna bean (a terrible skin irritant)
wa	of
wadudu	insects, pests, creepy-crawlies (*mdudu* in singular)
wakulima	farmers, cultivators
wakulima stadi	experienced or go-ahead farmers
yaya	child nurse, nanny, ayah
zawadi	gift, present

Glossary of Abbreviations
Used Within Text

awol	absent without leave
BOAC	British Overseas Airways Corporation (now British Airways)
CMS	Church Missionary Society
COI	Central Office of Information (in Britain)
cv	curriculum vitae (personal history summary sheet)
DC	District Commissioner
DDT	Dichlorodiphenyltrichloroethane (type of insecticide, now largely banned in Britain)
EAC	East African Community
EALB	East African Literature Bureau
EAR&H	East African Railways & Harbours
EASP	East African Sisal Plantations (a sisal estate on the edge of Kilosa)
EPCC	Eastern Province Cotton Committee (section of the lint & Seed Marketing Board)
eta	estimated time of arrival
GT	Government Transport or even Government of Tanganyika (all Tanzanian government vehicles have these registration letters)
HH	His Highness
JCB	(J. C. Bamford) the trade name for a very versatile type of tractor much used by building contractors
KAR	Kings African Rifles

LRAM	Licenciate of the Royal Academy of Music
LT	London Transport
MATIT	Ministry of Agriculture Training Institute, Tengeru
MATIU	Ministry of Agriculture Training Institute, Ukiriguru
MCIT	Member of the Chartered Institute of Transport (professional transport qualification)
MOTH	Memorable Order of Tin Hats (South African equivalent of the Royal British Legion)(ex-Services club)
mph	miles per hour
MSC	Manpower Services Commission (now defunct by UK government direction)
NRC	Northern Region Research Centre
OSAS	Overseas Service Aid Scheme
PCV	Public Carriage Vehicle
PGCE	Post Graduate Certificate of Education
PSV	Public Service Vehicle (ie a bus or coach) (now call a PCV)
PTC	Provisional Training Course (for scouters)
PWD	Public Works Department
QC	Queen's Counsel (a lawyer)
RAF	Royal Air Force
RATP	Régie Autonome des Transports Parisiens (Paris transport system)
SAR	South African Railways
SEA	Senior Executive Assistant (administrative grade)
TAMTU	Tanganyika Agriculture Machinery Testing Unit
TANESCo	Tanzania Electricity Supply Company
TANU	Tanganyika African Nationalist Union (Julius Nyerere's political party)
TPDF	Tanganyika/Tanzania People's Defence Force (ie the army)
UDI	Unilateral Declaration of Independence
ufs	under flying seal (a system within